PROGRESSIVE AND CONSERVATIVE RELIGIOUS IDEOLOGIES

This book explores the surprisingly disruptive role of religion for progressive and conservative ideologies in the tumultuous decade of the 1960s. Conservative movements were far more progressive than the standard religious narrative of the decade alleges and the notoriously progressive ethos of the era was far more conservative than our collective memory has recognized. Lints explores how the themes of protest and retrieval intersect each other in ironic ways in the significant concrete controversies of the 1960s – the Civil Rights Movement, Second Feminist Movement, The Jesus Movements, and the Anti-War Movements – and in the conceptual conflicts of ideas during the era – The Death of God Movement, the end of ideology controversy, and the death of foundationalism. Lints argues that religion and religious ideologies serve both a prophetic function as well as a domesticating one, and that neither "conservative" nor "progressive" movements have cornered the market in either direction. In the process Lints helps us better understand the complex role of religion in cultural formation.

To Kate, Sarah and Lucas
In whom wisdom, love and laughter reside in abundance

Progressive and Conservative Religious Ideologies

The Tumultuous Decade of the 1960s

RICHARD LINTS
Gordon-Conwell Theological Seminary, USA

ASHGATE

Published by
Ashgate Publishing Limited
Wey Court East
Union Road
Farnham
Surrey, GU9 7PT
England

Ashgate Publishing Company
Suite 420
101 Cherry Street
Burlington
VT 05401-4405
USA

www.ashgate.com

British Library Cataloguing in Publication Data
Lints, Richard.
Progressive and conservative religious ideologies : the tumultuous decade of the 1960s.
1. Religion and culture. 2. Nineteen sixties. 3. Ideology – Religious aspects.
I. Title
201.7–dc22

Library of Congress Cataloging-in-Publication Data
Lints, Richard.
Progressive and conservative religious ideologies / Richard Lints.
p. cm.
Includes bibliographical references and index.
ISBN 978-1-4094-0643-3 (hardcover : alk. paper) – ISBN 978-1-4094-0644-0 (ebook : alk. paper) 1. United States – Church history – 20th century. I. Title.
BR526.L498 2010
261.70973'09046–dc22

2010021505

ISBN 9781409406433 (hbk)
ISBN 9781409406440 (ebk)

Printed and bound in Great Britain by
MPG Books Group, UK

Contents

Acknowledgments

This book about the strange role of religion in the 1960s feels as if it has been a work in process since the 1960s. Like so many other writing projects, this one has been carried on in a love-hate relationship with the author. The decade was too rich and full ever to do it justice, and yet it was too rich and full ever to leave it alone. Mining its strange twists and turns kept opening new vistas, which in turn were never as straightforward as they appeared. What follows may be considered the midpoint of a conversation with the decade. It is not the final word. It is rather intended as set of questions that looks at the decade in a different sort of way than our collective memory of the decade suggests. My hope is that it will lead to yet more new questions and unexpected insights about ourselves and the ironic role of religion our own age.

I am deeply grateful to Albert Borgman, David Kelsey and David Tracy for their willingness to read through large chunks of the manuscript at earlier stages. They have left footprints on my own life in ways that are inevitably manifest in this book. I am appreciative of their wisdom even when I have not taken it to heart. In very different ways, they appear between the lines of this work, though I can safely assure them that they are not in any way responsible for the flaws that remain.

I am appreciative of the staff at Ashgate, and to Sarah Lloyd and Ann Allen in particular for taking on this project and for seeing it through to conclusion. They have manifested efficiency and kindness, two virtues that often do not go together in our times.

I am also indebted to long standing department colleagues David Wells, Jack Davis, Paul Lim and Gordon Isaac, and to newer colleagues Adonis Vidu, Patrick Smith and Peter Anders. They have been wonderful friends and engaging conversation partners. They have heard far more of the 60s than probably desired, but have been faithful friends in encouraging me to see this project to its proper conclusion. Their collegiality has made this a better book than it otherwise would have been. Two pastoral colleagues have also been very much a part of the conversation that has helped me reflect on the strange role of religion in the public square. To Preston Graham and Rick Downs belong thanks for the countless conversations about things that really matter, many of which are mentioned in the book.

Gratitude should also be expressed to the Administration and Trustees of Gordon-Conwell Theological Seminary for extending parts of two sabbaticals while this project was underway. Two deans along the way, Ken Swetland and Barry Corey, deserve special notice for their encouragements and support. They have survived their tenure as deans, as thankless a task as exists in academic communities, but whose work and support is absolutely central to the calling and mission of the community of scholars.

The material in the book has been the topic of several courses. As is normally the custom it has received wonderful scrutiny and unrelenting questioning in those contexts and is a better work because of it. My research assistants along the way deserve a special mention as well for their help. To Jeremy Mullins, Blake Arnoult, Michael Keller, Mickey Sanchez, and Megan Defranza are owed thanks for carrying on far too many tedious tasks while each remaining unfailingly kind.

It is hard to estimate how many hours and how much emotional energy was spent in conversation with my family about the myriad of topics in this book. Ann and Sarah and Lucas and Kate all learned more about the 60s than they probably thought wise and likely were glad that the 60s had come to a close, even if this book never seemed to end. For Ann's patience and perseverance with me and commitment to me, I am eternally grateful. Like the 60s, Lucas, Kate and Sarah have turned my world upside down and helped me see things in strange new ways. Their wisdom has come in unexpected ways and their love of an imperfect father continues to surprise me. To them this book is dedicated.

Introduction
The Problem of Naming

> The ground on which we are standing has been profoundly shaken, and most of us feel it in our bones.
>
> Peter Berger[1]

The popular imagination strongly confirms Berger's sentiments half a century after the tumultuous decade of the 1960s. The shadow of the decade has proven long indeed. Memories of Kennedy's assassination in 1963, or King's "I have a dream" speech as a part of the March on Washington earlier that year, or The Beatles appearance on the Ed Sullivan show in February of 1964 all seem seared in the American consciousness. It was a decade when pop culture exploded on the American scene. Everything from bell bottom jeans to long hair was suddenly "in." It was a time of loud colors, of loud music and loud protests. In retrospect these protests against the status quo had deep roots in an established American consciousness of protests.

An underlying reality which has not often been the subject of critical scrutiny has been the role of religious conviction in the era.[2] Let me state the obvious first. The role of religious belief in the decade was complex. Kennedy was the first Roman Catholic president in U.S. history. Martin Luther King was a fiery black Baptist preacher. God was pronounced dead in 1965 while over 90 per cent of Americans professed active belief in God through the decade. Young people exited the doors of mainline denominations in shocking numbers through the decade while many other young people entered into an abiding religious faith through conservative parachurch youth ministries. Religious conviction was imprinted on our coins ("in God we trust") and seemed ever present on television as well. Religion served as the foundation of protest in the Civil Rights Movement, and as the establishment against which protest was lodged by the student radicals in the New Left Movement. Prophets of secularity declared that religion would

---

1 "A Call for Authority in the Christian Community," *Christian Century*, 98 (27 October 1981), p. 1257.

2 Two significant exceptions to this generalization are Ronald B. Flowers *Religion in Strange Times: The 1960's and the 1970's* (Macon GA: Mercer University Press, 1984) and Os Guinness, *The Dust of Death: The Sixties Counterculture and How It Changed America* (Crossway, 1994). I follow several clues in Guinness in the treatment of a "third way" as suggested by Guinness' original title: *The Dust of Death: a Critique of the Establishment and the Counter Culture, and The Proposal for a Third Way*.

soon vanish, while campus evangelists saw fields white unto harvest. Traditional religious denominations diminished while denominations loyal to traditional religious belief experienced enormous growth. Rock music signaled an age of free love, lots of sex and even more drugs—not exactly religious-friendly themes. But rock music also spawned the era of Jesus music. It had the same rhythms of the Beatles or the Rolling Stones, but entirely different lyrics. The folk rock genre of the late 1950s and early 1960s was the music of protest, but a protest which led some into religious vocations and others away from any and all religious institutions. At times, religion seemed the enemy. At other times religion seemed to be the vehicle of protest against the enemy. The role of religious conviction was anything if not ironic when one scratches below the surface of the easy generalizations of the decade. It was not simply a matter of being for or against religious conviction. Part of the mythology of that era which persists today suggests that religious belief is always and only a conserving force in culture or that liberalizing tendencies in culture always spring from anti-religious forces. Understanding the ironies and the complexities of religious belief beyond these simple generalizations might aid our own ongoing discussion of the role of religious conviction in the public square.

Part of the fabric of our humanity resides in the quest to understand our times and ourselves. This search is a project both humbling and ennobling. It often results in a greater appreciation of our collective human identity, including our religious identity, and yet also unveils fundamental flaws of human character and cultures. An accurate awareness of ourselves is also elusive, it being far easier to understand others than ourselves. In this regard it is hard to name ourselves though we instinctively keep on trying.[3] It is easy to stereotype others, most especially when it comes to the religious perspectives of others. It is also easy to stereotype those who stereotype others. Our public discourse about religious conviction could use a healthy dose of honesty and humility, virtues not in great demand in our times any more so than was the case in the 1960s. Confusion often breeds hostility. Understanding does not always foster sympathy, but without understanding, there can be little real empathy for those with whom we have real differences.

This is nowhere clearer than in the debates about the role of religion in the public square over the last several decades. The "naked public square" theorists supposed that America would be far better off if religion could be privatized. Inevitably this brought a backlash against the naked public square which revitalized conservative religionists and brought the Religious Right onto the front pages of our public discourse. Sensitive and sensible people yearned for a different way to configure the public square than simply those opposed to religion, and those desiring to dominate with religion. There had to be alternatives. Seeing the religious complexity of the 1960s is part of this project of understanding ourselves and others better. Religious belief is never as simple and straightforward as it may appear, but neither is it so complex that it ought to be relegated to esoteric

---

[3] David Tracy, "On Naming the Present" *Concillium*, no. 2 (1990) writes of the present age as one that cannot name itself.

discussions behind closed doors. It is a vital and vibrant part of our humanity and the religious ironies of the 1960s bear this out.

I will argue that the complexity of religious conviction in the 1960s is illuminated by the fruitful and equally frustrating complexity of another cultural matrix, somewhat now out of vogue in scholarly circles, though it continues to be all the rage in pop culture mediums—that of modernity and postmodernity. The categories of modernity and postmodernity have been the subjects of significant controversy and overly abstracted discussions. At their simplest these debates have been about how we are to understand our times and ourselves. The postmodern age, whatever it is (or was?), is a contested age. When did it start? Is it still present? And importantly, what is/was it? Most significant for my argument is the way in which religious conviction problematizes categories of cultural interpretation even as it serves as one of the main story lines within our cultural interpretations. Does religion serve the interests of the status quo? Hoes does religious conviction become democratized and pluralized by the forces of a post-1960s world, or are these forces themselves shaped and framed by religious conviction? At the level of popular imagination, the post-1960s period has been about a culture war over moral and religious issues. The actual and complex role of religious belief in the 1960s might help us think "outside the box" of the culture war rhetoric we have inherited from the 1960s.

The culture war rhetoric grew out of a period of intense cultural upheaval, nowhere more evident than in the decade of the 1960s. The discourse on postmodernity is another way to understand that cultural upheaval. At times this alternative discourse illuminates the religious complexities in that upheaval, if also at other times, can downplay the significance of religion in culture. Talk of postmodernity is inevitably wrapped up with the debate about its predecessor construct, modernity. The terms themselves suggest a simple chronological relationship. Postmodernity follows after modernity. And modernity is but a stage (of progress) after its predecessor ages. Yet the discourse about these ages belies a merely sequential analysis. Postmodernity does not simply follow modernity but rather exposes the structures of the earlier age by providing a new set of lenses through which we look at ourselves and our past. We see things differently because we are looking for different things and in part because things are different.

The debates about cultural interpretation are contested along several different fault lines. Should we primarily investigate the great ideas or the social structures of our times? Are cultural constructs about aesthetics or the arts or sociology or politics or philosophy or perhaps some combination of all of them? The debates are notoriously ambiguous if nothing else in this regard. What are the core elements of the constructs? Is cultural change driven by changes in technology? Is it wrapped up with the growing breadth of democracy? Where does the imprecise concept of pluralism fit? Point your finger too quickly at one aspect, and no sooner does much else of significance drop out. Try to include too much, and inevitably the claim appears less of an argument and more of a prejudice. Recognizing this reality is part of the fruitfulness and frustration of these debates.

The matter is complicated even further (as everyone now seems well aware) by the fact that cultural interpretation means many different things to many different people.[4] It is a notoriously expandable activity, at times including so much under its rubric as to be virtually unintelligible. So for example, the language of postmodernity seems ubiquitous in pop culture, but serious definitional analyses are confined to a few culture studies monographs. Everyone might know where the term "postmodern" belongs in a sentence, though most would be hard pressed to know why it belongs there. It is one of those words whose frequent usage masks its great ambiguities.

These debates seem useless to some and to others a matter of great urgency. There are many careful thinkers who now disdain the language of postmodernity.[5] They suppose that it is too expansive to bring clarity to a culture's discourse about itself. The construct has proven too malleable to be useful for them. And yet ironically the language of postmodernity seems to others too narrow to fit the breath and diversity of contemporary cultural experience. Not everyone experiences the present age in similar fashion and the dominant themes are not dominant to everyone. By including too much under its umbrella, it became too easy to defend one's own prejudice in its usage. By not accounting for enough differences in the cultural narratives, it is not an adequate descriptor for many that were allegedly included within its story line.

And yet what other name shall we give to our age? How shall we name ourselves if not with these cultural descriptors? There are not many alternatives on the horizon. Perhaps "post-industrial" or "late capitalism."[6] But these terms argue for a central cultural force which shapes all else, and likely do not (nor do they intend to) weave together all of the disparate aspects and elements of the contemporary. The language of postmodernity, whatever else it is, is expansive. It tries to connect as many dots as possible while reminding us why not all the dots get connected. It is also not merely a description but a prescription. For this reason it is a contested cultural map.

---

[4] See Zygmunt Bauman, *Intimations of Postmodernity* (London: Routledge, 1992).

[5] The archetypal postmodern thinker, Richard Rorty, himself suggests that the term be abandoned. He writes:

> Post-modernism has been ruined by over-use. I have no idea what the philosophical views of Nietzsche and such post-Nietzschean philosophers as Heidegger, Derrida or Foucault have to do with recent changes in architecture and painting. Nor do I see what they have to do with the new and frightening socio-political problems that confront us. Yet the terms "post-modernism" and "the post-modern epoch" and "post-modern thinking" are being used to bring all of these together. The result of this colligation is a confusing blur, and blurriness seems a good reason for avoiding these terms, *Truth, Politics and Postmodernism* (Assen: Van Gorcum, 1997).

[6] Cf. Fredrick Jameson, *Postmodernism, or The Cultural Logic of Late Capitalism* (Durham: Duke University Press, 1991).

Few suppose the postmodern age (whatever it was/is?) is over. There is not another successor era, post-postmodernity, dawning. And so, before abandoning the debates about postmodernity, it might be important to remember that every age has sought to understand its own differences and continuities with the past and has done so in ways that generate further debate and reflection. The discourse about postmodernity was/is an attempt to grapple with major themes within our present cultural narrative by contrast with previous cultural narratives. It may be ambiguous but any and all attempts to name ourselves will invariably lean in that direction. Any attempt to narrate our present experience will inevitably be incomplete as well, but that ought not prevent us from grappling with and disagreeing about its central motifs, events, and consequences. There is no other way to illuminate our central assumptions and intuitions in the moral and religious debates of our time. There is no other way to understand why the "normal" is normal to us, nor to realize that the "normal" has not always been normal. Importantly it may help us understand why what is normal to some, is not normal to others in that same time. The discourse about postmodernity is nothing more than an attempt(s) to understand ourselves, illuminating our cultural intuitions and assumptions while remaining (respectfully) incomplete. The very complexities and ambiguities of that discourse is why it may prove insightful in wrestling with the place of religious conviction in a time of great cultural change.

By most accounts the chronological origins of postmodernity understood as a broad cultural construct and historical narrative, lie somewhere in the turmoil of the 1960s.[7] The term postmodern actually appeared first in the 1930s, but the sweeping change from modern to postmodern is most often associated with the climatic decade of the 1960s.[8] It was a time of cultural upheaval and generational conflict. It was the decade marked by a clear "before" and "after."[9] Its chronology was structured not so much by dates but by events which could not be contained within any accepted cultural hermeneutic. A new interpretation seemed requisite to understand the times—for "the times, they were a changing."[10] It was an

[7] The number of writers attributing the birth of postmodernity to the decade of the 1960s is stunning though with rare exceptions, there are virtually no concrete historical arguments to situate the rise of postmodernity in the 1960s. A sample of writers who note in passing the significance of the 1960s in the emergence of postmodernity include Andreas Huyssen, Cornel West, Todd Gitlin, Gerhard Hoffman, David Tracy, and Fredric Jameson.

[8] Hassan attributes the first instance of usage to Federico de Onis in the 1930s. See Ihab Habib Hassan, *The Postmodern Turn: Essays in Postmodern Theory and Culture* (Columbus: Ohio State University Press, 1987).

[9] Maurice Isserman and Michael Kasin, *America Divided: The Civil War of the 1960s* (New York: Oxford University Press, 2004) link the traumatic character of the 1960s to the Civil War of the 1860s and the disruptive forces unleashed throughout American culture.

[10] Bob Dylan's period defining song, "Blowing in the Wind" (1962) captured this sense of transition. On Dylan's significance to the cultural revolutions of the 1960s see David Pichaske, *A Generation in Motion: Popular Music and Culture in the Sixties*

era of great hopes and great tragedies. The mood of the country underwent an unmistakable change in the decade. The 1960s was a significant era because America's collective memory remains so indelibly imprinted by it. It was also a contested decade marked by impassioned causes and impassioned people. There was a clear sense that at the end of the decade, the ground upon which America stood had been profoundly shaken, and most Americans knew it deep down in their bones.[11]

In what follows the discourse about postmodernity is overlaid on the collective memories of that tumultuous decade, the 1960s.[12] There was something unusual and unusually important about the crises of that decade that brought to mind the transition of eras, a changing of the cultural and conceptual guard. The discourse about postmodernity is reflective of the 1960s, a decade all about new fads which quickly emerged and just as quickly faded but whose fascination with fads signaled something far deeper.[13]

Postmodernism is, more than anything else, a reaction to the 1960s. It is post-Vietnam, post-New Left, post-hippie, post-Watergate. History was ruptured, passions have been expended, belief has become difficult; heroes have died and been replaced by celebrities. The 1960s exploded our belief in progress, which underlay the classical faith in linear order and moral clarity. Old verities crumbled, but new ones have not settled in.[14]

Conceptual fads are often place markers for periods of transition before "new verities settle in." The fads of the 1960s burst onto the scene with a vengeance against the old order, but were quickly replaced by newer fads. The only constant in this era, the old adage suggests, was change itself. In retrospect, this appears as an indicator of the revolutionary character of the crisis. The crisis character of change became a characteristic of the decade itself, or so it seemed.

(New York: Schirmer, 1979) and Bruce Pollock, *When the Music Mattered: Rock in the 1960s* (New York: Holt Rinhart and Winston, 1983). Dylan himself was ambivalent about his role in the cultural revolutions of the 1960s. He expressed these thoughts poignantly in the first volume of his autobiography, *Chronicles* (New York: Simon and Schuster, 2004).

[11] Berger, "A Call for Authority in the Christian Community."

[12] There are suggestive hints of this intersection in Gerhard Hoffman, "The Sixties and the Advent of Postmodernism," in *The Sixties Revisited: Culture, Society and Politics* edited by Jurgen Heidekin, Jorg Helbig and Anke Ortlepp (Heidelberg: Universitatsverlag C. Winter, 2001). Hoffman is concerned to see themes of postmodernism as emerging from the legacy of the 1960s. By contrast, the present work is intended to trace the themes of postmodernity into actual concrete events and ideological controversies of the 1960s.

[13] Todd Gitlin notes that the debates about postmodernity are particularly engaging for that generation of boomers born between the end of World War II and the mid-1960s. It has held a trendy fascination with that segment of the population fascinated by trends. In this it is a construct born of a peculiar cultural experience and which may be more difficult to understand outside of that cultural crucible. See Gitlin, "Postmodernism Defined, At Last!" in *The Utne Reader* (July/August 1989).

[14] Gitlin, "Postmodernism Defined:" 58.

Against this backdrop, the religious complexities of the 1960s may provide a lens to better see the significant religious and ideological shifts of the entire last half century. The 1960s brought questions about human identity and human interpretation to the fore in such a way that they might help us understand the different ways those issues played out for the rest of the century, religiously and irreligiously, and our peculiar penchant for asking the questions in the way that we now take for granted.

The intersection of the two projects (postmodernity and the 1960s) is neither incidental nor accidental. Without supposing these are meta-constructs which are all inclusive in their reach, the following work is an extended attempt to illuminate the surprising role of religion and ideology in contemporary culture by situating the questions in the concrete realities of the 1960s and by paying attention to the ironies and ambiguities to which postmodern theorists have drawn attention. It is my hope that the discussion of modernity/postmodernity will aid in understanding the religious complexities of the 1960s and that selected cultural and religious crises of the 1960s will illuminate the ongoing complexities of religion and ideology in the half century since. Situating the discourse of postmodernity with its emphasis upon irony and ambiguity in an actual historical setting will illuminate the concrete complexity of religious belief and hopefully illuminate some of its surprising dimensions. And by interpreting the events of the 1960s this way, the decade's lasting influence will become more intelligible and its legacy more secure though more surprising. It may also help in some small way to interpret our collective cultural experience of religious controversies more thoughtfully and sensibly.

This volume is then a detective story and thereby an attempt to interpret the meaning of events of our recent past. The "events" under consideration are mostly those of the great controversies of the late 1950s and early 1960s. The controversies are woven together into an intelligible whole by challenging common stereotypes about the way religion and ideology interacted. It is important to situate the events in their historical context and pay attention when appropriate to the peculiar character of those historical and social contexts. The first two chapters then embark on a detailed examination of conceptual frameworks and common themes. Considerable time is spent in Chapter 1 on the conceptual themes which came to the fore in the discourse of postmodernity/postmodernism. In Chapter 2 the unique shape and ethos of the 1960s is examined. In both of these early chapters the mirror is pointed at the other chapter.

The third chapter on the Civil Rights Movement is pivotal in sketching out the initial overlap of religious protest and religious retrieval. The revolution of the 1960s burst forth in the 1950s with the advent of the Civil Rights Movement as an identifiably coherent protest movement. Its success was owing to its ability to retrieve religious themes from America's past which effectively challenged the status quo. It also contributed to the bursting of the bubble of naïve optimism so characteristic of America at mid-century.

The succeeding two chapters (4 and 5) chart two important elements of the progressive wing of the revolution of the 1960s: the New Left and the Feminist movement. Neither of these two was as coherent as the Civil Rights Movement, while both were profoundly indebted to the protests of the Civil Rights era. Both of them clearly illuminated the changing ideology at the heart of the 1960s and yet were built on surprisingly conservative foundations. They were deeply suspicious of the central intuitions of modernity and cynical about the mythology of progress central to America's identity. Both seemed on the surface hostile to religious belief, though both had enduring consequences by which religious conviction would play a more central and contested role in the public square.

In Chapter 6, attention is turned to a central crisis in the discipline of philosophy at the outset of the 1960s but not widely noticed until postmodern theorists trumpeted it in the 1980s and 1990s. This was the death of logical positivism and the consequent demise of foundationalism as its central assumption. This is an important episode to examine because of its centrality in later religious discussions and because of its importance to the demise of modernity's reliance upon human reason. It also challenged the relegation of religious conviction to the sidelines. Serious intellectual inquiry would henceforth abandon the secular mythology of progress. Its replacement mythology was still unclear.

In Chapter 7 a widely trumpeted but largely misunderstood religious controversy serves as the focus. The Death of God movement was widely heralded as marking a turning of the eras, but just as quickly dismissed by many who had thought it initially important. The paradox at the heart of the movement was that in pronouncing God's death, the movement unwittingly helped restore religious vitality, though of a distinctly ironic and ambiguous variety. Many social prognosticators at the outset of the 1960s assumed that religious spirituality would wither and fade under the pressures of increased secularization. After God's death had been pronounced, it was surprising to see that God made a comeback by the end of the decade.

The early work of Alisdair MacIntyre in the 1960s serves as a case study in Chapter 8 in the transition from secular optimism to religious realism. MacIntyre's religious conversion did not occur in the 1960s. He was a resolute atheist during the decade. But his uneasy conscience with respect to the unbridled secularism signaled the dawn of a new attitude towards all things secular. Declaring the god of establishment religion to be a "nobodaddy," MacIntyre nonetheless reckoned in a prescient manner, that a secular worldview offered nothing better.

The final chapter looks at the surprising story of evangelicalism in the 1960s. Long understood as a conserving force militantly opposed to liberalizing tendencies, the reality is much more mixed. The democratizing tendencies within evangelical movements pointed at strong analogies with protest movements at the opposite end of the religious spectrum. When it co-opted the "radical" rhetoric of the movement in the 1960s, evangelicalism proved to be an important force for change in the decade. This change was not motivated by a yearning to return to simpler and more traditional ways. Rather it was a clarion call to make religion relevant to the changing social conditions of 1960s America by standing against the authorities of the day. That made it a surprising ally with secular foes of religion in the fight against the establishment powers of the 1960s.

The conclusion to this volume may be simply stated: the 1960s were not very simple. The religious complexity of the age helps explain the complexity of the age that followed and against which the 1960s is illuminated. As David Tracy has written, "in our embrace of ambiguity, we live in an age that cannot name itself."[15] Yet the age that cannot name itself ably understands that we are no longer what we once were. Times have changed. And the 1960s was a watershed era that changed everything, or so it seems.

---

15 David Tracy, "On Naming the Present."

PART I
Protest as Upheaval and Retrieval

Chapter 1
Revolutions and Ruins: The 1960s and the Paradoxes of Interpretation

> There is a good deal of anxiety about the direction of American life. In fact there is reason to fear that America may be entering a moral and political crisis.
>
> Susan Sontag (1966)[1]

Introduction: The 1960s and the Emergence of Postmodernism

An archeological search into the eruption of ideological forces in the 1960s is difficult because the original formations are often hidden beneath layers of emotional scars still present from that tumultuous decade. In this regard, the sixties remain a time deeply covered by a shroud of passion.[2] It was a time of great catharsis for America and most especially for those whose lives became identified with the radical changes occurring in that era. Those who experienced the decade first-hand rarely ever remember it with indifference. Few have ventured to write about the tumultuous decade without a profound recognition of their own disturbing experience in that period.[3] It was a time, both beloved and despised. It was a radical era with radical causes, carried on in radical ways by radical people singing radical songs.

Learned reflection upon the decade bears out a sense of eruption and upheaval. The decade has been variously referred to as the "Fourth Great Awakening,"[4]

---

1 "What's Happening in America?" (1966) reprinted in *Styles of Radical Will* (New York: Picador, 2002), p. 193.

2 William Chafe, remarks about his own personal experience in the 1960s and consequently of the difficulty of writing about the decade, "I want to acknowledge the degree to which one's own personal history does shape the histories we all write, the insights we have, but also the blinders we wear that may keep us from seeing some things, because we are perhaps too heavily involved in them." In his "The 1960s: The Critical Decade for Postwar America" in *The Sixties Revisited: Culture, Society and Politics*, edited by Jurgen Heidekin, Jorg Helbig and Anke Ortlepp (Heidelberg: Universitatsverlag, C. Winter, 2001), pp. 3–24.

3 The two best first hand accounts from opposite ends of the ideological spectrum are Peter Collier and David Horowitz, *Destructive Generation: Second Thoughts About the Sixties* (New York: Summit Books, 1989) and James Miller, *Democracy is in the Streets: From Port Huron to the Siege in Chicago* (New York: Simon and Shuster, 1987).

4 William McCloughlin, *Revival, Awakenings and Reform* (Chicago: University of Chicago Press, 1978) and Sydney Ahlstrom, "National Trauma and Changing Religious Values" *Daedalus* (1978) 107: 13–29.

"America's cultural revolution,"[5] "the secular revolution,"[6] "the savage sixties"[7] "the destructive generation,"[8] "the nervous generation,"[9] "the seismic sixties,"[10] "America's suicide attempt,"[11] "the slum decade"[12] and "the age of rubbish," a phrase the late intellectual historian Richard Hofstadter promised he would use as a title if he ever undertook to write a history of the United States during the 1960s.[13] As the titles suggest, the radical character of the decade suggested a radical break from the past and yet an uncertain future. The straightforward question to begin: Why were the changes radical?[14]

Politics is the conventional key that often unlocks the interpretive door in this period and therefore presidential politics inevitably are foundational to the collective written memory of the decade.[15] Vietnam and the four tragic public assassinations (John and Robert Kennedy, Martin Luther King and Malcolm X) are most often seen through this lens. The "story" of the decade is normally narrated in terms of radical political events and in part this is accurate. But the radicalization of politics surely is part of a much larger story. Everything from music to students to sex to architecture to religion had "radical" subplots, which explained their significance in and for this period. "Radicalization" was the strange social glue which held the 1960s together, one of whose manifestations was in politics but by no means wholly defined by politics.

In the decades that followed, this radicalization was often interpreted with the tools of the culture war typology. This supposed that the conflicts were essentially political in nature and that these conflicts happened along a right-to-left

---

5 Gibson Winter, *Being Free: The Possibilities of Freedom in an Overorganized World* (London: MacMillan, 1970).

6 Harvey Cox, *The Secular City* (New York: Macmillan, 1965).

7 C. Eric Lincoln, *The Black Church Since Frazier* (New York: Schocken, 1974).

8 Peter Collier and David Horowitz, *The Destructive Generation: Second Thoughts about the Sixties* (New York: Summit Books, 1989).

9 Roderick Nash, *The Nervous Generation* (Chicago: Rand McNally, 1970).

10 Os Guinness, *The American Hour* (New York: Free Press, 1992).

11 Paul Johnson, *Modern Times* (New York: Harper and Row, 1983).

12 Richard Rovere as quoted in William L. O'Neill, *Coming Apart: An Informal History of America in the 1960s* (Chicago: Quadrangle Books, 1971) p. 427.

13 Cited in *America in the 1960s*, edited by Ronald Lora (New York: Wiley, 1974) p. vii.

14 The most complete chronicle of the "radical decade" can be found in *The Sixties in America*, 3 vols, ed. Carl Singleton (Pasadena, CA: Salem Press, 1999). This is a three volume encyclopedia of key events, texts, movies, people and themes from the 1960s.

15 The best broad cultural history of this period, Allen J. Matusow, *The Unraveling of America: A History of Liberalism in the 1960s* (New York: Harper and Row, 1984) manifests this bias. David Farber, *The Age of Great Dreams: America in the 1960s* (New York: Hill and Wang, 1994) also places national politics at the center of the story of the 1960s. Farber does ably place politics in a broader social context and also begins to wrestle with the global context of America in the 1960s.

(conservative to liberal) spectrum. The common stereotype has claimed that the "radical" movement of the decade was decidedly from the left against the right. The defining issues along this spectrum were political and most especially having to do with political authority. "Who would determine the fate of the nation?" seemed an ever present question looming over the cultural horizon in the decade. The radicalization of the decade was interpreted as an attempt to wrest (political) control away from the traditional forces of government (and to a lesser extent the church). The narrative of this radicalization appeared to suppose that the real action in the decade was fundamentally progressive, orienting itself towards yet greater freedom from institutional controls.[16] The conservative side of the decade was primarily a reaction against this push for freedom. Or so a standard culture war typology suggested.

There is an important paradox in the interpretation of the 1960s. The nature of this paradox has lied behind the central interpretive question of the decade—was the Sixties a decade of promise or peril? Did the decade mark the ending of an era and thereby the establishment of a new age or did it mark a climatic crisis for a secular society and thereby hearken the nation back to its roots? Was it a decade for optimism or pessimism?

The traditional answer has been—it depends upon your perspective? If you were a progressive you viewed the sixties as a time of hope—the old establishment paradigm was collapsing and a window of opportunity for a new age of racial, gender and ethnic liberty and equality had been opened. If you were a traditionalist you viewed the sixties as a time of horror which thankfully woke the faithful up and launched us into a search for and a potential recovery of significant aspects of the nation's Judeo-Christian heritage. Neither the conservative nor progressive interpretations of the 1960s adequately accounts for the complexity of the religious realities of that age though they manifest a vital component of the paradox. The crises of the sixties were at one and the same time animated by a retrieval as well as a criticism of the past. The retrieval of the past could be used for liberal and progressive causes as well as conservative ones, suggesting that "liberal" and "conservative" may not be sufficiently rich enough categories to explain the complexities of the decade. There were different thrusts and perspectives in the retrieval of older submerged subplots in America's history as a means of criticizing the general direction of that history. Appearing as polar opposites on the surface, diverse movements could equally protest the tragic distortions of America's

---

[16] In an otherwise extremely illuminating essay, Gerhard Hoffman, "The Sixties and the Advent of Postmodernism," in *The Sixties Revisited: Culture, Society and Politics*, edited by Jurgen Heidekin, Jorg Helbig and Anke Ortlepp (Heidelberg: Universitatsverlag C. Winter, 2001) accepts this fundamentally progressive reading of the decade. She writes: "The new paradigm substituted old humanism, the traditional loyalties, ties and associations, with a new humanism characterized by openness, possibility and freedom," p. 193.

identity. They might equally view themselves as outsiders to the nation, while also believing they possessed inalienable rights to be insiders.[17]

On a standard reading of the decade, the so called "right hand side" of the spectrum was committed to conserving the past including its traditions, customs, moralities, authorities and so on. The left hand side of the spectrum, by contrast sought to distance itself from the past locating the promise of the future in the freedom from the past. The political dimension of the culture wars suggested the central split right to left, had to do with this issue of authority, and specifically the authority to frame the political destiny of individuals. Traditionalists were interpreted as seeing the meaning of life as a "given" and therefore public institutions of control (government) were called to protect the older order.[18] Progressives were interpreted as seeing political destiny as fluid, emerging from each individual's own creativity.

Appearances sometimes were deceiving. The rhetoric of the culture wars was present in the decade and there can be little doubt that the cultural tension was often experienced (as well as interpreted) along a right-to-left spectrum. But overshadowed is the reality that both the right and the left saw themselves as outsiders during the decade. The radicalization of the decade occurred at both ends of the spectrum.[19] The relative success of each was determined in large measure by their ability to portray the revolt as one against the establishment. The establishment was interpreted as too liberal by conservatives and too conservative

---

[17] Most interpretations of the 1960s written in the 1970s emphasized these themes of alienation. However they mostly failed to see the alienation operating in more than one political or religious direction. Representative of this view were: Sydney Ahlstrom, "National Trauma" and William G. McCloughlin, *Reform, Revival and Awakenings*. Studies written in the 1980s focused on both of the diverse ends of the religious and political spectrum but tended to see the conflict as primarily a progressive effort versus a conserving traditionalism. These studies generally failed to see the conserving elements of the progressive movements and the progressive elements in the conservative traditions which appear to operate with the polarization thesis in view: Robert Wuthnow, *The Struggle for America's Soul: Evangelicals, Liberals and Secularism* (Grand Rapids: Eerdmans, 1989) and Langdon Gilkey, *Society and the Sacred* (New York: Crossroad, 1981).

[18] A helpful criticism of this stereotype of conservatives in the 1960s can be found in Sheldon Wolin, "The Destructive Sixties and Postmodern Conservatism" in *Reassessing the Sixties: Debating the Political and Cultural Legacy*, edited by Stephen Macedo (New York: Norton, 1997), pp. 129–58. See also John A. Andrew, *The Other Side of the Sixties: Young Americans for Freedom and the Rise of Conservative Politics* (New Brunswick, NJ: Rutgers University Press, 1997).

[19] Lisa McGirr is exactly right when she claims that there were "not one but two variants of radicalism [which] characterized the 1960s." She has in mind the progressive radicals and the conservative radicals, neither of whom saw themselves as part of the establishment. See her "Conservative Politics in a Liberal Age: A History of the Right in the 1960s" in *The Sixties Revisited: Culture, Society and Politics*, edited by Jurgen Heidekin, Jorg Helbig and Anke Ortlepp (Heidelberg: Universitatsverlag C. Winter, 2001), pp. 451–68.

by liberals but the tools of dissent belie a facile characterization of either side as simply "right" or "left." The movement of disestablishment of the 1960s had many sides to it and all sides used analogous strategies against their common enemy—establishment liberalism. In this regard, criticism of the establishment was not homogenous, but enormously complex and varied. To use another metaphor, the cultural conflict of the 1960s was triangular in shape. The missing element in the standard bipolar culture war typology is the "middle."[20] The establishment was the power broker denying the fundamental goals of both right and left, and equally despised by both ends. Its pragmatism was resented on the right by those who believed in transcendent values and feared governmental influence over individual confession and conviction. The critical realism of the establishment offended those on the left who believed in the promise of each individual and feared the government protected the rights of too few individuals. In other words the story is more complicated than the standard typology permits, though the resilience of that typology points at an enduring truth, America's identity was indeed under siege in the 1960s and afterwards.[21] The character of that revolution is the point of the present work, as I've suggested, and will later argue the depiction of the revolution may be helpfully enriched by the constructs of modernity and postmodernism.

The revolution encompassed a culture war but was not exhausted by it. The concern is, therefore, less with a social chronology of the 1960s, than it is an interpretation of the decade against the backdrop of stereotypes as a way to better understand the complexity of the decade. The intent is to see the forest in spite of the familiarity of the trees, or maybe to see some trees that haven't been seen because of the familiarity of the forest. Paying attention to the religious dimension of the revolutionary episodes in the decade reveals how ironic the forces of protest actually were. At the very height of modern secularity, religion of many varieties made surprising comebacks. Even while God was declared dead on the cover of Time Magazine in 1965, the Jesus People with their long hair and rock music provided a striking reminder that the young generation could be both radical and religious. The decade was a conflict of values but those values were not easy to predict by their cultural styles. Religious values in particular were rooted in diverse religious communities and arose from deeply conflicted theological schemes with

20 The language of "middle" itself is deceptive for it supposes a cultural calculus can be applied to the any and all questions with a resulting equation permitting the points to be plotted on a simple line to delineate the relative positions of everyone involved. The puzzle is much more complicated than this. The simple point here being stressed is bipolar analyses of the decade mistakenly omit at least one complicating factor—the establishment middle.

21 Cf. Michael Elliot, *The Day Before Yesterday: Reconsidering America's Past, Rediscovering The Present* (New York: Simon and Schuster, 1996). Elliot writes from the "middle." He defends the establishment's vision as the only effective means around which the nation could rally. From this vantage point, the sixties wreaked havoc on America's Golden Age. It represented a splintering of the nation. Elliot confirmed the disestablishment thrust of the 1960s and deeply regretted it.

differing approaches to cultural engagement which made it hard to determine the sides by the color of the (cultural) uniforms.

There are two significant and complex components often overshadowed in the traditional political narrative by which the story of the 1960s has been remembered. These are disestablishment and democratization. The disestablishment of the 1960s, in retrospect, was the abandoning of modernism with its emphasis upon technique and mechanization and the embrace (in a qualified sense) of postmodernism with its emphasis upon irony and ambiguity. The surest sign of this in the 1960s was the pervasive loss of hope, which had been engendered by the project of modernity. The nation witnessed the apparent collapse of its own salvation history (otherwise known as cultural progress) in this period. The cloak of liberalism, which had clothed the nation since early in the twentieth century, appeared to come apart at the seams. Disestablishment was inevitably accompanied by disillusionment. The patient (America) got sick somewhere in the decade and almost everyone could feel its effects, though they may have (violently) disagreed as to its cure. Ironically, the patient had never appeared stronger than she did as the decade began. The nation's victory in World War II, the economic boom of the 1950s and the massive new space program each held out the promise of an endlessly bright future. But by the end of the decade, the future seemed by contrast rather bleak. The race riots, the War in Vietnam and Watergate all conspired to burst the bubble of hope. The nation began to doubt itself, questioning not only its moral virtue but also its long perceived manifest destiny as the melting pot of cultures. Increasingly it appeared the melting pot had boiled over and everyone seemed scorched by it.

The legacy of disestablishment in American history is a well established pattern, but in the 1960s, political and religious enemies sought together to remove the powers that be. These powers-that-be represented an entrenched authority fundamentally at odds with the goals of the outsiders. Almost everyone thought of themselves as an outsider, each in their own way thinking of themselves as a victim of America's past. When the move to disestablish was combined with a prophetic impulse, the nation was brought to a breaking point. The Civil Rights Movement and the New Right in very different ways each relied on resources of sacred values to push their agendas against a secular pragmatism of the entrenched establishment. The prophetic rhetoric of both movements was rooted not only in their role as outsiders but also in their recovery of older notions of transcendent truth. They each delivered harsh criticism of America's compromises with big business and the commercial establishment. They might have held starkly different visions of the future but their prophetic edge proved too powerful for the sustaining of a flaccid and optimistic secularism. Even as some theologians celebrated the age of secularity, some secularists decried its anti-religious character. The roles played out in a century old warfare between science and religion were quietly reversed as the history of science was unveiled as religious-like in its fundamental commitments, and religion reentered the public square with a vengeance. At the end of the 1960s the nation no longer seemed sure of where it was going, though clear that it needed to change.

A second complicating theme in the story of the 1960s was democratization. A persistent thread that appeared woven throughout America's past was its protection of individual freedoms. The nation was continually "moving west" in its own mind, conquering new frontiers by the courage of rugged individuals. Not until the 1960s was there a realization that many groups had been trampled upon in America's history as the means of protecting the rights of privileged individuals to go where they pleased. The consciousness raising of the sixties brought a realization to the nation that not all of its citizens had been treated equally and not everyone could claim the protections of its laws. It appeared that the nation of individuals excluded a great many individuals. As the 1960s progressed, it unleashed furious arguments about including those formerly excluded. People of color, women and even religious conservatives had all experienced life as outsiders to the corridors of American power. They (and others) experienced the conflict between American ideals and American reality. Each in turn believed that democracy had failed, while each also argued for a greater democratization of the public square. And each of them, in different ways, sought to retrieve elements of America's past as a way to change America's present.

The Narrative, the Meta-Narrative and the Paradoxes

Life had been changing in very significant ways between the Great Depression and the Radical Decade. The revolution in the nation's topography started as people poured forth from small towns and the countryside to take up jobs being created in the emerging metropolitan areas. The movement westward mounted at an accelerated pace as the new life of California ceased being a Hollywood dream and became an attainable reality. The national highway system was built and cars became produced (and sold) on a massive scale mobilizing an entire population. This new found mobility added greatly to the consumer-culture by allowing increased shopping at strip malls also encouraged by the significant rise in disposable income during the decade of the 1950s. With the rise of a white collar economy, men (and women to a smaller degree) now had career paths to follow which not only took them away from their home towns and placed them in far away locations but also created social ladders they were expected to climb.

Increased mobility greatly effected the black population in this period as well. As a result of the War effort in the early 1940s, employment opportunities for the sizable rural black population shifted to larger urban areas both in the northeast and mid-west and to a lesser degree in the south. It was not accidental that the mass protest movements for civil rights originated under the leadership of several blacks employed as porters on the train system, individuals who saw the possibilities of life in diverse parts of the country.[22] And black clergy, who were among the best educated in the rural south, gave focus and energy to the civil rights protests.

There can also be no doubt that the sharp rise in birth rates from 1940–55 created enormous and unprecedented social pressures in America during the 1960s. An unprecedented population "bubble" reached adolescence (and early adulthood) in the decade of the 1960s, and many social institutions showed scant ability to cope with the new cohort. The educational institutions in particular had great difficulty in absorbing this vast new generation.[23] Between 1960 and 1972 the number of college students increased from 3 to 7.5 million. The numbers of college students increased so rapidly in the 1960s that the traditional socializing processes were rendered ineffective. It is fair to say that the members of this vast new generation taught each other, rather than being taught by adults.[24] Youth culture became a distinct culture in its own right, complete with unique fashions, music, slang and most especially a distinctive set of values. By the end of the 1960s, the yearly periodical indices disclosed three to four times as many words being written about youth as were written in all the decades combined prior to the 1960s. And that statistic reflects the growth of a superstition that the story of the age was in some large measure the simultaneous appearance of two ages, two worlds—one belonging to young people and the other to those who weren't so privileged to be young. The prime influence on behavior and feeling in both worlds was the attitude toward the other.[25]

---

22 See Larry Tye, *Rising from the Rails: Pullman Porters and the Making of the Black Middle Class* (New York: Henry Holt and Co., 2004) and Milton Viorst, *Fire in the Streets: America in the 1960s* (New York: Simon and Schuster, 1979) for background to some of the lesser known figures of the early civil rights protests of the 1940s and 1950s.

23 Norman Cantor cites the remarkable growth in new state colleges and community colleges during this period as evidence of the system's ability to digest the cohort but maintains that this new educational system little understood the impact of extending education in such short order to such a large cohort of the population. He notes a government report authored by Archibald Cox, professor of law at Harvard and later to become the special prosecutor during the Watergate affair, in which Cox concluded that the greatest blame for the student riots at Columbia University in May 1968 could be traced to the deplorable conditions of the student dormitories and the abominable diet at the student cafeteria. The sheer growth in student population at Columbia was not adequately cared for and resulted in radical solutions masked as radical social protests. See his *Twentieth Century Culture: Modernism to Deconstruction* (New York: Peter Lang, 1988).

24 Cantor argues that the generation coming of age in the 1950s on the other hand, was abnormally conservative and conformist. Because there had been a very low birth rate during the Great Depression, the population that reached maturity around 1950 was abnormally small. This facilitated their easy control and socialization by adults. Or so Cantor argued.

25 Benjamin DeMott makes this point powerfully in a essay entitled, "The Sixties: A Cultural Revolution" in *America in the 60s*, ed. Ronald Lora (New York: Wiley, 1974), pp. 433–47.

Personal income rose dramatically in this period as did corporate profits. The "bureaucratization" of the American economy also occurred in this period. In 1940, 26 per cent of Americans were self-employed. By 1960, less than 16 per cent were self-employed. In 1960 more than 38 per cent of the population drew paychecks from corporations larger than 500 people. From 1950 to 1960 the payrolls of local and state government increased 52 per cent. At the end of that period government employment accounted for 1/8th of the total non-agricultural workforce. And in 1956, for the very first time in American history, white collar workers outnumbered blue collar workers.

The ideology of American liberalism in the 1940s and 1950s sought to reject all forms of totalitarianism and affirmed a realistic democratic creed. It recognized the complexity of reality, the ineradicable sinfulness of human nature, the corruption of power, the virtues of pragmatism and gradualism and the narrow possibilities of all human endeavor.[26] It was optimistic about the future but cautiously so. The Great Depression was too significant a part of its memory for it to be otherwise. The collective sense of national suffering hung over this generation like a dark ever-threatening rain cloud.

This brand of liberalism seemed to be strangely out of place in the 1960s because it failed to come to grips with modernity, with that type of affluence generated by the technological and bureaucratic revolutions of the post-war period. In that period of rising expectations, liberalism promised too little and delivered too much. It preached honesty, thrift and delayed gratification all the while promoting the tools and infrastructure of a mass culture which all but denied these moral realities. It talked about making the world safe for democracy only to misunderstand the democratic impulse it unleashed in the neglected sectors of American society.[27]

In its wake, liberalism left two unhappy cousins, both of which were deeply committed to different parts of modernity and thereby able to withstand the death of liberalism though in radically different ways. The left hand side of the revolution pinned its hopes on human potential by way of participatory democracy while the right hand side committed itself to human potential by way of religious individualism. Both saw human freedom at the heart of the crisis and thereby were centrally concerned whether individuals were free to pursue ends they themselves deemed important.

---

[26] Names associated with this variety of chaste liberalism were: David Riesman, Daniel Bell, Reinhold Niebuhr, John Kenneth Galbraith, Sidney Hook, Dwight Macdonald, Richard Rober, Lionel Trilling, James Wechsler, and the editors of the Partisan Review.

[27] The growing chorus of criticism in the 1950s foreshadowed the cultural crisis that would come in the 1960s. The following influential titles give some indication of the direction of this criticism: *The Lonely Crowd* (David Reisman, 1958) *The Affluent Society* (John Kenneth Galbraith, 1958), *The Technological Society* (Jacques Ellul, 1954), *The Organization Man* (William Whyte, 1956), *The Power Elite* (C. Wright Mills, 1956), *Life Against Death* (Norman Brown 1959).

The battle for the recovery of human freedom was launched because the institutions of culture mitigated against finding human meaning external to the individual. The movement from fate to choice was unwittingly imposed upon the radical wings of the revolution by the very institutions against which they were rebelling.[28]

Disestablishment and the Search for a New (Countercultural) Home

The counterculture had both a left and right wing to it and both clearly saw the enemy not in ideological terms but in cultural terms. The conservative wing of the counterculture was as deeply populist, as profoundly committed to participatory democracy and as extreme in its commitment to diversity as SDS or SNCC or any other of the organs of the New Left. Both shared an antipathy to big business, government by the elite, and the Protestant establishment. Both spoke through the modern medium of rock music and both thought of themselves as a distinct "generation." As Gerald Howard aptly remarks:

> All of a sudden it was the lower orders who were creating the new styles and setting the fashion, society and art worlds on their heads—a new democracy of culture. The distinctions between high and low culture, the *haute monde* and the *hoi polloi*, became impossibly blurred.[29]

In the 1960s, many felt like America was no longer home. Traditional American ways neither communicated security nor significance to a generation born in the aftermath of World War II. The Vietnam vet returned home only to find he was little appreciated for his heroism. The yippies, the hippies, the Jesus people, and the Black Muslims all felt like strangers in a strange land. The common thread in all of these narratives was a sense of cosmic alienation from their America, that land which had, by virtue of its existence, granted value and meaning to all of its citizens.[30] The place seemed now a foreign and at times an evil land to these outcasts. The wrinkle in the story was that these foreigners waged a war as if this land was rightfully their home.

Their common objectives allowed both conservative Christianity to grow and liberation theologies to gain prominence because the revolution of the sixties was yet another episode of disestablishment, of America finding a new home.[31] There

---

28 See Peter Berger, *The Heretical Imperative* (New York: Anchor Books, 1979).

29 *The Sixties* (New York: Washington Square Press, 1982), p. 15.

30 I have borrowed the term "cosmic alienation" from William Becker but put it to slightly different use. See his, "The 1960s and Today's Vision of America," *The Christian Century*, 29 May 1985.

31 One further, though ironic, indication of this lay in the experiences of many Roman Catholic youths of this period. They rejoiced and quickly adapted to the death of the Latin mass and the emergence of the folk mass. Enthusiasm also accompanied the permission to

had been too little room for distinctive religious commitment in the immediate post-war period though it is surprising nonetheless that the 1950s witnessed the highest percentage of individuals attending church in American history. To the Jesus people and early feminist theologians, church attendance was evidence not of a robust religious faith, but of institutionalized control of religion by ecclesiastical bureaucrats. In the 1960s religion was searching for a home outside of the church.

The Secularization of Theology

Another paradox of religious life in the 1960s concerned the secularization of theology in the academy and the apparently overt emphasis upon the supernatural in emergent religious groups (including the cults) of the 1960s. The paradox was this: If theology was radicalized in the 1960s, why did the most radical of theologies in the period (the death of God theology) last such a short period? Why did liberation theologies emerge at the end of the decade as viable alternatives to the death of God theologies? Why did conservative campus ministries explode in the decade while university cultures became more hostile to religious faith? The answers lied in part in the reality that theologies no longer led culture but were becoming the servants of culture. The "cultural elites" no longer occupied chairs in the religious departments of the major universities. Instead the shapers of culture (and importantly the religious elements of culture) were those able to rally large segments of the population to an awareness of their own rights.[32]

The death of God was a fad in the 1960s lacking a substantive and sustained conceptual integrity and therefore offered only a limited appeal in the academy, which was after all its only natural environment. Therefore it was able to be "used" for purposes beyond its ideological capacity, to challenge the status quo and thereby awaken the consciousness of many oppressed minorities in the world, students, women, people of color, religious dissidents, even charismatics. As was the case in the Second Great Awakening, the religious outsiders in the 1960s took center stage, in part, because of the success of their democratic impulses in the face of institutionalization.[33]

---

eat meat on Fridays. At the outset of the decade, these youths experienced life in America as outsiders. By the end of the decade, they had found a new home, by way of a new president, a new music, and a new openness to things American.

[32] I want to be careful not to claim that this phenomenon had no historical precedent in North America. It surely did and therefore the claim here is that the cycle of populist religious leadership is most likely repeating itself as it had in earlier periods of America's religious history.

[33] Though Nathan Hatch in *The Democratization of American Christianity* (New Haven: Yale University Press, 1989) does not draw the parallel directly between the Second and Fourth Great Awakening, his framework for understanding the Second Great Awakening seems well suited for the Fourth Great Awakening as well.

At the heart of the radicalization of theology in this period was the rejection of an older Barthian emphasis upon the transcendence of God. The radical secularization of theology which the "Death of God" movement trumpeted sounded the death knell to theology done in the manner of the early twentieth century. Near the heart of the evangelical and charismatic response to the Death of God movement was a resolute unwillingness to cognitively negotiate the transcendence of God. But it was not thereby an implicit affirmation of the older notions of God's transcendence. The evangelical and charismatic movements, as well as the diverse movements of liberation theology were deeply anti-institutional, driven in large measure by a contextual understanding of the presence of God. For the revolutionary movements of the 1960s God was not known in the atemporal, timeless fashion of neo-orthodoxy. God was known at the center of an individual's unique and unrepeatable experience. God was found not "out there" but "in here."[34] In the hands of the evangelical and charismatic movements God's transcendence was reinterpreted as a divine presence different from the individual but known preeminently in the experiences of the individual.

To borrow Steven Tipton's term, religious protests against Protestant neo-orthodoxy manifested a sense of being an "alternative religion," by which they neither repeated the traditions from which they arose nor completely abandoned them. Rather they were reinterpreted to allow the adherents to make sense of their lives in the America of the 1960s. Though theology was being radicalized in the academy, the cognitive denial of God's transcendence remained in the Academy and therefore highly institutionalized. Cognitive bargaining of a different sort was rampant in the counterculture of the 1960s. The Death of God theologians still spoke in decontextualized fashion about a God who no longer mattered. What emerged after this theological fad was not the abandoning of God, but rather the suffusion of God into the very fabric of personal experience, in particular the experience of those who stood outside the mainstream of culture. The democratization of God's presence was neither voted upon nor legislated, though the music of the era amply recorded it. Neither the academy nor mainline churches were genuine alternatives for the counterculture in the 1960s. The funeral procession gathering in culture was not for God. In the oft repeated phrase of Robert Fitch, "the real candidate for interment is a lesser chap by the name of Liberal Protestantism."[35]

The movements of liberation and the evangelical and charismatic movements were genuine alternatives to the status quo. In reality the battle over the death of God was not a cognitive battle but rather a battle about institutional authority and on this reading evangelicalism was as firmly countercultural as were the liberation movements related to race, gender and ethnicity. The neo-orthodox theologies of Karl Barth and Reinhold Niebuhr in the 1950s emphasized the depravity of human nature and its

---

34 See David Wells' study, *God in the Wasteland* (Grand Rapids: Eerdmans, 1994) for an astute treatment of the cognitive bargaining inherent in evangelicalism's alliance with modernity and their compromising of the transcendence of God.

35 Robert E. Fitch, "The Protestant Sickness," *Religion in Life* 35 (autumn 1966): 503.

tendency towards corruption which became manifest in the will to power and the place of pride in human actions. Allied with this was their fear of politics and mass action and emphasis on law and social restraint as a means of holding down the fanaticism latent in political passions. Astonishingly all these concerns and cautions vanished in the radical religious writings of the 1960s of the Death of God movement as well as in the large scale crusades of Billy Graham. New optimism about human nature and human powers began to appear. What emerged were theologies far more optimistic about human nature, and yet driven by a deep sense of the corruption of American culture. This was as true of the Jesus people as it was of black theologians.[36]

The Tools of Modernity

A final interpretative puzzle of the 1960s concerns the control of knowledge in the age of the information revolution. This manifested itself most especially with the appropriation of television in this era. The newly ubiquitous presence of the media assured that the sense of cultural crisis would be larger than life, that "crisis" itself would become a defining aspect of 1960s' existence. A simple consideration of the statistics reveals the almost inevitable cultural upheaval caused by the emergence of television in this era. In 1947 there were 10,000 TV sets in American households. By 1960 there were over 40 million. By 1965, 94 per cent of all American homes had a television whereas a decade earlier, less than 50 per cent did.[37]

The cultural conflict of the 1960s may have appeared to have been fought over rival ideologies about the nature of society but in reality the battle was "staged" as entertainment each week on television. The Kennedy-Nixon debates at the outset of the decade reinvented political campaigns as exercises in image control and therefore gave rise to increasing cynicism about government. J.F.K. was the first genuine media-produced President and his assassination had all the characteristics of live drama produced on television.[38] Nixon, himself was brought down during

36 Writing at the end of the decade, Peter Berger commented:

> the celebration of secularity that came to the fore in the theology of more recent years, of which John Robinson's *Honest to God* and Harvey Cox's *The Secular City* were popular high points, naturally turned to more cheerful anthropological perspectives. The moral mood came closer to an endorsement of "enjoy enjoy!" than to the earlier recommendations to be as anxious as possible. The social world was once more seen as an arena of purposeful action for human betterment rather than as a quagmire of futilities. *A Rumor of Angels: Modern Society and the Rediscovery of the Supernatural* (New York: Doubleday, 1970), p. 64.

37 This is reported in William L. O'Neill *Coming Apart: An Informal History of America in the 1960s* (Chicago: Quandrangle Books, 1971) and William E. Leuchtenburg, *A Troubled Feast: American Society Since 1945* (Boston: Little Brown and Co., 1973).

38 Revelations linking the assassination to the mob and the labor movement only add to the "drama" of the event.

the Watergate controversy in such ignominy because of the care of the Senate and House subcommittees' production of the investigation as a TV event. The disenchantment, which the nascent baby-boomers had in the 1960s, was profound but surreal, presented live each night on television and enacted in student protest movements on campuses distant from any real conflict.

The Vietnam War would have been a very different war if it had been fought under the media guidelines of World War II or the two Gulf Wars. The graphic scenes from Vietnam brought into the living rooms of America each night on the national news programs served to underscore the brutality of war and therefore its meaninglessness.[39] Television shaped the way America viewed the War and framed the existential questions of meaning about the war for American youth.[40]

Television not only shaped the cultural crisis but was part of the crisis itself. The protest over government policy in Southeast Asia was spearheaded by a vocal minority, largely the SDS and other organs of the New Left.[41] Though the protest centered on the morality of war, the underlying tone of the resistance movement centered on the informational authority (or secrecy) with which the war was waged. The media and the New Left, whose purposes were often subtly intertwined, were cultural agents fundamentally protesting the right to know. The crisis loomed over the American landscape, not because the American heritage was ambivalent about the morality of war, but rather because that same heritage contained deep ambiguities about the morality of knowledge and information, ambiguities that were skillfully exploited by the mass media in the decade. The movement for participatory democracy in the 1960s and the information explosion went hand in hand, though both were undermined by their modern by-product, mass culture.[42]

---

39 See Michael J. Arlen, *Living Room War* (New York: Penguin Books, 1982).

40 See Walter H. Capps, *The Unfinished War: Vietnam and the American Conscience* (Boston: Beacon, 1982) for the lingering moral dilemmas posed by the war.

41 The very best history of the New Left can be found in Maurice Isserman, *If I Had a Hammer ... The Death of the Old Left and the Birth of the New Left* (New York: Basic Books, 1987). For helpful accounts of the protest against the war see, Todd Gitlin, *The Sixties: Years of Hope, Days of Rage* (New York: Bantam, 1987) and Larry Berman, *Planning a Tragedy* (New York: Norton, 1982).

42 The debates about mass-culture were legion already in the 1960s but had little effect on the phenomena itself. The British commentator, Andrew Hacker, lamenting the "radicalization" of mass-culture, said of the 1960s:

> The very dangers and discomforts of American life result from removing controls that once lifted the minds and movements of those now unsettled by current conditions. Tensions and frustrations are bound to arise when 200 Million human beings demand rights and privileges never intended for popular distribution. It is too late in our history to restore order or re-establish authority: the American temperament has passed the point where self-interest can subordinate itself to citizenship. Calls for enlightened attitudes and concerted action will continue, but with little ultimate effect. Our history shaped our character, and that history will now run its course. *The End of An American Era* (New York: Atheneum, 1968), p. 8.

The language of mass culture in the 1960s was rock music. Many commentators have noted that rock music was able to bypass the normal channels of institutional information control and thereby created a mass following connected with causes.[43] But if rock music served the interests of protest, it also undermined them as well, especially in its alliance with capitalism.

The rock 'n' roll generation having grown up on popular culture took images very seriously indeed; beholding itself magnified in the funhouse mirror, it grew addicted to media which had agendas of their own—celebrity-making, violence-mongering, sensationalism.[44]

Ed Sullivan transformed an obscure singing group from Liverpool overnight into a dominant cultural force among the youth of the country. It was a craze that served to clearly mark out the generation gap. It also spurned on a new consumer subculture, which eventually lacked the moral resources for effective protest.

Legacy

There were genuine culture wars fought in America during the 1960s between conserving and progressive forces. The surprising reality is that conservatives could be viewed as progressives in the defense of the liberty of conscience against the tyranny of the federal bureaucracy. And further, progressives could be viewed as conservative in retrieving elements of the original ideology of individual rights defended by the founding fathers. The culture wars moved in several different and surprising directions. The divergent political/religious glosses of the 1960s were overlaid upon a complex and common foundation. The 1960s produced opponents on divergent ends of the political and religious spectrum from one another, but in remarkable ways, there was also actually a synthesis of older polarized ideologies manifest in movements wearing very different political and religious garb while underneath being uncommonly similar.[45]

---

43 See Bruce Pollock, *When the Music Mattered: Rock in the 1960s* (New York: Holt Rinhart and Winston, 1983).

44 Todd Gitlin, *The Sixties: Years of Hope, Days of Rage* (New York: Bantam, 1987). With unusual perceptiveness from a central player of the 60s, Norman Podhoretz writes in his autobiography, *Breaking Ranks: A Political Memoir* (New York: Harper and Row, 1979):

> I doubt if this kind of hypocrisy had ever before reached the brazen and comical heights it did in the sixties, when a whole new breed of hustlers (rock stars, publishing tycoons, drug dealers, and other enterprising entrepreneurs) amassed huge fortunes by preaching against "the rat race," "materialism," "consumerism," and "middle-class values" in general, while providing entertainment and other services to a new mass market defined precisely by its repudiation of such values, but still prosperous enough thanks to parental allowances and grandparental trust funds, to enrich those catering to its particular tastes (p. 13).

45 I am indebted to Steven Tipton's significant work, *Getting Saved From the Sixties* (Berkeley: University of California Press, 1981) for this point about a concluding

The enduring lesson of the 1960s reflected in all the paradoxes above is that appearances are sometimes deceiving. Or to put the matter in our context, the culture wars could be fought in part because of a common (though often unseen) commitment to the social structures of modernity and the nature of public discourse that arose from them.[46] Protesting the consequences of modernity was often performed with modern strategic forces. The platform of protest allowed divergent voices to protest, each using the same megaphone of modern media. It was a media that was constitutionally allied with the very forces against which the protests were lodged. Every side sought to bypass the institutional controls on information by going straight to the people, using democratic means against the modern democratic state, all the while being constrained within the commercial limits of that public discourse. And each side wanted a slice of the American dream—material well being in the here and now, while protesting the greed-based system of commercialism which perpetuated moral decay. In this respect the religious and cultural protests were often undermined by the very structures used to protest the status quo.

The revolutions of the 1960s were initiated by a profound cultural dissatisfaction with the ideological forces of modernity (hope in science, optimism regarding material and moral progress, the autonomy of reason) which in turn produced a forceful critique of them (science as contributing to war, the collapse of the notion of progress in the face of oppression, and the intrinsic prejudice of the status quo). Yet the very success of these revolutions depended to a great extent upon the culture-shaping institutions (technology, mass media, democracy and urbanization) which provided the social context for the ideological forces being condemned. This resulted in the apparent failure of the cultural revolutions of the 1960s to slow the progress of the ever encroaching social and institutional forces of modernity: technology, democratic capitalism and urbanization. One might go so far as to suggest that the revolutions of the 1960s actually prepared the way for the institutionalizing of the previous cultural outsiders: the ethnics and the evangelicals.

If we may refer to our era as "postmodern," it may also justly be referred to as "high modernity." In the present age there are no signs that modernity has lost any

---

synthesis. This is a controversial conjecture and it must be nuanced in important ways. So for example, Langdon Gilkey notices this synthesis as a distant possibility but believes the polarization thesis still adequately explains religious realities. See his *Society and the Sacred*. Even Harvey Cox, that notorious trend watcher, supposes that evangelicalism cannot be understood as a simple retreat from the progressivist vision and revolution of the 60s though he still does suppose there are in reality two fundamental ways to respond to the death of neo-orthodoxy—either in a conservative/evangelical or a progressive/liberationist fashion. See his, *Religion in the Secular City: Towards a Postmodern Theology* (New York: Simon and Schuster, 1984).

46 This is especially clear in the best treatment of the culture wars, James Hunter, *Culture Wars: The Struggle to Define America* (New York: Basic Books, 1991).

of its vital strength. The powers of modernity still rule the West (and increasingly the non-Western world). That most modern (and Western) of beasts, television, continues to spread its tentacles across the entire globe with a message of freedom and democracy but also convenience, commercialism and the cult of the self. It continues to motivate the masses both to protest and to servile consumerism. There are remnants of the counterculture of the 1960s which continue to question some of these values but the real change has come in the synthesis between the collapse of the Enlightenment ideology and the increasing power of tools which first came of age in the industrial revolution. Culture may no longer think of science as the cultural savior but not because technology is less pervasive. Optimism for the future may have been replaced with a profound confusion but there still remains within our culture an inability to take the notion of limits seriously. Though "reason" may no longer be autonomous in the older Enlightenment sense, there is still every indication that modern education is the key to success.

If modernity had been so profoundly criticized in the cultural revolutions of the 1960s, why is it that modernity seems largely unaffected and American culture barely takes notice? How is it that we live in an age that may be characterized as "postmodern" and "modern?" By my reckoning the conundrum is only a conundrum if cultural interpretation simply cuts and pastes together simple chronological events rather than construing the task as interpreting complex movements sometimes in conflict which are also often subconsciously overlapping. To that we turn in the next chapter.

Chapter 2
The Identity of Crisis: Postmodernity and the 1960s

> Some men see things as they are and say why. I dream things that never were and say why not?
>
> John F. Kennedy

Introduction: Ideas of Dissent and the Culture of Dissent

The cultural upheavals of the 1960s were undoubtedly forms of protest against a perception about the "way things are." Dissent against the perceived establishment was the obvious storyline that bound the protests of the decade together on American soil. The obviousness of the claim suggests it needs little justification. The argument to follow is that the dissent of the 1960s was itself a dissent against central intuitions and structures of modernity—a revolt against the moral emptiness of affluence, the mechanization of human nature and the imperial nature of the American establishment. It was a dissent against a liberal establishment, but the dissent came from more than one direction and the role of religion in the dissent was quite complex. The optimism of the American spirit came under withering attack during the decade. Flags were burned. Draft cards were torn to shreds. Race riots destroyed whole cities. It felt to some as if the nation was being turned upside down. To those on the cultural bottom, it must have felt like the weight of the (established) world was finally off their backs. To those in power, it must have felt as if the country was coming apart at the seams.

Contrary to our collective memory of the decade, the dissent against the establishment came from many diverse angles, much of which was inspired by religious conviction. At other points religious believers protected the status quo with all their might. The complex story of religion in the decade suggests that religious conviction provided the resources for cultural dissent, it also even provided resources to stifle cultural dissent. A great irony of the decade (and one which continues to play itself out in America public life) is that religious conservatives in the 1960s were often the most vociferous in their protest against the establishment while many religious liberals often protected the status quo. Undoubtedly there were also religious conservatives protective of the establishment and religious liberals deeply engaged in dissent. And there were many with religious convictions who would not fit easily along the conservative/liberal spectrum. The standard cultural war typology of religious conservatives versus secular progressives does not tell the full story.

Surprising in the decade also was the relative success of the dissent in the face of establishment powers. To understand the success of the dissent requires the realization that dissent necessarily took place at two different levels. The widespread "cultural dissent" of the 1960s required an "ideological dissent" to legitimate claims against the status quo and to provide any chance of abiding significance. There was a conceptual narrative in addition to the cultural narrative which legitimated society's intuitions about the "way life is" and about "the way life could be." The conceptual narrative may not have been the prime motivation behind the intuitions, but without a conceptual story the intuitions would not have taken collective hold in the wider culture. Ideological debate and dissent provided the intellectual grid map(s) that appeared to mark out the terrain in which the culture lived out its intuitions.[1] The two were not related in precise causal fashion. At times great ideas led the way but more often than not, they served as justifications for the notion of change in the wider culture. They provided a plausibility to the emergence of trends which otherwise might have been stopped in their tracks. And true by contrast, cultural shifts took place often presaging a race of ideas intended to play catch up with the concrete reorientations of life.

This is to suggest that the cultural revolution of the 1960s was under girded by an antecedent and sometimes subsequent ideological revolution and it is that ideological change which we most closely identify with the language of postmodernity. The cultural upheaval was much more noticeable at the time and retains a privileged place in the popular memory of the era. The ideological upheaval of the era is not as well understood nor as well connected to the cultural shifts which took place on the surface. Religious belief and behavior was one of the significant connections between the changes taking place on the surface and below the surface.

Caught in the matrix of ideological dissent and cultural change was religious belief and behavior in the 1960s. Sometimes religious conviction halted change. At other times religious conviction propelled changes. The all-too-easy characterizing of religious conviction as a "conserving force" does not match with its reality in the decade. The public square was configured by an establishment often at odds with diverse religious communities, even as other religious communities were protected by the status quo. The ironies of these realities are often lost in our collective memories of the era.

---

[1] One could argue that conservative politics in the early 1960s was oriented towards the battle of ideas and that progressive politics often took ideas for granted turning them into political slogans for mass consumption. A conservative like William F. Buckley not only saw conservative politics as an outsider to the Nixon-Kennedy election debates, but that the establishment was about to falter because it lacked genuine intellectual firepower. Buckley often echoed the sentiments of Richard Weaver's dictum: "Ideas Have Consequences." See John A. Andrew, *The Other Side of the Sixties: Young Americans for Freedom and the Rise of Conservative Politics* (New Brunswick, NJ: Rutgers University Press, 1997).

The economic boom of the post-War period brought remarkable affluence to America and also appeared to make religious belief somewhat irrelevant. So arose the debates about secularization and the role of religion in the public square.[2] Most prominent (though not most rigorous) among the ideological debates in this vicinity was the Death of God movement. It was strikingly populist in tone if esoteric in its jargon. It was a movement that retroactively sought to justify the new found secularity of the nation. Little noticed, then or now, was that the movement's defense of secularity was primarily an affirmation of the actual secularizing process of the economic changes already well established. The movement was trying to legitimate a cultural change that had already taken place. So it was with other ideological debates of the time. They followed broader cultural changes rather than serving as a portent of things to come. In this they were trying to make sense of changes already taking place in popular culture.

The reverse is also true at times in the era. Slavery and segregation were indelibly imprinted on the minds of Black Americans at mid-century while largely ignored by the establishment white culture. The religiously conservative Black Church served as the primary fuel to protest the treatment of blacks in American culture at mid-century. The Civil Rights Movement was in the first instance primarily a religious movement given legitimization by its retrieval of traditional Christian themes of the dignity of all human persons and the yearning for the justice of God in human communities. It did not hurt the cause that the burgeoning new world of television brought the painful economic realities of black life into the family rooms of ordinary Americans night after night. Ideas mattered situated in the right cultural contexts.

It is the unique matrix of ideological dissent, cultural change and religious belief that I want to narrate by examining several key episodes of the 1960s. At times the focus will be on concrete movements of dissent with a distinctly religious or irreligious tone (such as The Civil Rights Movement and The Second Feminist Movement). At other times the focus will be the great ideological battles with important implications for the religious conviction (for example the rise of the New Left and the Death of Foundationalism). On both scores, the attempt shall be to weave these apparently contrasting narratives together into a (relatively) coherent whole as a means to understand our sense of the "before and after." It is important to situate the ideological debates in the concrete "lived protests" of the time and to explain the enduring significance of the cultural upheavals by taking note of the ideologies which persisted beyond the popular protests.

---

2 Surely this is an overly simple summary, but there can be little doubt that affluence and religious belief were tied together in inverse order throughout the twentieth century. The same can be said for higher education and religious belief in the twentieth century. On the former point, see Robert Wuthnow, *God and Mammon in America* (New York: Free Press, 1994). On the latter point, see George M. Marsden and Bradley J. Longfield, eds, *The Secularization of the Academy* (New York: Oxford University Press, 1992).

Postmodern Preliminaries

Most of the debates surrounding the character of postmodernity have to do with its relationship to modernity. Is the postmodern a repudiation of the modern or a radical extension of the modern?[3] The answer to those debates hinges on how one defines the modern period. Adjudicating when modernity begins and ends is somewhat arbitrary by virtue of the complexity of history. Time periods are not cleanly marked by signs popping out of the ground. More often they are marked by events of significance which make demands that cannot be interpreted away. If not entirely, epoch-defining events are self-interpreting, at least in part. Certain events are of such a magnitude that they "jump off the pages" of history, redefining history in its wake. The American Revolution and the Civil War were obvious cases in point. Revolutionary historical events resist the normal narrative structure of a society's life and thereby alter its own self-perception.

The issue is made more complex realizing that postmodernity is less of a chronological construct than an ideological construct. It is less a claim about a time period than about a mood with regard to wider events of social significance. It concerns convictions about the gravity of developments in technology, economics, and politics in the latter part of the twentieth century.[4] Its convictions are rooted in historical episodes without being merely historical. The chief manifestations of postmodernity were first in art and architecture.[5] Its defense emerged most clearly in the work of sociologists and philosophers.[6] Its prophetic voices dispersed the construct across a multitude of pop culture platforms. In each of these, postmodernity was/is concerned less with what happened, than why it happened and what it meant when it happened. It is an interpretation of history rooted in history's own sense of itself.[7]

---

3 For a helpful review of the respective arguments see Johannes Willem Bertens, *The Idea of the Postmodern: A History* (New York: Routledge, 1995). The debates are cast in theological terms helpfully in the collection of essays edited by Claude Geffre and Jean-Pierre Jossua, *The Debate on Modernity* (London: SCM Press, 1992).

4 See Albert Borgmann, *Crossing the Postmodern Divide* (Chicago: University of Chicago Press, 1992) and Thomas Carmichael and Alison Lee, eds, *Postmodern Times: A Critical Guide to the Contemporary* (DeKalb, IL: Northern Illinois University Press, 2000).

5 See Paul A. Bove, "Preface: Literary Postmodernism," in Paul A. Bove, ed. *Early Postmodernism: Foundational Essays* (Durham: Duke University Press, 1995).

6 One of the earliest (and it remains one of the most influential) expositions of postmodernism is found in the philosopher Richard Rorty's work, *Philosophy and the Mirror of Nature* (Princeton: Princeton University Press, 1979).

7 There is a significant (but small) debate within literary circles as to whether postmodernism can be construed as a historical construct. The dispute concerns whether periodizing the concept neglects the manner in which all of history is reinterpreted. See Kathryn V. Lindberg and Joseph G. Kronick, eds, *America's Modernisms: Revaluing The Canon* (Baton Rouge: Louisiana State University Press, 1996).

In each of the disciplines where the discourse of postmodernity was/is raised, there appeared a growing realization that the world had changed, or at least our understanding of the world had changed. We thought differently about how our understanding of the world related to the world itself. For a host of reasons, fundamental assumptions about this relationship changed. Certain intuitions were no longer taken for granted while new convictions quite suddenly were taken for granted. Part of the equation was that the world (of technology, economics and politics) changed, but a larger part of the equation was that fundamental assumptions about the world changed.

Few doubt that humans can do much more than was thought possible fifty or a hundred years ago, let alone a millennium ago. Our tools are much more powerful and their power is more widely available across a larger segment of the population. Those tools have made life far more efficient and have brought greater affluence by comparison to previous ages. Efficiency and affluence impact the way we relate to others and how we think about ourselves. Television reshaped our sense of belonging no longer to a neighborhood but to a whole world. Jet travel greatly shrunk our sense of distance while the computer shrunk our sense of time and space. So much more could be done and done quickly. A striking fact of these modern tools and one not always noticed is the way in which they reorder the inner consciousness, the way they exert enormous social pressure to reshape our perceptions of the world.[8] This is to say that we think differently about the world we live in because of the world we live in.

This critical dynamic of human identity is important in any discussion of the cultural context. Naively, some suppose the world has changed while they have remained relatively unchanged. The world may be filled with technological innovations undreamt about fifty years ago, cyberspace-related toys, space-travel gadgets and advanced medical tools, but the greater change has occurred in how individuals relate to that world, what they think about themselves and last but surely not the least the ways in which their religious faith has been transformed. These changes do not affect everyone in precisely the same way, nor is there a universal set of assumptions that everyone now shares as a result of living in the

[8] Tools and technology are central to the description of postmodernity that follows. The story could have begun elsewhere. However, technological shifts have been so dramatic in the last century as to provide a reasonably efficient way to start the narrative. The linkage between technology and the reordering of grand cultural norms is very well established in the literature by now. See: Jacques Ellul, *The Technological Society*, translated from the French by John Wilkinson (New York: Alfred Knopf, 1964); Albert Borgmann, *Technology and the Character of Contemporary Life: A Philosophical Inquiry* (Chicago: University of Chicago Press, 1984), David Harvey, *The Condition of Postmodernity: An Enquiry into the Origins of Cultural Change* (Oxford: Basil Blackwell. 1989), Neil Postman, *Technopoly* (New York: Knopf, 1992), David E. Nye, *Narratives and Spaces: Technology and the Construction of American Culture* (Exeter: University of Exeter Press, 1997).

present world. However, the undeniable power of modern tools lie as much in their power upon us as the power they give us.[9]

Discussion of the tools of the contemporary world leads in two directions, towards the explanation of the tools themselves and conversely of their general impact upon humankind. By now several trends seem clear. The tools of our time have forced a unique interaction between a wider diversity of cultures of the globe and with far greater intensity. These tools have also empowered individuals in a manner that (relatively) frees them from the constraints of older institutions. These tools are made available to individuals as consumers in an economy of market networks. Respectively, these phenomena are those of globalization, democratization and commodification, each in turn being central to the large conceptual changes of the last half century.

Globalization

Globalization is the realization that individuals are citizens of the globe even if their passports do not manifest it.[10] They inhabit a planet of enormous cultural diversity. That is impressed upon them each day.[11] Most take this for granted though it was not always this way. Advances in transportation powered the rise of the colonial empires in the fifteenth and sixteenth centuries. National economies were transformed as a result and the epoch of world exploration commenced. European civilization grew dominant for the very reasons that they exploited these new realities. The advent of sustained cross-cultural interactions was fueled by the new modes of transportation and by the volume of trade carried along the routes of the colonial empires of England, Portugal and Holland. The globe was growing ever more intertwined as the Europeans economically exploited more and more of the globe. Ironically the globe also grew smaller as people groups came into far more pervasive and persistent contact with the Europeans. The loss of the limitations of geography also slowly eroded the European's sense of identity, while in the 1960s it cemented an American's sense of identity. The melting pot mythology of American history seemed uniquely suited to the era of jet travel, the television and Civil Rights.

---

[9] Ellul, Jacques, *On Religion, Technology, and Politics / Conversations with Patrick Troude-Chastenet*, translated from the French by Joan Mendès, France (Atlanta, Ga.: Scholars Press, 1998). See also Albert Borgmann, *Power Failure: Christianity in the Culture of Technology* (Grand Rapids, MI: Brazos Press, 2003).

[10] The most able treatment of the distinction between global and national cultures is *Global Culture: Nationalism, Globalization and Modernity*, ed. Mike Featherstone (London: Sage Publications, 1990).

[11] Peter L. Berger, and Samuel P. Huntington, eds, *Many Globalizations: Cultural Diversity in the Contemporary World* (New York: Oxford University Press, 2002).

In general terms, the industrial revolutions of the eithteenth and nineteenth centuries introduced major changes to transportation (coal fired engines, steam-powered trains and ships) and created new economies of scale within the western world.[12] Exploration continued at a furious pace across North America. Western civilization spread its tentacles yet further, taming the "uncivilized" world. Monopolies were built with the acquisition of new tools and capital markets were greatly expanded. The limits on human achievement seemed to lessen in proportion to the increase in technological advances. Modern domination was a function of the power of the tools, unfortunately manifest also in the domination of whole people groups for economic and political reasons. The plantation economies of cotton and sugar in the southern United States were the most notable evidence of this domination and the most persistent in the post-Colonial imagination.

The transportation revolutions of the twentieth century (automobile and plane) reordered population patterns into suburban/urban frameworks as well as serving to economically deepen the divide between the first and third worlds. The tools of transportation helped to modify central assumptions about time and space. Westerners were less likely to think of themselves as "tied down" to a space or time. The trip across America had taken nearly eight months at the beginning of the eighteenth century, and merely two weeks by the end of the nineteenth century. By the 1960s it could be accomplished in less than a day. By the 1960s Americans were also becoming more fully citizens of the world, able to fly to Cape Town or Calcutta with the same ease they could get to California. They were also able to watch the events of the entire globe unfold before their very eyes with the widespread distribution of televisions in the period immediately preceding the 1960s. The narrative of progress served to legitimate this brave new world where the old boundaries and limitations were melting away into thin air.[13] Anything seemed possible—and quickly.

But if the twentieth century dawned with the spirit of optimism and triumph, it is also true that spirit quickly dissipated in the 1960s. Reflecting now a half century past the 1960s, it is safe to say that the events of the twentieth century were not kind to American optimism. The two World Wars, most especially World War II with the holocaust, the Cold War and its accompanying tensions, the tragedies of Vietnam and Watergate along with the assassinations of John F. Kennedy and Martin Luther King, each contributed to the cracking of the edifice of self-assurance. The demise of the colonial empires in the 1960s also signaled a waning of the triumphal spirit of the West, even if television extended the West's commercial and cultural influence more pervasively than any colonial empire could

---

[12] Albert Borgmann argues in compelling fashion that the era of modernity was the era of domination most clearly characterized in the building of the American railroads in the nineteenth century. See his, *Crossing the Postmodern Divide* (Chicago: University of Chicago Press, 1992).

[13] Marshall Berman reflects this imagery in his cultural history of the late twentieth century, *All That is Solid Melts into Air* (New: York: Simon and Schuster, 1982).

have.[14] The new superpowers of the twentieth century had held out hope of a new world order but now fell under a moral suspicion in the rest of the world, precisely because of their superpower military might. Great modern military tyrannies came crashing down before the twentieth century was over but not before the world realized the danger of the weapons of mass destruction, whoever controlled them. As the globe grew ever smaller, so did the fragility of human co-existence. The spirit of the 1960s framed a protest against the (dangerous) powers-that-be, while also concluding that there were no other ideal alternatives. The end result: a culture bordering on the cynical.[15]

Personal security seemed much more precarious the more life changed and the quicker those changes occurred. Convictions about who "we" were also changed as the melting pot of American culture increasingly added new ingredients to the soup. America was becoming less distinctive with the blending of so many cultures and the increasing awareness of cultural differences. Identity seemed deeply rooted in the strangeness of this new set of cultural interactions, increasingly highlighting the differences of religion, ethnicity and gender. Americans were citizens of a globe, which was both decreasing in size (with the power of technology to span it) and increasing in size (with the awareness of its cultural differences). What were Americans to think about themselves? Who were they supposed to be? How were Americans supposed to relate to the "other?" These questions animated the original debates about postmodernity in America, suggesting not that the modern world of technology had changed, but that somehow human identity had changed in the midst of the modern world.[16]

All of this pointed to a much deeper "pluralization" of modern life or what may be called a "pluralist impulse." At mid-century most Americans were well aware of the many diverse cultures that inhabited the earth. It may have been an unprecedented awareness though it was less conscious and more visceral. Each evening the entire globe was brought into a family's living room through the vehicle of the national news. Far away lands like Vietnam and Russia were no longer very far away. American neighborhoods slowly began to manifest this global character as well. No longer was the blend simply that of Scotch Presbyterians residing beside Irish Catholics. Indonesian Muslims and Sri Lankan Hindus were likely to be neighbors if you lived on the East or West coast. The old world European neighborhoods were true only in mythological form. Economies were likewise increasingly global in structure—interest rate rises in America were

---

[14] Harold MacMillan, the British Prime Minister gave his famous "Wind of Change" speech in 1960 in Cape Town, South Africa, announcing the beginning of independence for the African colonies of Britain. By the end of the decade most of the African nations were free from colonial rule.

[15] See Dick Keyes, *Seeing Through Cynicism: A Reconsideration of the Power of Suspicion* (Downers Grove, IL: IVP Books, 2006).

[16] Succeeding chapters on the Civil Rights (3), The New Left (4) and Feminism (5) will lay out this argument in much greater detail.

tied (if indirectly) to economic structures in the Far East as well as ethnic tensions in the Middle East. This "global village" was presented as a reality which did not initially require philosophical justification or reflection. The medium simply asked for the acceptance of its reality, not a requirement to think about it. The pluralization of life must be embraced if only because that's the way life is.

When the phenomena of this "global village" became internalized, people began to think not simply of diverse religions, but rather of religion as diverse. Religion appeared to relate not to something "out there" but rather to the inner experience of individuals, otherwise how could we possibly adjudicate the conflicting truth claims of the diverse religious traditions. Some religious thinkers inevitably protested the move towards pluralization and provided significant dissent from the powers-that-be on this. When Eisenhower declared in 1954, "Our Government makes no sense unless it is founded on a deeply held religious faith, and I don't care what it is," many viewed it as an affirmation of the establishment of religion so ambiguous and pluralized as not to permit real genuine religious conviction. The civil religion of the political establishment at mid-century seemed to some hopelessly enamored with a religion so subjective as to prohibit any concrete religious tradition speaking with conviction into the public square. Evangelicals and Roman Catholics created whole new television networks in this period because they had been officially prohibited by the FCC from having any air time on the three main public television networks. By outward accounts conservative, evangelicals and Roman Catholics nonetheless were excluded from the fraternity of pluralized civil religion. They forcefully protested the homogenization of religion as the best means to protect the breadth of religious traditions. They may have articulated different versions of "old time religion" but they were persuaded concrete religious traditions must be given a voice in the modern world.

Under the pressure of "pluralization" a fragmentation of religious and cultural experiences was affirmed if somewhat cautiously. Too many feared a return to the religious wars of seventeenth and eighteenth century Europe if religion was allowed out of the cultural closet. In this regard there was increasing pressure to pluralize both institutions and plausibility structures, giving no one religious group significant authority or voice. The contested outcome of the strategy was the embrace of relativism—all religious traditions being considered equally true. Some openly embraced this reorientation of religion, while others sought to navigate around it. All sides recognized the intractability of the conditions that gave rise to the dilemma. Pluralization was accepted as a brute fact and the consequent loss of confidence in a religious consensus engendered by it proved to be a most significant issue in American public discourse.[17]

---

[17] Lasch, Christopher, *The True and Only Heaven: Progress and Its Critics* (New York: Norton, 1991).

Democratization

If technology and transportation brought radical shifts to an individual's sense of place on the globe, equally great were those shifts brought about by the ripple effects of the modern politics of democracy. The American Revolution had been a revolt narrowly constrained by the issues of taxation and representation. Yet it was part of a much larger revolt against institutions of authority that had governed nations previously. In America, democracy was never simply a political theory about the election of governing officials. Its sweep was far wider and its reach far more profound. It has been a cultural framework that unified many disparate social elements. It was the displacement of the privilege of a few to lead by the right of everyone to lead themselves. It prized individuals and was suspicious of established institutions. In this wider and deeper sense, democratization was the diffusion of authority into the populace at large. Authority dispersed was better than authority collected, or so most people throughout American history generally believed.

In this regard, the American experience had less to do with the specifics of democratic polity or formal theories of economics than with the infusion of authority, especially of a commodified form, across popular culture. As a democratized culture, America worked to deny the intrinsic distinctions of class, refusing to believe that any one group was better than another. Virtue was associated with the ordinary or common person rather than elites and was better expressed in the simple vernacular than in complicated and abstract prose. As a result, institutional constraints of individual freedoms have been viewed with distrust and populist leadership was more effective than learned and reflective leadership. The correct solution to virtually every problem of note lay embedded in the people's choice.[18]

The American revolution was an experiment whose central force was the individual, and whose moral integrity was championed against the forces of institutionalization. The revolution was a fight for freedom, freedom from the controls of the institutions of the old order—a centralized church, a hierarchical government, and an economic caste system. In each of these spheres, the moral authority of the individual was prized over that of institutions.

The central threat to the power of individuals during the era of modernity in America has been economic institutions rather than ecclesiastical or political ones. With the rise of the new tools that fueled globalization, came also the increasing "reach" of new forms of institutions, the centralized bureaucracies that sought to organize and administer human relations for economic benefit, often as a mirror image of the new tools. In these bureaucracies, people related to each other as parts of a large machine, efficiently and predictably. Early into the twentieth century, most Americans took the functional organization of society for granted, as the unproblematic context of life. People were no longer craftsmen but increasingly

---

[18] See Nathan Hatch, *The Democratization of American Christianity* (New Haven: Yale University Press, 1989) Ch. 8.

specialists within a bureaucracy. By the 1960s the "system" of human relations created its own form of protest, a therapeutic revolution.[19] Feeling powerless to control the bureaucracy, people inevitably turned inwards hoping to control their own subjective resources. This translated into a longing for self-esteem and significance. Significance was defined as the ability to fully express one's deepest self. It was to be freed from the constraints of externally defined standards. It was the freedom to pursue what one really wanted. At bottom it was an attempt to reestablish the foundational authority of the individual.

The tug-of-war between the individual and the institution was also reflected in the reorganization of life into separate spheres: workplace and home, work and leisure, white collar and blue collar, public and private. The division of life into these separate functional sectors permitted the individual a safe haven (in the latter spaces) from the pervasive influences of institutional dynamics. Domesticity, love, and intimacy increasingly were viewed as outside the realm of institutional realities.[20] Inside the institution, specialization increased and functional identity became greater. Outside the institution the individual could express their true selves.[21]

The problems inevitably lay in the intersections of these spheres. Individuals had to relate across the borders. They had to play different roles at different times during the day. And they weren't always entirely sure where their ultimate loyalties lay. Under such conditions the major dilemmas of life appeared as negotiating a reliable and harmonious balance among the various sectors of life. But these negotiations were difficult and exhausting. The sustained and continual crossing of the borders led to a thinning of the self, no longer were people sure of who they really were underneath all their different roles.[22] It was as if a person were simultaneously a resident of the United States and also Cuba. Each morning they got on the jetliner and flew from Boston to Havana and each evening flew back the other way. They instinctively knew the one country was large, affluent and religiously ambiguous and the other a deeply devout and rigidly socialist country. In the one world all of the talk centered around the latest immoral behavior of politicians, movie stars or sports celebrities. In the other world all the talk centered on fidelity and devotion to the latest mandates of Castro. In the one world, money was everywhere. In the other country, poverty was everywhere. Living in these two worlds simultaneously would produce what sociologists might call "cognitive dissonance." Psychologists might have called it "schizophrenia", philosophers

---

19 See Philip Reiff, *The Feeling Intellect.* (Chicago: University of Chicago Press, 1991) and David F. Wells, *Losing Our Virtue* (Grand Rapids, MI: Eerdmans, 1998).

20 An early work by Christopher Lasch captured this diagnosis well, *Haven in a Heartless World: The Family Besieged* (New York: Basic Books, 1977).

21 This is the argument of the now classic work by Robert Bellah and associates, *Habits of the Heart Individualism and Commitment in American Life* (Berkeley CA: University of California Press, 1985).

22 Christopher Lasch, *The Minimal Self: Psychic Survival in Troubled Times* (New York: Norton, 1984).

might have referred to it as a "fundamental conflict of world views." But most people would experience it simply as a mess. So was the cultural experience of crossing the borders of segmented lives.

As a means of coping with the tension intrinsic to these border crossings, individuals became therapists and managers of themselves. As their own manager, their task was to organize human and non-human resources available to them so as to improve their position in the marketplace. Inside organizations their role was to persuade, inspire, manipulate, cajole, and intimidate those around them so that their own sense of importance to the organization increased. They were attempting to measure up to criteria given by the marketplace and specifically laid out by those in control of the organization. In most modern bureaucracies there was always somebody "above," whose expectations determined the success of one's managerial tasks, including the chief executive who had a board to which they answered in principle. On the institutional side of the self-identity question, the individual always was looking over their shoulder for approval, and scrambling to make sure that approval persisted. The problem was the number of factors over which they had no control but which nonetheless directly affected their success or failure. Managing oneself was hard enough, but attempting to manage other people who were neither so predictable nor controllable proved to be the greatest obstacle to enduring institutional satisfaction.

Given that the management of one's own institutional image was precarious, individuals sought to find a more enduring significance elsewhere, at home or at leisure or among friends. These spheres appeared at times to be protected from the whims of the marketplace. These were private spaces promising to give a measure of self-fulfillment. Here each individual dealt with resources largely internal to themselves and were free to pursue their own intuitions about personal satisfaction. It was the essence of the therapeutic task to find those private spaces where self-esteem could be found in the unbounded pursuit of one's own enjoyment.

These public and private roles often contrasted sharply as symbolized by the daily commute from the green suburban settings reminiscent of rural life to the industrial technological ambience of the workplace. But as with the commute in traffic, so with the daily commute from private to public and back, most knew the trip was long, tiresome and frustrating. It was an emotionally draining task each day to drive with the rest of the nameless commuters on the highways and back-road short cuts. It was even harder to keep the two worlds emotionally linked though they were financially joined at the hip. Without the material rewards of work, the pursuit of leisure was impossible. The stress therefore tended to flow in one direction, from work to home, from work to leisure, from work to relationships. How was one to know how to act in this complicated set of negotiations? What became clear in the modern world, was the ambiguity of an individual's identity in this segmented culture.

An individual not only had more choices to make, but was bound to make so many choices in life, it appeared many of them were artificial. Many have argued that movement from fate to choice was/is characteristic of modern consciousness.[23] The vast array of things possible with the advent of the industrial and technological revolutions made it appear that individuals could do virtually anything their heart desired.[24] They were not bound by the fates of history any longer.[25] The power of their tools created so many more choices than could have been imagined by any earlier civilization.

Consider the international traveler who carried these choices on their person in symbolic form in the 1960s. At the airport, they could change their plane ticket and fly to Paris instead of London. With the advent of easy credit in the 1930s and 1940s, they could use that little plastic pearl of great price to get currency at either destination they chose. Their money was tied to a stock market whose gyrations rippled from New York to Tokyo to London. All these choices however, represented only a small slice of an enormously larger array of choices that were part of the taken-for-granted fabric of their lives as the second half of the twentieth century got underway. There were choices of occupation, choices of place of residence, choices of marriage partner, choices of the number of one's children, choices of one's vacation destination. The list went on almost endlessly with regard to the external arrangements of life. But there were other choices, inner choices that also deeply touched the consciousness of individuals. These were the choices of life-style, the choices of religious preference and choices of moral norms.[26] "Choice" became the operative mental category in modern life and "freedom" was its politically popular translation.

The more choices the more reflection. The individual who reflected became more conscious of themselves. They turned their attention from the objectively given outside world to their own subjectivity. As people did this, two things happened simultaneously: the outside world became more questionable and their own inner world became more complex.[27] People became more suspicious of any solution that appeared as the "only" one. The hegemony of truth itself came under severe scrutiny. Individuals also came to experience themselves as being alone in a way that was unthinkable in traditional cultures, deprived of the social solidarity of their collectivity, uncertain of the norms by which life was to be governed and

---

[23] Peter Berger is the most notable of the sociologists who have argued this. See his *The Heretical Imperative: Contemporary Possibilities of Religious Affirmation* (Garden City, N.Y.: Anchor Press, 1979).

[24] See Albert Borgmann, *Power Failure.*

[25] The modern technology associated with birth control permits, nay demands, that one side of the debate be labeled "pro-choice"—indicative of the sociological reality of modernity. Undoubtedly the language of "choice" is also embedded in the subjective turn in morality, viz. that morality arises primarily from the human subject.

[26] Other examples abound. The abortion debates have been caste in terms of "choice" as is the controversy over sexual preferences in the last decade.

[27] Peter L. Berger, *Modernity, Pluralism and the Crisis of Meaning: The Orientation of Modern Man* (Gütersloh: Bertelsmann Foundation Publishers, 1995).

finally uncertain of who or what they were. Individuals became the center of all choices but they were often an empty center.[28] Being overwhelmed by the plethora of choices became more pervasive as the number of choices themselves grew ever greater. There were too many choices to make and too few criteria to make them.

Religion both exploited the language of choice and was appalled by it. Evangelicals made much of the language of a "personal decision for Jesus" while also eschewing the freedom of choice accorded to teenagers regarding sex and drugs in the decade. Black Churches rallied around the language of freedom hearkening back to traditional themes of the American revolution while effectively protesting the legacy of the American experiment on race relations. Women began to protest the constraints on their choices against the backdrop of what they believed was the religiously inspired hierarchy of the "traditional family." The home was no longer a safe haven for them but rather a place of quiet desperation. It was ironic then that Pentecostal and charismatic churches were in the vanguard promoting the ordained role of women in the church. These theologically conservative, culturally backward traditions were surprisingly very progressive on gender roles.

Commodification

One of the central historical processes of the twentieth century was the triumph of the commodity form.[29] Cognizant of the number of choices to be made in the modern world, people were often reduced to making choices motivated in large measure by their role as consumers. They chose because of the ubiquitous pressure to act as buyers of some perceived set of goods. From this perspective, objects received their primary value as objects for sale to someone else. Objects were perceived as commodities. When those objects were then placed into a carefully crafted network of rationalized exchange of goods, a full blown commercialization took place. In the modern period, commodification and resultantly, commercialization took on a relentless and carefully calculated life of their own, reaching their zenith when everything imaginable was a marketed commodity. Practically speaking there were no objects that were not bought and sold by the end of the 1960s. Commodification metastasized into every cell of human life. Even a short list of things available in commodity form by the 1960s reaffirmed the pervasive character of the commercialized character of modernity: food, water, house, clothes, insurance, information, leisure and entertainment, education and information. Inevitably people began to think they could buy a part of their own identity, be it with their purchase of clothes or cologne, a house in the

[28] Kenneth J. Gergen, *The Saturated Self: Dilemmas of Identity in Contemporary Life* (New York: Basic Books, 1990).

[29] Cf. George Ritzer, *Explorations in the Sociology of Consumption: Fast Food, Credit Cards and Casinos* (London: SAGE, 2001) and Stephen Fjellman, *Vinyl Leaves: Walt Disney World and America* (Boulder: Westview Press, 1992).

suburbs or a vacation on Miami Beach. Purchasing power was easily interpreted as the power of self-fulfillment.

The original rationality of the markets in colonial America lay in terms of wider distribution of goods and the maximization of profit for society in general. The initial phase of doubt regarding this economic rationality appeared when manufacturing capabilities outstripped the apparent demand for the commodities that could be produced in the industrial revolution of the nineteenth century. Too many goods could be produced for the number of people who actually thought them useful. The crisis became a crisis of demand. It was solved in part by the introduction of personal consumption on a mass basis. The great expansion of personal credit, the explosion of advertising and the creation of "desires" for commodities early in the twentieth century all contributed to the eruption of a new kind of democratized capitalism. Part of the promise of this new economic system was abundance. In America (white) citizens had been assured of certain political rights but as the nation fought its way out of the Great Depression in the 1930s and experienced the boom years of the 1950s, most everyone believed they had a right to acquire as much of the material goods being spewed forth from the nation's factories as they could. This meant that people's energies were primarily directed towards their fulfillment as a consumer. The original vision of economic rationality was replaced eventually by the unleashing of desire as the ultimate motivation for every choice. What every person wanted (or were persuaded by marketers that they wanted) they deserved. Desires became ends in themselves. People were seduced into thinking all their desires were worth satisfying, especially those desires trumpeted in the marketplace of mass culture.

The irony of this pervasive commercialization was that the desires themselves eventually were commodified. The fulfillment of desires was achieved by paying attention to those desires that could be fulfilled with the available goods. The narrowing of fulfillable desires was a function of the market. People purchased the gratification of their desires in part by locating those desires that could be gratified by means of an economic transaction. The market responded less to consumers, than consumers responded to the market.

What was uniquely characteristic at mid-century and beyond was that personal consumption oriented itself increasingly towards images or symbols rather than concrete objects. Actual wealth was not as important as the status and image of wealth. In the 1950s the color of one's stove, or the size of the wings on one's Cadillac manifested one's significance. In the 1960s with the dramatic increase in jet travel and disposable income, the location of one's vacation home became a new status symbol.[30] The symbols of status became a substitute for any enduring substance. The crafting of a self-image was an all-important activity and that image was itself a function of a consumer appetite for consumption. It was a driving

---

30 Gary Cross, *An All Consuming Century: Why Commercialism Won in Modern America* (New York: Columbia University Press, 2002), p. 179 argues that by 1960 two million Americans already owned a second home, a sharp increase from the previous decade.

impulse behind many of the choices of life. Consider the dominant marketing images that emerged from the media from the mid-century onwards; McDonalds, Walt Disney World, the Caribbean, the Concert, the Shopping Mall, the Football Game. These new symbolic worlds have only a tangential relation to reality, though reality has in part been redefined by the images. These marketing images include powerful forces that compel individuals to purchase the image, somehow supposing that their well-being is enhanced by their purchase. The common assumption that goods were purchased for a certain utility, e.g. cars purchased as reliable means of transportation, now seems naïve. The perception nearer the truth was that goods were purchased for their association with symbolic goods of significance, security and power. Cars were sold situated in beautiful landscapes connoting peace, or with scantily clad women connoting lust fulfillment, or with speed connoting power. Each of these betrayed the purely functional purpose of the car as a mode of transportation. Each in turn reshaped how people viewed their significance in a commodified culture.

But all was not peaceful in a world of abundance. Benjamin Braddock was the reluctant anti-hero of the 1967 blockbuster film, *The Graduate*, played memorably by Dustin Hoffman.The character of Benjamin was a recent graduate from college and embarking on life as an adult. He was exploited and seduced, much to his own delight, by his father's business partner's wife. At one of the high points of the film during a cocktail party, Ben was given advice by his father's business partner to "go into plastics." Hoffman provided a puzzled look on his face even while the audience recognized the blatant symbolism of the advice. The burgeoning new manufacturing industry came to represent the superficial character of the adult world to a generation raised on abundance. "To be plastic" meant to be shallow and artificial and to lack a depth of character. It was a stinging indictment of the young generation on the culture of affluence which their parents had fought so hard to create. The sharp rebuke of consumerism by the most affluent generation in American history served as one of the great ironies of the brave new world of the 1960s. Having everything was not everything it was cracked up to be.

The Postmodern State of Mind

The contours of the cultural narrative rehearsed above may be generally familiar by now, though still contested. The ideological story is undoubtedly less familiar though it follows a mirror outline in a decidedly ironic fashion. One of the central interpretive turns in that story in the second half of the twentieth century had been the reversing of the order of influence between ideological conviction and social reality. Most contemporary social theorists suppose ideas do not float free abstracted from social realities but rather are intimately tied to concrete social realities. The dominant direction of influence is from social structures towards the great ideas of the time. Knowledge is thought to be socially constructed in this sense. What a person "knows" is a function of the cultural conversation in which that person is embedded. The conversation of knowledge is constrained by the dominant social dynamics of an era. The conversation is always a contextualized discourse, rooted and grounded in social assumptions and practices. In our time and place, the contexts of globalization, democratization and commodification most clearly frame the conversation. It is those forces which are "taken for granted." It is those contexts which influence fundamental assumptions about the way the world is. Our common intuitions now suggest that ideas cannot be abstracted from their concrete contexts. These intuitions are pre-philosophical and not a result of a long and extended argument. They may more nearly be said to capture the tone or the mood of our thinking as distinct from being consequences of our through processes. In this sense it may be better to speak of the postmodern state of mind than a postmodern ideology.[31]

A central tenet of Enlightenment modernism was a sharp distinction between high and low culture.[32] The older (pre-modern) hierarchies of church, monarchy and class were abolished and were replaced by a new order. In the new order, ideas reigned. In particular the ideas of neutral and unbiased thinkers were privileged. A disinterested scholar was thought to be in a far superior position to knowing the world as it really was than any religious cleric or political appointee of period. The crisis of older authorities, which the Renaissance, the Reformation and the Enlightenment had heralded still constrained the democratization of ideology in a significant manner. Authority still lay in the hands of a cultural elite, but increasingly in the nineteenth and early twentieth centuries that authority was reserved primarily for the intellectual guild. The postmodern state of mind by contrast reflects a deep resentment towards any version of ideological elitism. There is something intuitively disturbing about the older (modern) claim that knowledge can be privileged and controlled by any intellectual or cultural elite.[33] The results of the revisionist historical treatments of older (modern) intellectual elites provided a substitute story about their character and status. There were new critical lights casting doubts upon the political and social motives of these elites and which thereby placed them in a far less heroic and noble light. The consequence was democratization of knowledge and information in the last

[31] This phrase is borrowed from Zygmunt Bauman, "The Re-Enchantment of the World, or, How Can One Narrate Postmodernity" in *Intimations of Postmodernity*, reprinted in *The Bauman Reader*, Peter Beilharz ed. (Oxford: Blackwell, 2001), pp. 188–99. Bauman defends the claim that there is no "system of ideas" in postmodern social theory, but rather a recognition of the complex habitat of social conditions in late modernity which we now refer to (rightly) as postmodernity.

[32] I take this to be Andreas Huyssen's central filter through which he understands the consequent leveling effect of postmodernism. See his influential work, *After the Great Divide: Modernism, Mass Culture and Postmodernism* (Indianapolis: Indiana University Press, 1986).

[33] Michel Foucault, *The Archaeology of Knowledge and the Discourse on Language*, trans. A.M. Sheridan Smith (New York: Pantheon Books, 1972).

half century. And here one of the ironies of the postmodern discourse manifests itself clearly. The revisionist histories about the origin of our habits of mind in the hands of prominent social theorists have remained distinctly esoteric in style and substance.[34] The democratization of ideas has been prosecuted by distinctly abstract and esoteric writings of the guild. The allure of the new social theories belied their indebtedness to an older style of intellectual elites.[35]

Any universal claims about postmodern state of mind must inevitably be qualified, as most theorists are fond of doing themselves. There are many different postmodern states of mind. They come in a variety of shapes and sizes. They also come in varying degrees of confidence with respect to fundamental intuitions. Moderate postmodernism is skeptical about too much skepticism. Radical postmoderns are skeptical about too little skepticism.[36] Both affirm a prior hubris on the part of those who controlled access to the corridors of information and knowledge. They all seem to agree that it is important to be suspicious about received opinions, though in varying degrees it is also important to retrieve prior opinions that may have been overlooked. How much to retrieve? How much to cast out? The varying divergent theorists vary greatly on this matter. But all of them in one way or another seem to have lost confidence in the human knower as an objective and neutral rational agent.[37] This older confidence is now largely discredited, cast into the Humean flames of rejected epistemological opinions. With the belief in objectivity gone, the morality of the autonomous self has been placed in the grave as well.

For a variety of reasons, the obligations that once appeared to fall on the shoulders of all humans as rational agents, has been replaced by a tradition-specific or culture-specific morality.[38] Radicals suppose that all morality is itself socially-

---

[34] Foucault's history of mental disorders is exemplary in this regard. See his *The History of Madness* (London: Routlege, 2006, originally 1961).

[35] See David Lyon, *Postmodernity*, second edition (Minneapolis: University of Minnesota Press, 1999).

[36] The language of "moderate" and "radical" is questionable and simplistic though necessary for the purposes of description. I take Michel Foucault, Jean-Francois Lyotard, Jean Baudrillard, Mary Daly and Richard Rorty to have inspired radical postmodern states of mind, whereas Hans Georg Gadamer, Umberto Eco, Alasdair MacIntyre, Cornel West and Carol Gilligan to have inspired (markedly) different moderate postmodern states of mind. It is a contentious claim to include feminist and African-American traditions of scholarship under the more general rubric of postmodernism. However separate the historical trajectories of these diverse traditions may be, there are important insights, which they each share and which contribute in significant ways to the construct presently under discussion.

[37] This is most forcefully argued in the feminist traditions of epistemology. See Linda Nicholson, ed. *Feminism/Postmodernism* (New York: Routledge, 1990) and Rae Langton, "Feminism in Epistemology: Exclusion and Objectification," in *The Cambridge Companion to Feminism in Philosophy*, ed. Mrianda Fricker and Jennifer Hornsby (Cambridge: Cambridge University Press, 2000), pp. 127–45.

[38] Alasdair C, MacIntyre, *Whose Justice? Which Rationality*? (Notre Dame, Ind.: University of Notre Dame Press, 1988).

constructed, even those norms which apply to knowledge. Knowledge emerges in the perspective of the knower (or the knowing community) rather than from the world "out there." The knower can never get outside of their own perspective to see the world "as it is." In fact there are some that suppose the concept of "truth as mirroring the world" is merely an artifact from an earlier misplaced optimism about human perception.[39] To radical theorists, every interpretation is an assertion of the will rather than merely a claim about the way the world is.[40] Moderate theorists suppose that the earlier confidence in human rationality too often masked fundamental (ir)religious and political assumptions about the world.[41] Being honest about the influences of those assumptions may not undermine the claims to knowledge, but it ought to greatly temper the arrogance of the claims. Epistemic humility and toleration are watchwords to most theorists that use/d the discourse of postmodernity.[42]

Most of these theorists are also wary of the pretentious focus on the self as the substantive center of reality. The self has withered under the pressure of modernity and now appears sustainable only in a greatly modified form.[43] The self is now either too empty or too saturated to bear the conceptual weight it once did.[44] In its place has come either a renewed interest in community (individuals-in-relation) or a claim that the self is merely a bundle of desires whose driving interest is preservation and power. On the former reading, there has been a renewed appeal to notions of the "common good" which are not rooted in a common humanity nor in a meta-narrative, but rather emerge from the community's own interests. On the latter reading, there is neither a universal category of humanness or of self. Both body and soul are socially-constructed and emerge only within the Western interest of introspection as a restraint on external authorities.[45] The claims about the self

39 Richard Rorty's *Philosophy and The Mirror of Nature* is the most prominent early work to put forward this thesis. Rorty and his intellectual ties to the 1960s are discussed at length in Chapter 6 of the present work.

40 Michel Foucault, *Power/ Knowledge: Selected Interviews and Other Writings, 1972–1977* (New York: Pantheon Books, 1980).

41 Cf. Cornel West, *Prophetic Thought in Postmodern Times* (Monroe, Me.: Common Courage Press, 1993) and *Beyond Eurocentrism and Multiculturalism* (Monroe, Me.: Common Courage Press, 1993).

42 See Umberto Eco, *The Limits of Interpretation* (Bloomington: Indiana University Press, 1990) and Stefan Collini, ed., *Interpretation and Overinterpretation*, Umberto Eco with Richard Rorty, Jonathan Culler, Christine Brooke-Rose (Cambridge: Cambridge University Press, 1992).

43 The work of Anthony Giddens is important in this regard. See his *The Consequences of Modernity* (Stanford, CA: Standford University Press, 1990) and *Modernity and Self-Identity* (Stanford CA: Standford University Press, 1991).

44 See the masterful essay by Calvin Schrag, *The Self After Postmodernity* (New Haven: Yale University Press, 1999).

45 Judith Butler, "Variations on Sex and Gender" in Seyla Benhabib, and Drucilla Cornell, *Feminism as Critique* (Minneapolis: University of Minnesota Press, 1987).

rest upon prior assumptions about the nature, meaning and power of language. The act of speaking of the self is the act of self-creation. Alternative cultural accounts of personhood provide assurance that cultures can get along quite well without universal (Western) notions of selfhood.[46]

There has been no greater concern among theorists who use/d the discourse of postmodernity than the concern about language. The revolutionary character of the last half century is rooted in the linguistic turn taken in the middle of the twentieth century.[47] The positivist conception of knowledge as built from the ground up out of impressions and ideas was abandoned. Words replaced ideas and became threads in which the fabric of knowledge was woven. No longer was it acceptable to think of knowledge like a pyramid built upon some unshakeable foundation. The search for this foundation (be it in the Bible as envisioned by Medieval and Reformation thinkers or in science as modern thinkers were convinced) had been abandoned. Every belief was potentially (and ought practically to be) revisable. The epistemological enterprise was less like building a house than it was like engaging in a conversation or telling a story.[48] There was no longer a sure and certain foundation upon which the natural or human sciences rested. Knowledge was fluid and flexible and always revisable.[49]

Many of the radical postmodern thinkers rejected the onto-theological tradition, which supposed that there was a stable world out there simply waiting to be described as it really was.[50] That discredited view of things supposed both that God was the guarantor of the stability of the world and that God was another piece of furniture of the universe. But there was no such thing as an objective perspective from which to know whether language actually "hooked up" to the world. And God, if there was such a being, was not an object let alone like any other object in the world. At the heart of the critique of earlier conceptions was a conviction that language is nothing more than a set of conventions that permits (more or less) a certain set of practices rather than a set of mental mirrors reflecting

---

46 Featherstone, Mike. *Undoing Culture: Globalization, Postmodernism and Identity* (London: Sage, 1995).

47 This is charted well in Richard Rorty, *The Lingustic Turn: Recent Essays in Philosophical Method* (Chicago: University of Chicago Press, 1967/1988).

48 Richard Rorty, *Truth, Politics and Postmodernism*. See also Fred Newman, *The End of Knowing: and the Rediscovery of Development in the Performance of Conversation*. (New York: Routledge, 1997) and Peter Levine, *Living Without Philosophy: On Narrative, Rhetoric, and Morality* (Albany, NY: State University of New York Press, 1998).

49 The death of foundationalism is helpfully summarized in Robert Audi, *Epistemology* (New York: Routledge, 1998). Its death is summarized and defended most clearly by Michael Williams, *Groundless Belief: An Essay on the Possibility of Epistemology* second edition (Princeton, NJ: Princeton University Press, 1999). The story of its death in the early 1960s is told in Chapter 6 of the present work.

50 Mark C. Taylor, *Erring: A Postmodern A/theology* (Chicago: University of Chicago Press, 1984).

objects in the world. Words derive their meaning not by reference to things "out there," but in relation to a system of words, a culturally devised system.

There are many moderate contemporary theorists leery of such reductionistic claims about language, namely, that language "never" hooks up to a world out there. But most philosophers of language are convinced that words do not function merely as mirrors, their only meaning being their referential capacity. Words outside of a language make little sense and language outside of a series of practices is not very meaningful. Language does indeed help one get along in the world and in this regard performs many diverse functions, the least of which may be to refer to things in the world. Paying attention to the uses of words may help one see the way in which language is rooted in particular and peculiar contexts. Paying attention to diverse contexts, helps increase appreciation for the malleability of language and its resilience as well. The history of usage will often unveil much about the culture and the people that used the language. It will also reveal real and substantial differences among cultures as to how they make sense of the world and their experience in it.

Intrinsic to the mood in the post 1960s period has been the rejection of a unified science and correspondingly of a unified religious interpretation. Appreciation of a deep pluralism emerged in the aftermath of the death of the "world out there." Interpretations may be more or less adequate, but never ultimate. They never finally grant a window onto all of reality and therefore are always partial and finite at best. In that light, respect for the plurality of visions ought to be sustained, not simply as a civic virtue but as a matter of philosophical principle.

Unexpectedly, the toleration of pluralism has gone hand in hand with a vigorous and sustained sense of protest against oppression and exclusion. It has been not simply an intolerance of intolerance (though it is) but a deeper intolerance of those forms of social organization and behavior which do not respect the diverse identities of individuals. There has been no absolute moral principle to guide this prophetic stance, but it is ever more clear that many who call themselves postmodern, do not see themselves as passive observers in the messy world of human interactions. Ideology, though always relativized, must nonetheless not be privatized. It ought to contribute to the public discussion and this it cannot do if it simply echoes those convictions of the mainstream culture in which it speaks. The postmodern state of mind is often vigilant in its suspicion of received opinions and practices. The prophetic tone of postmodernism is surprisingly rooted in its fundamental commitment to pluralism.

A Preliminary Postscript

The preceding preliminary characterizations of social structures and conceptual intuitions have been intentionally and inevitably broad and ambiguous. Social structures and ideologies are never easily correlated though neither are they ever completely unhinged from each other. Postmodernity is a very large umbrella under which multiple social modalities of the "contemporary" have been placed. A considerable amount of tension exists between the various elements under the umbrella. The tensions themselves are often thought to be part of the "contemporary" which fit under the umbrella. Explaining those tensions and granting to them a sense of the "ordinary" is a function of our own ideological constructs. These constructs are then nothing more nor less than the attempt to make sense of individuals and their experience of their own "contemporary."

Surely not everyone interprets the "contemporary" in complementary ways. The manner in which the experiences of life are to be situated into an interpretive framework is itself radically contested. Any framework belies the intractable conflicts at the heart of the experience of the "contemporary." What is rarely contested about the contemporary, however, is the connection to a peculiar past that began in some concrete sense in the 1960s. The before and after of that decade defines the "contemporary" indelibly for us. The conflicts of our era emerged in large measure in the debates about the meaning and legacy of the era of the 1960s. It was a decade of conflict and it gave rise to a set of conflicting interpretations. We ought not to be surprised that piecing together the puzzle of that religious and social landscape will itself be full of surprises. Movements as diverse as feminism and evangelicalism manifest similar democratizing tendencies at their heart—and therefore bear some ideological resemblance to each other even while shouting at each other from distant political horizons. The Civil Rights was a progressive movement whose core arguments were entirely traditional. Charting those ideological surprises is possible only when we let the original contexts ask their own questions, rather than imposing a "one size fits all" template upon them.

Being careful to recognize the ideology in the revolt against ideology, and the orthodoxy in the revolt against all orthodoxies, it is also important to notice that there will always be fault lines of divergence and significance in any contemporary context. The argument that follows is concerned not so much with which side of the fault line is theoretically more stable, but rather to see in the concrete details of the 1960s, the reason the fault lines have erupted in their present form and also why the fault lines themselves appear as socially constructed interpretations which may not account for all they suppose. Suspicions ought to be present if "left and right" emerge as a totalizing spectrum. That fault line may explain some of the cultural realities of the 1960s but it also masks many others. Indeed so much of our public discourse is constrained by the typology of "left and right" as to belie its relatively recent origin and its complexities. Understanding the conditions of concreteness may shed some light on the diversity of fault lines and the manner in which religious conviction problematizes even the most well known of those fault lines. And it may just be true that discovering different fault lines will lead to a more adequate interpretation of the concrete events of the 1960s. It is to those concrete events of the 1960s we now turn.

PART II
Protest and Irony

Chapter 3
The Stirrings of Change: Civil Rights and the Ideology of Race

If ever America undergoes great revolutions, they will be brought about by the presence of the black race on the soil of the United States,—that is to say, they will owe their origin, not to the equality, but to the inequality, of conditions.

Alexis De Tocqueville (1840)[1]

Introduction

The first set of cataclysmic events that launched America into the seismic 60s was quite assuredly the Civil Rights Movement. Before the rise of the New Left and the politics of protest it represented, there was no more major cultural upheaval in this era than that associated with the Civil Rights Movement.[2] The struggle for civil rights was a defining episode of the American experience in the early 1960s. In rich and ironic ways the struggle for civil rights was surprising in its retrieval and use of religious conviction in the struggle for equality. It overturned that optimism of modern secularity that supposed all the nation's problems could be solved with greater attention to technique and organization. And ironically the Movement itself was catapulted into existence in the first place by a religious hope grounded in the conviction that all individuals had equal dignity given by their Creator. This "equal dignity" argument was also strangely tied to the deep secular hope of the age of increased material prosperity.

The Civil Rights Movement brought with it the beginnings of "identity politics," which supposed race (and class to a lesser extent) was a defining element of one's orientation in this world and of one's relationship to the rest of society. The struggle for civil rights also cast grave doubts on the notion of an objective

---

1 *Democracy in America*, as cited in Cornel West, *Race Matters* (Boston: Beacon Press, 2001), p. 95.

2 This chapter assumes that there is a definable and organized movement and not simply a loose coalition of diverse interests represented in the struggle for civil rights during this period. Though there was no formal membership in the "Movement," there was quite clearly a sense of being a part of the Movement. Most historical treatments of the Civil Rights Movement take this for granted. See, for example, Peter Levy, *The Civil Rights Movement* (Westport CT: Greenwood Press, 1998) and Robert Weisbrot, *Freedom Bound: A History of America's Civil Rights Movement* (New York: Norton, 1990).

American perspective which could speak for all and which represented every citizen. As America learned painfully through the struggle, not all perspectives were created equal and not all Americans experienced life in equal ways.

Protest against the status quo was the thread that bound together the Civil Rights Movement. It was a movement of dissent at its heart and for which the Movement had an enduring appeal on the American conscience during the last half of the twentieth century. It was also a dissent for which the American populace was little prepared and yet one deeply rooted in its own democratic traditions. It was a surprising protest movement if only because its moral framework was thoroughly American. Its claims were rooted in the "inalienable rights" of the Constitution and its base was found in the church. It was a movement of protest rooted in the American tradition of protest.

It was also a movement that clearly signaled the end of an era and the beginning of a new era. There was a distinct "before" and "after" connected with the Movement. The "modern" experiment of segregation came to an end (all too slowly) and a new "post" modern era of race relations began. There is no more clear ideological marker of the changing of the ages than the Civil Rights Movement. This suggests it ought to help frame the significance of our present cultural moment, whatever we decide to call it. An old era ended and a new one has begun.

The central defining forces of postmodernism were at work in complex ways in the phenomena which was the Civil Rights Movement. Democratization, pluralism and the technologies of consumerism each in their own surprising ways, were manifest in the era of Civil Rights. The democratic impulse was overtly the glue that held the Movement together. The underside of the renewed defense of democracy for the African-American community was the demise of the "melting pot" metaphor for American national identity. This led to the unforeseen politics of pluralism rooted in the intuition that racial and social diversities were more central to a person's identity than any common human experience. The presence and impact of television on the Movement would suggest the forces of consumerism would muddy the waters of the Movement as well.

The Social Narrative and Individual Stories

The origin of the Civil Rights Movement can be (and ought to be) debated relative to issues of economics, class, race, religion and politics, large social dynamics that are by nature complex and interwoven.[3] The Civil Rights Movement is not explainable apart from reference to the forces of urbanization, the influence of

---

[3] The language of "civil rights" came from its usage in the Truman commission report, "To Secure These Rights" (1947) to address the "Negro problem." Consequently the language of "civil rights" replaced the language of the "Negro problem" in national discussions. Truman was the first president to address the NAACP, and he used the language of "civil rights" from the report in his address.

northern labor movements, the emergence of new forms of mass communication and the profound disruption and social relocation caused by black participation in World War II. As well, undoubtedly, there were individual acts of heroism, (and cowardice) without which the Movement would not have happened. The interplay between larger social dynamics and individual actions must always be kept in mind.[4] Larger than life figures such as Martin Luther King or Thurgood Marshall or Malcolm X do not come onto the stage every day—and yet wider social events are not always present to inspire such individuals. Interpretations of revolutionary social movements ought not settle for a historicist determinism, which prohibits meaningful human action, nor so emphasize human decisions as to downplay the significance of social dynamics that are larger than any individual.[5]

As with the heroes in this story so with the villains. The social and political structures of oppression and discrimination proved to be ever so subtle, complex and more powerful than individual attitudes or actions and which could not be changed easily. Individuals such as Bull Connor or the Grand Wizard of the Klu Klux Klan served as lightning rods for the cause and figured prominently in the rhetoric of the debate. It was the interweaving of these individuals within the cultural system of the South (and increasingly apparent in the North as the 1960s progressed) that convinced many, nothing less than a social revolution was required for genuine and lasting change. The central focuses of the protests were the laws of racial discrimination.[6] The tragic irony of the civil rights protests against the Jim Crow laws was that it often prompted mob reaction by southern whites and police, revealing the genuinely lawless character of racism in reverse.

There remain important controversies regarding the complex interplay of events that led to the public explosion of the Civil Rights Movement. In the period immediately preceding the new national consciousness of civil rights, significant southern black leaders recognized that they would have to create sufficient chaos and disorder socially to be noticed by the national media. The nascent visual media also realized that the crisis character of the Movement would create significant interest before a national audience.[7] The black leaders understood that they would

---

4 See Peter Berger and Peter Luckman, *The Social Construction of Reality* (New York: Anchor Books, 1967) for a classic defense of this inter-actionist model of social analysis.

5 No finer treatment of individuals placed against the larger backdrop of the tumultuous times of the Civil Rights Movement can be found than Taylor Branch's two volume epic, *Parting the Waters: America in the King Years 1954–1963* (New York: Simon and Schuster, 1988) and *Pillar of Fire: America in the King Years 1963–1965* (New York: Simon and Schuster, 1998). See also the fine treatment of King in Stewart Burns, *To the Mountaintop: Martin's Luther King Jr.'s Sacred Mission to Save America, 1955–1968* (New York: Harper, San Francisco, 2004).

6 Voting rights and the rights of public access were the two most prominent discriminatory statutes.

7 See Anthony Lewis, *Portrait of a Decade: The Second American Revolution* (New York: Random House, 1965) for a review of the press coverage of the civil rights era. Lewis

have to make it more costly for white politicians (and the average black working person as well) to maintain the status quo than to accede to change. But this prophetic strategy depended upon significant moral and economic allies outside of the black community, allies that were far removed from the deep South. The political power of blacks in the North would be exploited to help enlist the political power of the federal government, the national Democratic party and northern middle-class public opinion. The early Movement leadership understood well enough that it would have to divide before it could conquer. It would have to divide southern white leadership from the safety of national and federal protection.[8] And in so isolating the white elites of the South, the Movement leaders held out hope that lasting change might be effected. A national movement, if still largely located in the black community in the South, emerged out of these insights and strategies. But these insights and strategies proved difficult to employ because of the older narrative of colonial slavery and its legacy.

The rise of the colonial powers in the fifteenth and sixteenth centuries carried with it the enormous expansion of the slave trade.[9] The rise of slavery in this period owed its origin in this period predominantly to economic forces. The central colonial powers, England, Holland and Portugal controlled the sea-lanes and therefore controlled international trade. Cotton and sugar were the two dominant commodities of international trade and were labor-intensive crops. The new colonial economies based on the international trade of sugar and later cotton, called for a greatly expanded labor force, which in turn provided the economic justification of the slave trade.[10] Native Americans were first tried as slaves on the emerging cotton and sugar plantations of North and South America. However, they had family structures in tact in the Americas, which made enslavement far more difficult and escape far easier. It was also not unimportant that European diseases decimated Native Americans. It soon became apparent to the colonial powers, and especially to the elite class of the new agrarian economies of the Americas, that

---

brings together much of the compelling coverage of the Civil Rights Movement from the pages of the New York Times and other national media outlets.

[8] For a clear statement of this strategy see Jack Bloom, *Class, Race and the Civil Rights Movement* (Bloomington, IN: Indiana University Press, 1987).

[9] Cf. John Thorton, *Africa and Africans in the Making of the Atlantic World, 1400–1680* (Cambridge: Cambridge University Press, 1992).

[10] Eugene Genovese, *Roll Jordan Roll: The World the Slaves Made* (New York: Vintage Books, 1976) writes:

> Southern slave society grew out of the same general historical conditions that produced the other slave regimes of the modern world. The rise of a world-market, the development of new tastes and of manufacturers dependent upon non-European sources of raw materials—encouraged the rationalization of colonial agriculture under the ferocious domination of a few Europeans. African labor provided the human power to fuel the new system of production in all the New World slave societies (p. 5).

the African kingdoms were easier prey, more willing to trade off each other, and dislodged from their social base, were economically far more efficient as laborers on the plantations.

Estimates suggest that nearly 10 million slaves were brought from Africa to America between the years 1550 and 1850.[11] Britain alone transported nearly 3 million slaves in the first 50 years of the nineteenth century. In 1776 alone there were 500,000 black slaves in the American colonies. In that same year there were almost 2 million slaves in Brazil. By the middle of the nineteenth century estimates suggest one in every four Africans was a slave.

By nearly all accounts, modern colonial slavery was quite brutal. The journey from Africa was carried on in sub-human conditions and a significant percentage did not survive the journey across the Atlantic.[12] A slave' was a slave for life, and the social cohesion and structures of support were sustained, if sustained at all, by the paternalistic attention (or absence thereof) of the plantation lords.[13] It was not insignificant that the average slave lasted little more than seven years on a plantation.

The economics of colonial slavery demanded the strongest, the brightest and the youngest men (and to a lesser extent, women) be taken from Africa. It was this more than any other reason which decimated the African population and to some extent changed the African social structures indelibly. The African tribal and family structures were largely destroyed and the social structures of the black community in America could never genuinely replicate the lost culture of Africa.[14] The "rootlessness" of the slave population would continue to haunt the black community in America throughout much of its modern history.[15]

---

11 For estimates of the volume of the slave trade see Philip D. Curtin, *The Atlantic Slave Trade: A Census* (Madison: University of Wisconsin Press, 1969).

12 Estimates suggest 25–40 per cent died on the Trans-Atlantic journey.

13 Eugene Genovese, *Roll Jordan Roll*, "[Modern] Slavery rested on the principle of property in man—of one man's appropriation of another's person as well as the fruits of his labor. By definition and in essence it was a system of class rule, in which the people lived off the labor of others," p. 3.

14 See Albert Raboteau, *Slave Religion* (New York: Oxford University Press, 1978) for sustained argument that African-American religion neither simply replicates African religion nor does it is merely adopt the European settlers' culture of religion. See also Sterling Stuckey, *Slave Culture: Nationalist Theory and the Foundations of Black America* (New York: Oxford University Press, 1987) and Matthews, Donald, *Honoring the Ancestors: An African Cultural Interpretation of Black Religion and Literature* (New York: Oxford University Press, 1998).

15 On this point see the compelling analysis of Orlando Patterson, *Rituals of Blood: Consequences of Slavery in Two American Centuries* (Washington DC: Civitas/Counterpoint Books, 1998). Patterson argues that the traumatic shifts of gender identity and gender relations resulting from colonial slavery persist in fundamental ways throughout the twentieth century.

With the formal and official abolition of slavery in North America after the Civil War, a new form of oppression arose throughout the south, segregation.[16] Many fiercely guarded prohibitions and exclusions defined the new Jim Crow order. The last two decades of the nineteenth century, which ended the era of reconstruction, were a period in which every southern state passed legislation effectively disenfranchising African-Americans and giving license to racial segregation in the public square. Whites and blacks were not supposed to drink or eat together in public nor in private. They were not to attend the same schools or churches or live in the same neighborhoods. Public facilities of every imaginable kind were restricted by race. And in nearly every industry, race was a defining factor for job advancement.[17]

The second stage of segregation occurred with the demise of the old southern economy, which had provided the earlier justification of slavery.[18] The cotton trade was changed dramatically with the invention of the cotton gin and the industrial revolution more generally brought about massive shifts in the black population from rural to urban contexts. Many social thinkers during the early days of the industrial revolution may have wistfully believed that urban life would encourage the equality of the races, but the jungle-like character of the northern ghettos belied this message at every turn. The social destruction of plantation slavery was replaced with a new and more entrenched kind of social dislocation, the industrial ghettos of the twentieth century. The continuing economic destiny of the black community still seemed bleak, even as the promise of modernity blossomed in many other sectors of American society.

One of the central precursors to the rise of the Civil Rights Movement was the migration of sizeable numbers of rural blacks to the urban areas of the North (and to a significant extent the South as well) during the first half of the twentieth century.[19] The migration began in the early 1920s after the massive destruction

---

16 Two fine works describing race relations during the Reconstruction period are: Leon Litwack, *Been in the Storm So Long* (New York: Vintage Books, 1980) and an older study by Thomas Clark and Albert Kirwan, *The South since Appomattox* (New York: Oxford University Press, 1967).

17 The early history of the reconstruction period remains an anomaly in light of what preceded and what followed. In many southern districts the 1870's saw a far greater proportion of elected black officials than even in the present day. This period, however, was effectively over by the end of the 1880s as a result of legitimization of the Jim Crow laws in the national courts.

18 For a helpful discussion of the character and effects of the segregation era see Allen Weinstein and Frank Gatell, eds, *The Segregation Era: 1863–1954* (New York: Oxford University Press, 1970).

19 The best scholarly treatment of this migration can be found in the collection of essays edited by Joe William Trotter, *The Great Migration in Historical Perspective: New Dimensions of Race, Class and Gender* (Bloomington, IN: Indiana University Press, 1991). See also the older study by August Meier and Elliot Rudwick, *From Plantation to Ghetto* (New York: Hill and Wang, 1976). The specifically religious dimension of the migration

wrought by the boll weevil plague and the floods of 1914–16 which had made life very difficult in the South. There was also a shortage of foreign immigration in the period between the World Wars along with an enormous increase in demands of northern factories for personnel. This resulted in 4.5 million black men and women migrating out of the rural south between 1940 and 1960.[20] During the 1940s, the number of blacks employed in agriculture dropped by 450,000, almost one-third of the entire black agricultural population. At the same time, jobs for blacks opened up in manufacturing, over 500,000; and in commerce, over 350,000.[21] By 1960, the black population had become 73 per cent urban, reversing the urban-rural ratio of six decades previous.[22]

This shift in the black population signaled a significant transformation of expectations and social structures within the black community. In the cities, blacks were concentrated and were thus able to partially reinterpret the structures of discrimination, which furthered their sense of social inferiority. It permitted the beginning of a "mass culture" devoted in large measure to African-American concerns. The move away from the agrarian and rural South towards the urbanized and bureaucratized North in the period between the World Wars was noticed by many economists and social historians at the time, but little did any realize the religious tensions that were thus created in the shift—from the rural parish to the large urban churches and even to the large secular self-help organizations. Nor did many understand the events it foreshadowed in the late 1950s and early 1960s.

World War II was a significant catalytic event in the history of the Civil Rights Movement. It opened up jobs for blacks, took them off the farms, and set them in the cities. It put guns in their hands and trained them to use the tools of modern weaponry. The war exposed blacks to education and to the world and made them more cosmopolitan. It also inspired a sense of courage for a cause in which many blacks were otherwise uninvolved. This would be reflected later in numerous collective deeds of heroism in the Movement.[23] The Second World War was a moral issue, however, which remained relatively removed from the pressing day-to-day concerns of most black Americans.

---

is well analyzed in Milton C. Sernett, *Bound for the Promised Land: African American Religion and the Great Migration* (Durham, NC: Duke University Press, 1997).

20 Maurice Isserman and Michael Kazin, *America Divided: The Civil War of the 1960s* (New York: Oxford University Press, 2000), p. 23.

21 Bloom, *Class, Race and The Civil Rights Movement* p. 60. Bloom also notes that cotton production was down nearly 50 per cent from the 1920s to the 1940s. This contributed as much as anything to the diversification of the agricultural economy in the South—and resultantly to the sharp changes in race relations that were built around the cotton industry.

22 Wills, David W., "An Enduring Distance: Black Americans and the Establishment", in William R. Hutchison, ed. *Between the Times: The Travail of the Protestant Establishment in America, 1900–1960* (New York: Cambridge University Press, 1989), p. 168.

23 Bloom, *Class Race and the Civil Rights Movement*, p. 128.

The NAACP (National Association for the Advancement of Colored People) had come into existence in 1909 under the leadership of W.E.B. Dubois, but its national prominence did not emerge until the 1950s. It was early in that decade that the leaders of the NAACP made a strategic decision to cease litigation against particular inequities of public resources simply because they were unequal. They reversed course and decided instead to bring suit against the institution of segregation itself as inherently unequal. Associated most nearly with this shift in strategy was the young and brilliant lead counsel for the NAACP, Thurgood Marshall. Later to land on the U.S. Supreme Court, Marshall effectively argued for an approach to segregation which was national in scope rather than merely regional. This provided a context for the marshalling of resources large enough to withstand the pressures of the status quo.

The first in the long and prominent line of cataclysmic events that are normally associated with the beginning of the Civil Rights Movement was the Supreme Court decision in 1954 outlawing segregation in public schools.[24] In "Brown vs. Board of Education" the court slowly began to overturn the troubling legacy of its 1898 decision of "Plessy vs. Ferguson" which approved of "separate but equal" railroad cars and by extension segregation of all other public facilities. In the 1954 decision, the High Court ruled as unconstitutional the "separate but equal" doctrine as it pertained to public education, specifically to the schools of Topeka, Kansas. The momentous decision of 1954 effectively overturned the legislative history of "Plessy" and returned the fourteenth Amendment to its original post-Civil War intent, to prohibit all state-sponsored forms of racial discrimination. It would be well into the 1960s before the actual laws of the land more robustly manifested this change. But with the "Brown" decision of 1954, the beginnings of the split between the federal government and the political establishment of the South emerged and would be successfully exploited in the decade ahead.

The first localized crisis that reached the attention of the nation in the beginning of the Civil Rights Movement was the televised trial surrounding the murder of Emmett Till in Mississippi in early 1955.[25] The young black teenager from Chicago, visiting his relatives in the small rural town of Money, Mississippi, addressed one of the white women in town with a customary "northern" greeting. Warned by several of the town's white citizens against this kind of behavior, Emmett was kidnapped later that night from his aunt's home and taken to an isolated spot outside of town and brutally murdered by the woman's husband and her brother-

---

[24] This has become a standard inaugural event in histories of the Civil Rights Movement. Harvard Sitkoff, *The Struggle for Black Equality: 1954–1992* (New York: Hill and Wang, 1993) representatively begins his account of the civil rights era in 1954 with the "Brown" decision.

[25] Cf. A. Whitfield, *Death in the Delta: The Story of Emmett Till* (New York: Free Press, 1988) for the best account of the whole affair.

in-law.[26] An all-white jury in the neighboring town of Sumner, Mississippi, under the glare of television spotlights nonetheless found the two white men not guilty. The outrage that was vicariously experienced through the television coverage began to stimulate a national conscience that had been largely submerged on these matters beforehand.

In 1956 Rosa Parks was a young African-American seamstress who also volunteered in the local office of the NAACP in the city of Montgomery, Alabama.[27] She had previously protested quietly against the rituals of segregation in the city and had gone so far as to organize the Women's Political Council of Montgomery to work against the Jim Crow laws. At their urging, the newly formed Montgomery Improvement Association took up consideration of the boycott of buses in Montgomery in mid-1956. At one of the first meetings of the Improvement Association, a new young pastor in town, Martin Luther King was chosen to spearhead the boycott. And with the refusal of Rosa Parks to give up her "whites-only" seat on the bus, the massive and traumatic boycott of public buses in Birmingham began. To support the boycott, nightly meetings were held in the Black Churches throughout the city to consider the cause and rationale for the boycott. At first, it was clear that the most effected part of the Birmingham population was the black community. They largely depended upon the bus system as the means of getting to work. Some of the most notable inconveniences were caused for the black maids of the city, forced now to walk many miles to work in the homes of the wealthy whites on the outskirts of town. Ironically, this proved fortuitous, for the success of the boycott depended to a great extent on many sympathetic white women in town, most of whom developed friendships, and to some extent even sympathy, with their black maids. The boycott also laid a significant basis for a deepening unity among blacks, whose expectations were fueled by landmark federal legislation against public segregation enforced everyplace except where it was intended the most, in the deep South.

The year 1957 marked yet another major step forward in the momentum for change throughout the South. Orville Faubus, the moderate governor of Arkansas (moderate only in the sense that he favored an implicit rather than an explicit political structure of racism) was pressured by the White Citizen's Council of the state to call in state troops to prevent nine black students from attending Central

---

26 *Eyes on the Prize* (1989) PBS Documentary, suggested that the critical evidence linking Till's murder to the defendants was the testimony of Till's uncle as he testified it was he who answered the door the night when the two white men came looking for Emmit. It was this evidence which surfaced in the trial but which was all but forgotten by the all-white jury in its deliberations. See also Carl Rowan, *South of Freedom* (Baton Rouge: Louisiana State University Press, 1997), pp. 170–71.

27 An instructive narrative of this remarkable woman and the story of her life can be found in Rosa Parks, *Quiet strength: The Faith, The Hope, and The Heart of a Woman Who Changed a Nation. Reflections by Rosa Parks with Gregory J. Reed* (Grand Rapids, MI: Zondervan Publishing House, 1994).

High School in Little Rock. As the television cameras captured the drama for a national audience, one of the young students, Elizabeth Eckford refused to give up and marched all the way to the front of the high school building. She was followed by an angry mob of students who, by their taunting captured on national television, encouraged enormous sympathy for the cause of civil rights throughout the country. The young lawyer for the NAACP, Thurgood Marshall, subsequently won a motion to have the case moved to federal court, since desegregation was already federally mandated. President Eisenhower met with Faubus in mid-September 1957 and assumed that Faubus would agree to the appropriate remedies. Instead Faubus simply removed the State National Guard and allowed the mob to control the situation. Eisenhower finally called in national troops and before a watching national audience, Elizabeth Eckford was finally permitted to enter the public high school. Days later, Faubus in a last act of desperation, ordered the schools closed because of the citywide unrest. They remained closed for months. The whole episode seared the conscience of the nation.[28]

The decade of the 1950s ended quite differently than it had begun. During the span of ten years, a national energy was created on the "race question," owing in large measure to the organizational skills of the Civil Rights Movement and to an attentive national television audience. And so it was not surprising that early in 1960 in the city of Nashville, Tennessee, a city with a tradition of being progressive yet still segregated, a planned and systematic group of student sit-ins occurred disrupting the entire economy of the city.[29] At nearby, predominantly black, Fiske University, Professor Jim Lawson had given seminars in non-violent resistance that attracted many of the activist black students. At the beginning of 1960, Fiske served as the staging ground for student protest in Nashville. It was from these seminars that students organized sit-ins at "whites-only" lunch counters throughout the city. Two weeks went by without incident but on 27 February 1960 mobs violently reacted. The city police restored order only by arresting many of the demonstrators and none of the mob. Alexander Lubey, a leading black lawyer for the Movement, took the case. John Lewis, a student at Fiske and later the founder of the Student Non-violent Coordinating Committee (SNCC) was convicted of disorderly conduct. He was fined $50 for the offense. When Lewis refused to pay

[28] In that same year, a case which received more national attention but which provoked less outrage was the case of James Meredith. He was a black student admitted to the University of Mississippi, but was later refused entrance to the University by the actions of the governor of Mississippi. Burke Marshall, the U.S. assistant Attorney General in charge of enforcing federal regulations of this sort—uttered the words: "This is the final gasp of the Civil War" in response to a question from the national media about the case. Meredith was finally registered at the University and went on to become a significant voice in the Movement. See *Eyes on the Prize*, tape 2.

[29] See Martin Oppenheimer, *The Sit-In Movement of 1960* (New York: Carlson Press, 1989). The best narrative account of the Nashville sit-ins is David Halberstam, *The Children* (New York: Fawcett Books, 1998).

he was sent to jail for 30 days. His jail sentence became the grounds for a citywide boycott of downtown stores. The boycott of the stores actually spread to include national chains. And on national television, the cameras captured the violence of angry white mobs seeking to take vengeance for the boycott. Little did they realize they were reflective of a system teetering on its last legs. Lubey's house was bombed though no one was injured seriously. The boycott in Nashville ended only after a public confrontation with Mayor Ben West by a large group of black students on the steps of City Hall, a confrontation captured well on television. Mayor West, before a national audience, reluctantly affirmed the right of blacks to be served at public lunch counters. The unrest was quelled, though the upheaval left a bitter taste for many mouths.

The young black preacher from Montgomery, Martin Luther King, who had by now organized and run several successful protest marches, was arrested in Atlanta early in 1960 at an arranged sit-in analogous to the student sit-ins in Nashville. King's arrest was much larger news than the sit-in itself. Evidence of this was the intervention of the new young President, John Kennedy into the case. Harris Wofford, a black assistant to Kennedy on the campaign trail, urged Kennedy to call Corretta Scott King the night her husband was arrested. Kennedy did and the conversation was leaked to the national media. In addition, Robert Kennedy, the president's brother who was also the U.S. Attorney General, intervened on behalf of his brother and called the judge presiding over case. With political pressure thus applied, bail was eventually set and King was permitted to go free. Many local white southern politicians resented the intervention of a President in such local matters, but had little choice but to accept Kennedy's intervention, if begrudgingly. Undoubtedly, there was much political gain for Kennedy in the eyes of the black community and increasingly in the eyes of the national media. Politics was both shaping public opinion and being shaped by it.

In that same year, 1960, John Lewis and others organized the Student Nonviolent Coordinating Committee (SNCC) in Raleigh N.C. under the auspices of the Southern Christian Leadership Conference (SCLC), an organization of established and older southern black pastors and civic leaders in 1957 under the leadership of Martin Luther King.[30] Ella Baker of the SCLC had urged SNCC to be independent of the adult organization but was not initially persuasive. She believed, rightly, that the youthfulness of SNCC leadership presented the greatest opportunity for

[30] A standard history of SNCC is given in Emily Stoper, *The Student Nonviolent Coordinating Committee: The Growth of Radicalism in a Civil Rights Organization* (New York: Carlson Press, 1989). See also Clayborne Carson, *In Struggle: SNCC and the Black Awakening of the 1960s* (Cambridge: Harvard University Press, 1981). The SCLC's history is told by David Garrow, *Bearing the Cross: Martin Luther King, Jr., and the Southern Christian Leadership Conference* (New York: Morrow, 1986). See also Thomas R. Peake, *Keeping the Dream Alive: A History of the Southern Christian Leadership conference from King to the Nineteen-Eighties* (New York: Peter Lang, 1987).

exposure in a nation captivated by youth.[31] SNCC did eventually break off from SCLC organizationally, and successfully combined the protest elements of two distinct but now overlapping constituencies, blacks and youths.

1961 was a turning year in many ways for the Movement. It was the year in which many young white students entered the civil rights fray and garnered a different kind of national publicity than was possible at that time by persecuted blacks. In May of 1961 the Congress on Racial Equality (CORE) organized a set of "Freedom Rides."[32] A team of black and white students got on two public buses in Washington D.C. bound for New Orleans. The buses were firebombed in Anniston, Alabama. Twelve riders were hospitalized and one of the buses destroyed. The Klu Klux Klan met the second bus in Birmingham. The FBI had advance notice of Klan actions but refused to act even when local police absented themselves from the scene. SNCC students from Nashville arrived to reinforce the riders in Birmingham. At that point the attorney general, Robert Kennedy, got involved. Governor Patterson of Alabama refused to guarantee the safety of the riders. However, in a meeting with Robert Ziegenthaler of Kennedy's staff, Patterson's public safety director chimed in, that if ordered, their safety could be guaranteed. The "Freedom Riders" boarded the bus under state and at least implicitly, federal protection. Outside of Montgomery, Alabama the state protection vanished. The bus was met by a mob on the outskirts of Montgomery and significant damage was done to the bus. Consequently, Martin Luther King came to Montgomery and led a rally at the First Baptist Church. A mob formed outside and a series of phone calls ensued between King, Kennedy and Patterson. Finally, late in the night, Patterson relented and sent in state guards.

The Freedom Riders mounted the bus now headed for Jackson, Mississippi. They made it successfully to Jackson only to be arrested under a deal struck with Kennedy. Kennedy had promised their safety would be guaranteed though they would be liable for breaking local laws of trespassing when they entered the whites-only area of the bus terminal. Over 300 people were arrested in the Jackson bus terminal that summer—until finally the Interstate Commerce Commission under pressure from Robert Kennedy outlawed rules of racial segregation of all interstate bus terminals. This was the clearest sign yet that federal laws guaranteeing equality between the races would trump any local laws of segregation. It was also the ironic result of democracy being protected, not by a vote of the majority, but by the imposition of centralized authority. This was a long standing tension within the American experiment of democracy and one which would continue to reverberate in unexpected ways in the 1960s.

---

[31] Charles Marsh writes: "SNCC brought to the civil rights movement youthful energy and a bold restless vision for social change more impatient and edgy than King's." "The Civil Rights Movement as Theological Drama—Interpretation and Application" *in Modern Theology*, vol. 18, no. 2, April 2002, p. 235.

[32] August Meier and Elliot Rudwick, *CORE: A Study in the Civil Rights Movement 1942–1968* (New York: Oxford University Press, 1973) is an older but reliable history of CORE.

The climactic year of the Movement was 1964. In August of the year prior, King had made his momentous "I Have a Dream" speech before 200,000 people during the March on Washington. There was a gaining sense of ascendancy to the Movement and to its central figure. It is striking to remember that major civil rights legislation was passed in the U.S. congress in the year following John F. Kennedy's death, under the influence of the newly appointed president, Lyndon Baines Johnson. Increasingly bogged down by the war effort in Southeast Asia, Johnson believed that his legacy would largely hang on his ability to bring racial reconciliation to a country with a tortured past on the issue. His legislative efforts however were soon overshadowed by the rising discontent with the pace of change in urban black communities in the North. This caught Johnson by surprise and likely would have surprised Kennedy had he survived the assassin's bullet. Both Kennedy and Johnson were liberal politicians in the pragmatic tradition using the rhetoric of classic morality while acutely aware of its tyrannical tendencies when left unchecked by realities on the ground.

The optimism for real and substantive change proved short-lived. A new era of pessimism and cynicism emerged with the events surrounding the murder of Medgars Evers in cold blood in Jackson Mississippi in the summer of 1964. Evers was the secretary of the NAACP in the state of Mississippi. He had championed the cause of James Meredith's admission to the University of Mississippi two years previously. Riots broke out shortly after Evers very public funeral. It was attended by well over a thousand though only a handful of whites. However, the national press was present and the national television cameras were capturing the episode for a nation increasingly aghast at the violence.

The largest and probably last significant non-violent public protest of the Civil Rights era began early in 1964 when four hundred and sixty-five thousand pupils in New York City staged a one-day boycott of school. That was nearly 45 per cent of the African-American enrollment in the New York City school system.[33] The nation was only slowly coming to grips with the reality that the plight of African-Americans in the North was not much better than African-Americans in the Deep South. Race riots broke out in many of the large urban jungles in the summer of 1964 and would rage for better than half a decade. These riots effectively paralyzed the moral debate over Civil Rights. In many ways these represented the last gasp of a Civil Rights Movement which had left the church and found itself now in the middle of bloody war fought more on anger than on hope. Individually and corporately unresolved anger led almost inevitably to despair. A culture enamored with moral despair would eventually become a culture of cynicism, one of the tell-tale symptoms of the cultural revolution underway.

The crowning moments of despair in the Civil Rights Movement came first in 1965 with the assassination of Malcolm X in New York City and then 3 years later

[33] See Anthony Lewis, *Portrait of a Decade*, p. 260. Lewis argued that the student boycott attracted national attention but proved to be largely ineffective in bringing about substantive change in the schools.

and most especially with the murder of Martin Luther King Jr. on his hotel balcony in Memphis, Tennessee. As Kennedy's assassination must be understood to have played a significant role in the loss of optimism in the experiment of modernity, so the assassinations of Malcolm X and Martin Luther King Jr., burst the bubble of hope at the heart of the early Civil Rights Movement. There was a darkness that settled over the landscape of Civil Rights protest, though that darkness proved to be the clearest indicator that times had changed—for good and for ill. No less than a second Civil War had been waged in the Civil Rights Movement and no less despair resulted from its moral victory. Or at least so it seems in retrospect.

Suspicion and Retrieval

The scars of the long and tumultuous fight for freedom in the African-American community undoubtedly remain and the legacy of the Movement is by no means a settled fact. Yet for all the ambiguity and the pain of that episode of American history, there is little question as to the moral clarity of the Civil Rights Movement and thereby of its ability to distinguish the past from the present in a prophetic and partially postmodern fashion.[34] The break with the past was sharp and profound and moral. The collective experience of Americans now, a half century after the Civil Rights Movement, seems barely able to comprehend what life must have been like before the struggle. For most the moral gains are now taken for granted. And yet the continuity with the past, often unnoticed, is vital in understanding the enduring significance of the Civil Rights Movement. The integral connectedness of the "before" and "after" of the Civil Rights era is evident in the moral and quasi-religious grounding of protest and the goals of inclusion of the protest.

The Movement was revolutionary in so many ways, but from another vantage point it was peculiarly and predictably American. Its historical trajectory was deeply rooted in America's past. The Movement formed important historical continuities with long standing American ideals of social democracy and restraint of institutional power in the face of individual rights. The Civil Rights Movement was also linked with other social conditions which permitted and perpetuated the struggle for social and racial justice, but which were themselves indifferent to the moral and religious dimensions of the Movement, most notably that of the new communication medium of television.

Of particular interest at this point are the analogies between the Civil Rights Movement and the theoretical construct of postmodernism as a means to highlight the patterns involved in cultural change. Most significant interpreters of the Civil

[34] The moral clarity of the Movement is most evident in the PBS documentary, *Eyes on the Prize* (1989). There is no pretence throughout this well-received and prize-winning documentary to a "morally neutral" reading of the events surrounding the civil rights movement. Segregationists are portrayed as uniformly morally negative and never is there any question about the virtue of the protest against segregation.

Rights Movement have paid scant attention to the conflicting themes within the postmodern typology as a grid to understand the divided legacy of the Civil Rights Movement.[35] Without reducing one pattern or paradigm into the other, it is important to note that there are interesting juxtapositions of the two that cry out for an attempt at correlation. The complex structural categories of postmodernism may illuminate aspects of the Civil Rights Movement heretofore hidden. In this fashion, this chapter will seek to suggest further complexities to the interpretation of this revolutionary period. Understanding the Civil Right struggle as a transforming moment in American history will also aid in the understanding the turn cultural transformations of the last half century, at least in their American instantiation.

The history of interpretation of the Civil Rights Movement is fascinating in its own right. The beginning of a hermeneutical framework for later commentary on the Movement began prior to the public stages of the Movement. In the early 1940s the Carnegie Foundation funded a major interpretive work by Gunnar Myrdal, *An American Dilemma*.[36] Myrdal laid the groundwork for the academic establishment of the problem of racism as indeed a "problem" and provided ample statistical evidence that all but banished any hope of an academically respectable segregationist response. Mrydal's study also served to weaken the alleged link between the broadly held but abstract belief in racial equality and the correspondingly concrete behavior it was supposed to engender. Belief and behavior were severed in reality as Myrdal's study amply testified. This was a turning point in the academy towards the "race question" as worthy of academic reflection and analysis.

Myrdal's study was followed several years later by the Rockefeller Foundation-funded study of V.O. Key, *Southern Politics*.[37] Key attempted to examine the specific political structures of southern states as they directly correlated to race relations. It was groundbreaking both for its analysis and for the interest it unleashed regarding the South's segregated culture by outsiders to that system.

In both of these early studies preceding the public phase of the Movement itself, the central interpretive question internal to the African-American community revolved around the conflicting models of black radicalism and black accommodationism. Here was the alleged "culture war" within the black community, resident at the turn of the century and now openly at odds with each other in the Civil Rights

[35] Though it is an apparent truism of our contemporary context that race is a defining issue of personal identity and therefore a particularizing element of postmodern sensibilities. Much more has been written on sexual identity and its particularizing aspects against the backdrop of postmodernism than on the questions of racial identity in the same context. Cornel West's substantial contribution is a notable exception to this rule. See his, *Prophetic Thought in Postmodern Times* (Monroe, Me.: Common Courage Press, 1993) and *Prophetic Fragments* (Grand Rapids: Eerdmans, 1991).

[36] The subtitle of the study gave clear indication of its purpose, *An American Dilemma: The Negro Problem and Modern Democracy* (Harper and Brothers, 1944).

[37] (New York: Alfred Knopf, 1949).

Movement. There were black radicals and there were black conservatives. Radicals, following in the tradition of W.E.B. Dubois, argued for aggressive and direct confrontations with the entire political system of segregation. Conservatives in the shadow of Booker T. Washington, argued for a renewed morality within the black community that would be the best enemy against segregation. This typology supposed the "problem" was either internal to the black community (conservatives) or external to the community (radicals).[38] In hindsight it seems fairer to say there were systemic issues internal and external to the black community, which were both supportive of and resistant to change. The forces within the black community (and the black church in particular) able to exploit those systemic issues for change came to the fore whilst also being exploited by them. Strangely, many of the forces which enabled substantive change were already deeply rooted in America's past even as were its exploitive characteristics.

The urgency of the Civil Rights protest was as old as the American Revolution in the eighteenth century. The structures of protest were deeply rooted in the patterns of democracy that grounded the American experiment from the beginning and which sustained it at crisis moments. Democracy was a political system but it was also an ideal that lay deep within the bosom of most Americans, even if it was in conflict with much of their behavior. The rights of individuals were a sacred trust given to the American people. Moral strength was defined in large measure by opposition to centralized authority and the demand for a dispersal of power. The peculiar suspicion of authority which lay behind the Reformation and the Enlightenment was itself one of the significant impulses behind the American experiment. Without supposing that retrieving these themes was either easy or simple, the moral authority of the Civil Rights Movement lay precisely in the extension of this core value of democracy to race relations in the twentieth century.[39]

The democratic impulse that had given birth to the American experiment in the seventeenth and eighteenth centuries lay behind the moral struggle of the Civil War in the nineteenth century and was the enduring theme that sustained the Civil Rights Movement of the twentieth century. Part of the narrative of America from the beginning has been its exaltation of individual freedoms. There can be little doubt that this narrative thread is an important link between the social upheavals of the eighteenth, nineteenth and twentieth centuries on American soil. What marked the upheaval of the 1960s as distinct was the surprising role of the rhetoric of "freedom" in that era. It was surprising precisely because most Americans assumed democracy was the established law of the land and was that for which America itself was in conflict in the Cold War against Communism. Little did most think

---

38 Instructive in this regard are two conservative black commentators on the plight of the black community in the shadow of the Civil Rights era. Both: Shelby Steele, *The Content of Our Character: A New Vision of Race in America* (New York: Harper Books, 1990) and Tom Sowell, Race *and Culture: A World View* (New York: Basic Books, 1994) draw attention to the internal factors of the problems which continue to plague the black community.

39 Cf. Cornel West, *Prophetic Thought in Postmodern Times*, Chs 1–3.

that America at the height of the Cold War was itself profoundly undemocratic? American attitudes in the first half of the twentieth century seemed to take it for granted that the "Negro problem" (as it was called throughout the early decades of the twentieth century) had been solved with the Northern victory in the Civil War of the 1860s. It was the hubris of modernity on American soil that supposed the real problems were somewhere else.

In this manner the Civil Rights Movement cast doubt on a unifying "morality tale" that held American history together. This "older" story supposed that American cohesion lay in the country's commitment to stand on the side of justice and human dignity. It was a story allied with the narrative of progress intrinsic to the American embrace of the democratic revolutions of the eighteenth century and the industrial revolution of the nineteenth century.[40] It was a story that made sense of politics in the American republic.

The exaltation of the individual against the tyranny of established institutions and the hope of a new future empowered by the tools of modern science seemed an apt overarching rhetoric to explain much of the American experience in its first two centuries of official existence. Individuals rather than the institutions of tradition were the heroes of American culture. Language was often cannibalized to serve the interests of the common person and public institutions were often viewed with great distrust. This story was also deeply moral in character and during most of the American past, it was an overarching religious meta-narrative that persisted across generations. Deep in the bosom of the American people lay the conviction that virtue and insight resided in ordinary people.

During the first half of the twentieth century, the prophetic power of the American ideal lay in the opposition it aroused to the tyranny of foreign governments around the globe.[41] The paradigmatic tyrants of the early twentieth century were Adolph Hitler and Joseph Stalin. They provided clearly defined moral boundaries and also a political will to subvert differences within the American people for a common (and greater) good. Nazism and Communism were ideological in their own right, but it was Hitler and Stalin that provided the concreteness necessary to mobilize an entire population on moral grounds. The defense of democracy was not limited to American shores. In this regard these global conflicts were waged as a form of moral protection to the American ideal.

That American ideal seemed utterly resilient at the end of World War II and the advent of America into superpower status legitimated the moral contentment with its own democratic ideal. However, it was not long before the first significant chink in its moral armor appeared with the emergence of the Civil Rights conflict. The Movement offered a fundamental challenge to the moral integrity of America, and thereby brought into question the moral boundaries of that "older" story. With

40 See Christopher Lasch, *The True and Only Heaven* (New York: Norton, 1991) for a valiant attempt to distill this American ideal into a readable narrative.

41 Paul Johnson, *Modern Times: A History of the World from the 1920s to the 1990s* (London: Phoenix, 1992) lays out this claim as exhaustively as possible.

the advent of the civil rights conflict, the enemy was not only on foreign shores, but strangely also in the very corridors of American power.

It may have seemed utterly surprising to some, but the struggle of the Civil Rights Movement surfaced a tension intrinsic to America's democratic past. The protest against tyranny was motivated in part by a moral suspicion of authority. But successful protest inevitably resulted in a new authority—one that likely created suspicion on the part of those governed by it. The cycle of protest repeated itself though often with a new set of concrete issues at stake. This may be referred to as the pattern of "established disestablishmentarianism" and it should be noted that it runs deep in the American psyche. Dissent becomes institutionalized in the next generation against the dissent of an earlier generation. This creates popular dissent against the purposes of the original popular dissent. Dissent rooted in individual rights became the only constant in public causes, speeded up in successive generations by revolutions in communication technology.[42]

The recognition of this cycle and the reluctant acceptance of its terms in part also characterize the ambiguity of a postmodern moral framework. The dispersion of moral authority among temporal and temporary subjects is considered virtuous if not also dangerous lest any individual or group consider themselves morally superior to others. It is the danger and the acceptance of the pattern of suspicion of authority as itself morally ambiguous though necessary that characterizes the contemporary ethos.

As the decade of the 1960s dawned, it seemed that moral clarity depended upon where one was standing, or more accurately, where one was standing relative to the corridors of power. The remarkable success of the Civil Rights Movement was its ability to engage an enemy that continued to think of itself as an ally in the struggle for democracy. The illusion of the ruling elites was simply in the conviction that America had already been sufficiently democratized. The shouts of those on the margins of society trumpeted so clearly by the new communications medium reminded everyone that a full democracy had not yet been achieved on American shores, even in the 1950s.

There was no ambiguity in the moral protest against tyranny, simply in the inevitability of the cycle of moral protest. Elite southern culture was surprised by the upheaval, supposing that democracy was essentially a political system rather than a cultural system as such. Even more surprising was the readiness most Americans displayed in the aftermath of the Civil Rights era to vicariously own the moral victories of the1960s regardless of their own sympathies during the struggle itself. It was a vicarious moral victory even as it was also a deeply dividing moral victory at the time. The echoes of the Civil War era in the Civil Rights era are unmistakable in retrospect, but only in retrospect. The abolition of slavery was a moral extension of the original American ideal and therefore could more readily be embraced by later Americans regardless of their moral location

---

[42] The religious dimensions of the pattern are well documented in Nathan Hatch, *The Democratization of American Christianity* (New Haven: Yale University Press, 1989).

during the struggle. And like the Civil War, the Civil Rights era tore the country apart even as it strove to put the nation back together. The cause was just, but it left the combatants morally exhausted. Reconciliation required neither abandoning the moral character of democracy, or the conflict intrinsic to democratic progress.

In this, the struggles themselves were part of the moral fabric in which the progress was interwoven. These were wars fought not simply for political ends, but in the eyes of the combatants, primarily for moral purposes.[43] The abolitionists of the 1860s and the freedom riders of the 1960s believed firmly that nothing less than the moral character of America was at stake in the respective struggles. It is not an exaggeration to suppose that the Second World War for Anglo-Americans possessed no greater moral clarity than the Civil Rights struggle was for African-Americans or the Civil War was for slaves and abolitionists. In the narrative of the twentieth century, The Klu Klux Klan and the White Citizen's Councils remain as indelibly clear examples of moral depravity every bit as heinous as Hitler and the Third Reich. The number of Jews tortured and killed in Hitler's concentration camps seemed to most Americans incomprehensible and reprehensible beyond description. But likewise, the contemporary reading of the narratives of African-Americans during the tenure of lynchings and segregation argues for a correspondingly overwhelming incomprehensibility and depravity. In both instances, totalitarian regimes were toppled with moral turpitude animated by a righteous indignation. So it is that the contemporary age looks back upon that earlier era as an age of disguised authoritarianism while recognizing the fragile character of the moral victory achieved in the revolution. It is fragile precisely because the moral framework necessary for the revolution is part of the fabric of the age against which one was rebelling.

The moral battle with totalitarianism fought during the Second World War was a chapter in the saga of modernity. The enemy was external, the terms of struggle were the control of land and people, and the weapons were technologically advanced. The moral struggle over Civil Rights was quite clearly of a different order. The enemy was internal and combatants on both sides largely accepted the terms of conflict (individual rights and human dignity). World War II brought a fundamental challenge to democratic freedoms across the globe. The Civil Rights Movement brought a fundamental challenge to democratic freedoms at home. The moral irony of World War II was represented in its final climatic violence at Nagasaki and Hiroshima as the means to usher in a new era of peace. The irony of the Civil Rights Movement was to affirm that the enemy's (racist) commitment to

---

[43] This is Alan Guelzo's claim about the enduring significance of Lincoln in the aftermath of the Civil War. Lincoln's ability (after an initial reluctance) to define the conflict in moral and religious terms integrated the drama into America's past while allowing moral progress. The danger was always to demonize one's opponents so as not to permit redemption and reconciliation. See Guelzo, *Abraham Lincoln: Redeemer President* (Grand Rapids, MI: Eerdmans, 1999).

freedom was superficial at best while also depending upon the cultural values of democracy erected by those very same enemies.

The difference in the terms of engagement in World War II and the Civil Rights Movement also illuminates their enduring significance. World War II seemed to manifest the moral superiority of the American ideal by means of its technological superiority. There was a clear intertwining of the narratives of moral and technological progress. By contrast, the Civil Rights Movement was fought without weapons of mass destruction. At its core, (or at least in its origin) the vision was non-violent, precisely in the hopes of creating yet greater conflict with the powers that be. The separating of moral progress and technological progress was central to the Movement. Those with the strongest weapons were viewed with greater moral suspicion on the grounds that those tools created an inevitable temptation for power and oppression. The Civil Rights Movement was both a repudiation of the power of modernity while also an affirmation of the democratic vision at the heart of modernity.

The ironies of difference in the two episodes extends further. World War II was fought with military weapons while keeping close control over information access. The Civil Rights Movement fought with different kinds of weapons, the tools of modern communication, hoping to overturn the traditional controls on information. World War II reminded Americans of their moral ideals. The Civil Rights Movement reminded Americans of their betrayal of their moral ideals. Maybe most surprising, the Civil Rights Movement made a far greater difference to the cultural life of America than World War II, though at the time the conflicts of World War II seemed to pose a far greater danger.

The enduring significance of the Civil Rights Movement is one important clue arguing for the link between the Civil Rights Movement and the inauguration of the postmodern era. Moderate postmodern culture is dubious about moral superiority in any absolute sense, all the while trumpeting the moral clarity of the issues. Moral significance is most often racially and ethnically particular as a reflection of those who had not experienced the fruits of modernity prior to the advent of the 1960s, for example, African-Americans, women and recent immigrants.

It is ironic that the memory of a segregated South may be dimmer in the minds of most Americans than the memory of the South under slavery. The movie and book publishing industries have effectively kept the Civil War as an integral part of the nation's story, as it has the global conflict of World War II. Much less so has it celebrated the Civil Rights Movement.[44] This is in large measure because the Civil Rights Movement shattered the utopian vision of America as the land of the free, and uncovered the systemic character of discrimination, far more problematic than that of individual discriminatory acts. The enemy in the Civil Rights era wore tall pointed white hats (an ironic color reversal from Hollywood's portrayal of heroes and villains) and it increasingly appeared the entrenched enemy lay within the

---

44 The recent spate of Civil Rights era sports movies, such as *Remember the Titans* and *Coach Carter*, is probably evidence to the contrary of this claim.

structures of American society. This distaste for self-criticism explains much of the entertainment media's dislike for the Civil Rights struggles, except insofar as it was originally able to televise this to an audience captivated by real life drama. Little noticed at the time, was the perception that America's bubble of optimism was beginning to burst right before its very eyes.

There are few today that suppose the institutions of slavery or segregation were ethically justifiable. The overwhelming majority of the population takes it for granted today that segregation as well as slavery was immoral and egregiously so. Those who disagree are extremists of a deplorable sort. That is pervasive in the contemporary cultural ethos in a manner that was not so evident prior to the Civil Rights Movement. Most of America sat on the moral sidelines during this great social crisis. Only later did many realize the magnitude of the changes wrought in the crisis. Only later came the realization that America had a moral blemish of sizeable proportions. It was this recognition that served as a (blurred) line of demarcation of the ages.

One of the central rhetorical devices of the Civil Rights Movements was its prophetic protest against discrimination all the while retrieving resources in American history and most especially church history, which cemented the American impulse to protest discrimination.[45] This is referred to now as a "hermeneutics of suspicion" and a "hermeneutics of retrieval." It gave rise unpredictably to a hermeneutics of cynicism as well. This cynicism was grounded in the very dynamic of suspicion and retrieval. For every retrieval there appeared to be equally great temptation towards suspicion. It was a vicious cycle that nonetheless persisted.

The significance of the Civil Rights Movement to our current cultural sensibilities is enormous and enormously complicated. The Movement was an episode both radically discontinuous with the past and revolutionary in its retrieval of the past. The struggle for civil rights appears as a sharp dividing line between the past and the present as momentous in many ways as the American Revolution in its time or the Civil War in its time.

The hymnody of the Civil Rights Movement harkened back quite distinctly to these earlier struggles, reinterpreting the past to meet the needs of the contemporary context. "We Shall Overcome" and "Free at Last" served as battle cries in the early 1960s though their roots lay much earlier.[46] In this manner, as in so many other ways, the Civil Rights Movement was about a hermeneutics of suspicion

---

45 Notable is Cornell West's work of interpretation of this impulse. He opens his work, *Prophetic Thought in Postmodern Times* with these words. "I think it is very important as we reflect on prophetic thought in postmodern times, in these very deep and difficult crises of our day, to always view ourselves as part of a tradition. A long and grand tradition trying to forge a sense of dignity and decency, keeping alive quests for excellence and elegance," p. 3.

46 See C. Eric Lincoln and Lawrence H. Mamiya, *The Black Church in the African American Experience* (Durham, NC: Duke University Press, 1990) Ch. 12. See "The Performed Word: Music and the Black Church" for an introduction to the hymnody of the Black church during the era of Civil Rights.

but was carried on effectively by a hermeneutics of retrieval, in particular the retrieval of those eminently enigmatic American notions of individual freedom and dignity.

Sacred Retreat and Secular Reform?

Interpreting the Civil Rights era requires that the role of religious belief and behavior be taken seriously. The place and presence of religious belief now well documented in the African-American community, was unmistakable from the Civil War to the Civil Rights eras.[47] And the role of religious conviction is important in mapping the Civil Rights era in the cultural landscape. There are complex relationships between religious belief, social protest and other core cultural values in the Civil Rights era. The relationships are not two-dimensional and they move in a multiplicity of directions, suggestive of a link with the complex picture of the emergence of postmodernism.

Early critics of the Black Church in the 1930s and 1940s charged that the Black Church was not politically nor socially engaged for protest. Gunnar Myrdal's study had argued in the 1940s that the Black Church had hindered a fundamental democratization of religious life, and thereby hindered the means for successful protest. He argued that church life was highly stratified among blacks, and membership in various denominations denoted specific class levels. In this regard, Black Churches mirrored the social stratification of white churches. On Myrdal's reading of the data, the Black Church was ineffective as an instrument of collective action to improve the position of blacks in American society.[48]

From a different angle though reaching similar conclusions, E. Franklin Frazier had argued that Black Churches became secularized in the migration from their original rural bases into the urban environment during the first half of the twentieth century.[49] During this period, churches showed signs of increasing concern with the worldly well being of their members and supported such "practical" organizations as the NAACP and the Urban League. In this sense Frazier supposed that the success of church lay in it becoming less religious and more secular. In contrast to Myrdal, Frazier argued that the churches, though secularized, could be effective

---

47 See Albert Raboteau, *Fire in My Bones: Reflections on African-American Religious History* (Boston: Beacon Press, 1995) for an accessible overview of the role of religion in the African American community over the course of U.S. history.

48 It must not be forgotten that Myrdal's study preceded the emergence of the Civil Rights Movement and should not be judged inadequate by virtue of not predicting the tumultuous events to come. The central point here is that he, and other critics of the black church of the era, failed to capture the richness and full texture of religious protests that were intrinsically a part of African American religious history.

49 See his *The Negro Church in America* (New York: Schocken Books, 1963).

agents of change. The point was still the same. Religion was otherworldly and could not justify social protest.[50]

Commentators into the 1970s continued to argue that religion was a conservative force within the black community. Some even argued that it simply further enslaved blacks to the ideology of segregation and inferiority. So for example Nelsen and Yokely wrote:

> After the Civil War, an attempt was made to throw off the yoke of religious enslavement and secure genuine autonomy in religious matters by forming independent black churches. This attempt, in retrospect, seems to have been little more than a gesture. As slaves left formal captivity, the church—their major means of institutional protest—became a captive of white society, the same determining power that had formerly enslaved its members.[51]

Myrdal had correctly noted that the Black Church was fundamentally an expression of the black community itself. What Myrdal and many other commentators failed to recognize was the ability of religious conviction in the Black Church to legitimate the "outsider" status required for successful social protest. It was this status in fact which the Civil Rights leaders successfully exploited.

Religion does not always under gird the establishment. By virtue of its transcendent claims it may at times provide for a prophetic impulse which challenges human authorities and structures. The powerful voice of Malcolm X was unintelligible apart from its deeply religious but anti-establishment character. Myrdal well recognized the capacity of the Black Church to provide a safe haven from a heartless world, but he mistook that for passivity against the powers that be. There can be little doubt that religious belief on American shores has the capacity for accommodation to the status quo by virtue of its desire to explain and justify human behavior. But the Marxist generalization (so prominent at mid-century in academic studies of religion) that religion is always and only a sedative in the face of tyranny and oppression proved mistaken in the Civil Rights struggle.

Most commentators did not view religious conviction in the Civil Rights era as a good predictor of social protest. This was another very surprising aspect to the tumultuous events of the Civil Rights Movement. Its protest was profoundly religious.[52] Compounding the mistaken interpretation was the

---

[50] As a black intellectual writing in the 1960s, Frazier also argued that the black church was anti-intellectual and significant only among the lower classes.

[51] *The Black Church in America*, eds, Hart Nelsen, Raytha Yokley and Anne Nelsen (New York: Basic Books, 1971).

[52] In what follows I am largely sympathetic with Albert Raboteau's reading of the role of religious belief in the Civil Rights era, with minor modifications. There is here greater interest in the intersection of Civil Rights and postmodern attitudes towards religious belief than Raboteau. See his *Canaan Land: A Religious History of African American*s (New York: Oxford University Press 2001).

supposed secularization of American culture that allegedly left little or no room for religious belief.[53] Against the backdrop of the economic boom of the post-War period, religious belief as viewed by many intellectuals, was supposed to wither and finally fade away. The forces of modernity would make religious belief obsolete, no longer necessary to sustain human purpose and progress. The standard interpretive grid suggested that religion would continue to decrease in significance as the technological and communication eras expanded. According to this reading of modern America, earlier generations employed God to justify superstition, irrationality, ignorance, tyranny, and dogmatism, but the world was increasingly freeing itself from those forces. Abandoning the claim that God was the prime mover of history, forced humanity, on this rendering, to take responsibility for the world, for the human plight, and to change society for the better.[54] In this scenario, a return to God would be ruinous to human intelligence and progress. Religious belief was permitted a private space but its place in the public square was no longer viable.

On this grid, black religious belief had the potential to endure only by virtue of the fact that the black community was thought to lag behind the larger white community in appropriating the fruits of technological and economic success. The Civil Rights Movement was judged successful in so far as it allowed the black community to share in the fruits of the secularizing process and distance itself from its former religious ways. Or so one reading of the narrative suggested.

The Civil Rights Movement was most often articulated in secular moral terms to the national audience watching on television. The fight for justice and equality was paramount in staking a claim before the wider (and largely white) culture. This was most often defined by material well being, job opportunities and preeminently by the right to vote. To many interpreters of the Movement this rhetoric was the obvious manifestation of the secularizing influences upon the Movement, and which many suggested allowed for the success of the Movement.[55]

---

53 Cf. David Lyon, *The Steeple's Shadow: On The Myths and Realities of Secularization* (Grand Rapids, MI: Eerdmans, 1987).

54 Chapter 4 details Daniel Bell's argument to this effect in the "End of Ideology" debate and Chapter 7 details the Death of God Movement as a particularly clear instantiation of this sentiment.

55 So for example Douglas McAdam, *Political Process and the Development of Black Insurgency 1930–1970* (Chicago: University of Chicago Press, 1982) highlights the rise of urbanization and the demise of a cotton economy as central forces in the origin of the Civil Rights Movement. Francis Piven and Richard Cloward, *Poor Peoples' Movements: Why They Succeed, Why They Fail* (New York: Vintage Books, 1977) argued that the increasing political power of the black community arose from changes in the federal governments agricultural policy which in turn granted African-Americans a secular legitimacy which they had not experienced prior. Michael Walzer, a leading member of the New Left in the 1960s, believed that the kind of mass nonviolent civil disobedience being practiced by the southern civil rights movements could serve as a guiding example for a revived American Left. Far from approaching the Civil Rights Movement in the role of instructors, radicals could

There is a significant element of truth in this. However, success is a relative term and requires significant qualifications. The legislative gains of the Movement were undoubtedly aided by the ability of the Movement to articulate clear secular goals. But the internal dynamism of the Movement that persisted at least until the mid-1960s was of a different order and of a decidedly religious character.

As suggested earlier, the culture shaping forces of television and technology were integral to the success of the Movement. They allowed access to the public discourse of the nation without the controls of southern elites. The Great Migration and the attendant boo weevil crisis of the 1920s also profoundly shaped the African-American community and church. The collapsing of the structures of the cotton economy brought significant shifts to the relationship of the black and white communities in the South. But the secularization thesis supposed that these secularizing forces were antithetical to religious conviction. The framework supposed a simplistic reading of religion. In retrospect, that reading of religion-in-modernity implicit in the secularization thesis was also reductionistic and did not account for the rich and complex relationship between economics and religion nor between politics and religion.[56] That model also did not adequately account for the deeply and diverse religious character of the Civil Rights Movement.

The Movement was deeply religious but it was not religious in the expected mid-twentieth century fashion. Its notion of religion was neither private nor impotent.[57] It was prophetic and also pragmatic. It was also very diverse. There were establishment Black Churches and there were fringe religious movements, and everything in between.[58] The Black Muslim Movements, now well documented,

---

learn from the example set by the civil rights movement. The black struggle in the South represented a new indigenous American radicalism, democratically organized, drawing on the creativity and spontaneity of ordinary people, dealing with issues of immediate concern and of transcendent values. See Maurice Isserman, *If I had a Hammer: The Death of the Old Left and the Birth of the New Left* (New York: Basic Books, 1987), p. 110.

56 On this point, see the argument of Mary Douglas, "The Effects of Modernization on Religious Change," in Mary Douglas and Steven Tipton, eds, *Religion in America: Spirituality in a Secular Age* (Boston: Beacon Press, 1983).

57 See Charles Marsh, *God's Long Summer: Stories of Faith and Civil Rights* (Princeton NJ: Princeton University Press, 1997) for a persuasive argument that the drama of Civil Rights was a peculiarly theological drama. Different faiths clashed with each other, but the history of the era cannot be written adequately without referencing the theological character of the conflict.

58 Baer and Singer develop a working typology of black churches that illuminates a good deal of this diversity, though it still underplays the religious character of the Civil Rights Movement in its diverse factions. See *African-American Religion in the Twentieth Century: Varieties of Protest and Accommodation* (Knoxville, TN: University of Tennessee Press, 1992). Though their portrait of the black church is largely negative, Hart Nelsen and Anne Nelsen, *The Black Church in the Sixties* (Lexington KY: University Press of Kentucky, 1975), argued for important differences among black churches on the issue of protest/

exerted a powerful and important influence upon the black community.[59] Black religious leadership took many different forms. No one paradigm fit them all, least of all a paradigm that flattens out religious belief as primarily passive and otherworldly.

The Black Church was the only stable and coherent institution to emerge within the ex-slave community after the Civil War and it remained the strongest and most cohesive force within the post-Reconstruction black community as well.[60] The decimation of the black family under slavery left a social void that was filled in part by Black Churches. The Church was the womb from which African-American culture was birthed in the twentieth century. Many Black Churches were revitalized in the segregation period, as they grew independent of the tight political controls of the white plantation masters.[61] As a result they began to exert a very different and more powerful voice upon the black community than was possible under slavery.

Black Churches in various ways, accentuated the reality that the black community was still an alien community in America. Sometimes this outsider status was accepted and sometimes it prompted subtle forms of protest.[62] Part of its "outsider status" was its own peculiar and enduring church structures, at whose heart was the ability to make sense of African-American suffering. The church was the center of consolation in a harsh and hostile world. An individual facing bereavement, physical pain or a dehumanizing world around them was unlikely to find solace anywhere save for the church. The haven against the hostile world was a religious one against an increasingly secular world.

Religious belief made sense of this "outsider status" as well by its belief in the overwhelming faithfulness of God despite the hardships of life. God's presence was real and immediate in stark contrast to the ineffable God of liberal theology at mid-century. The immediacy of God was a simple theodicy, able to give hope in the face of suffering. It may not have explained all the suffering, but it saw beyond

---

accommodation. They argued rightly that black religion in the twentieth century cannot be categorized in a uniform manner.

59 National attention was brought by *The Autobiography of Malcolm X*, with the assistance of Alex Haley. Introduction by M.S. Handler, epilogue by Alex Haley (New York, Grove Press, 1965). C. Eric Lincoln's classic work, *Black Muslims in America* (Grand Rapids, MI: Eerdmans, 1994, originally 1966) brought academic attention to the significance of the Black Muslim community for the religious landscape of the African-American community.

60 Raboteau, *Canaan Land*.

61 Baer and Singer note that there were many cases in which rural black churches during Reconstruction were highly dependent upon white patronage and thus rendered powerless to protest. See Chapter 2 of their *African-American Religion in the Twentieth Century*.

62 Baer and Singer writes, "Black Christianity in the U.S. from its birth in the camp meetings and hush arbors of the slave period, can best be understood as a dialectical unity of protest and accommodation." *African-American Religion in the Twentieth Century*, p. xvi.

suffering to a more enduring significance. To some commentators this could at times appear escapist, but the soul of the church under girded the dignity of every individual in it. The great secular ideals of modernity; the eventual triumph of natural science, the attainment of national independence—would not and could not sustain hope nor provide consolation when the pain of present realities was urging itself on the African-American community. But the church could and did. It was an ironic reversal, religion provided freedom from the burdens of modern secularity. This was especially true in the Black Muslim communities of the 1950s. It was this prophetic distance from mainstream culture that permitted the Civil Rights Movement to take the form it did. It was also the rebirth of the prophetic impulse against the dangers of secularity.

Two significant interpreters of the Black Church, Benjamin Mays and Joseph Nicholson had argued in the 1960s that there were "brick and mortar" reasons to think the church had real problems, but that there was also something very positive about the soul of the Black Church.[63] Black Churches were the most thoroughly owned and controlled public institutions of the African-American community. Under Reconstruction, the church was the lens through which African-Americans often viewed the wider world and their peculiar relationship to that world. Opportunities found in the church to be recognized and to be "somebody," had stimulated the pride and preserved the self-respect of many blacks who were not moored to a tradition of hope and likely would have been entirely defeated by the economic hardships of the post-cotton economy. Hope came, if it came, in the realization that there was solidarity with a community of equally oppressed individuals. The cause of freedom and social protest lay in the strength of this solidarity and the recovery of the prophetic vision of the Christian Scriptures. Religion was the framework around which the community was built. When it retrieved the elements of protest in its own tradition, the empowerment of large segments of the black community took place. Here lay the genuine though mostly untapped potential of the black ministry prior to the Civil Rights Movement.

The pastor of the Black Church during Reconstruction was like the pastor of the seventeenth century New England congregational church. They were the central political voice in town. At the very height of the movement to disenfranchise African-Americans after the Civil War, the number of black clergy increased more than three-fold.[64] Part of this increase must be attributed to the realization that there was a greater potential for influence from the pulpit than from any other vocation in the black community prior to the Civil Rights era.[65] There was also a

---

63 Benjamin E. Mays and Joseph W. Nicholson, "The Genius of the Negro Church" in *The Black Church in America*, pp. 287–91.

64 C. Eric Lincoln and Lawrence H. Mamiya state that in 1890 there were 5,600 Black Baptist pastors. By 1906 there were over 17,000. See *The Black Church in the African American Experience*, p. 28.

65 Taylor Branch notes: "It was far easier to make ends meet as a preacher than as a lawyer [in the black community] and far easier to serve humanity as a lawyer than as

great social prestige attached to the ministerial vocation in the black community in contrast with the white community.

It also must not be forgotten that African-American intellectuals were mostly preachers until well into the twentieth century.[66] Black intellectuals were much more willing to cooperate with Black Churches than white intellectuals were with white churches during this period.[67] Serious education was most often denied to ordinary blacks in churches by the segregationist character of public education in the pre-Civil Rights period. As a result the most educated vocation in the black community was the black preacher. It is not accidental that during the first decade of the Civil Rights Movement, black preachers were absolutely instrumental in the strategic decisions related to the cause. Among others, the list of most influential early Civil Rights leaders must include the following ministers: George Edmund Haynes, Gordon Blaine Hancock, Howard Thurman, Adam Daniel Williams, Ralph Abernathy and surely the most significant voice of the Movement was Martin Luther King, an ordained Baptist preacher.

It is not an exaggeration to say that there were critical links between the Black Church and the Civil Rights Movement at every major turning point through its first decade.[68] Black Churches were the social glue for the African-American community at the origin of the Movement.[69] In the black community there was

---

a preacher. Preaching was often seen as a way of making money, of securing financial security. Lawyering was more noble of a calling but much more financially risky. The exact opposite of the white vocation." *Parting the Waters: America in the King Years, 1954–1963* (New York: Simon and Shuster, 1988), p. 61.

[66] Baer and Singer, *African American Religion.*

[67] Van Harvey writes of the dilemma most theologians found themselves in during the 1960s as pertaining to Christian belief but no longer believing nor belonging to the Christian Church. Harvey's category of the "alienated theologian" captures this sense of distance between white intellectuals and the white church in his period piece, "The Alienated Theologian," in *The Historian and the Believer: Morality of Historical Knowledge and Christian Belief* (New York: Macmillan Press, 1966).

[68] Albert Raboteau notes, "The history of economic boycotts and political demonstrations by southern and northern blacks before the civil rights movement remains to be written. When it is, it will very likely confirm the conclusion of one recent study that the activism of black ministers and black congregations, as well as the legal struggles of the NAACP and the Urban League, laid the groundwork for the Civil Rights Movement that erupted in the 1950s." "The Black Church: Continuity within Change" in *Altered Landscapes: Christianity in America, 1935–1985*, ed. David W. Lotz (Grand Rapids: Eerdmans, 1989) p. 87.

[69] Aldon Morris, *The Origins of the Civil Rights Movement: Black Communities Organizing for Change* (New York: The Free Press, 1984). Morris' treatment of the Civil Rights Movement is unique in many respects, but most especially because of his contention that the Black Church was the central institution and engine for change during the era preceding and during the Civil Rights Movement.

no sharp sacred/secular dichotomy.[70] Prophetic church leadership (when it was present) was the prime moving force for change while reminding the black community that social protest was in part demanded by religious conviction. This may have been little understood by the national and increasingly secular television audience.[71] That audience seemed immersed in an ethos of secular progress which held out a place for religious belief as long as it was relatively private.

Religious conviction as the ground of social protest was also surely not universally present in Black Churches. It was more likely to happen in larger southern urban churches than rural churches. It was far more likely to happen with the leadership of a socially conscious black minister than without one. It was far more likely to happen after the Brown vs. Board of Education decision than before.[72]

Religious conviction in the Civil Rights era, viewed from one angle, was not a good predictor of social protest. And yet to the African-American community, the internal dynamic of the Civil Rights Movement was of a religious crusade. In this sense the Movement was profoundly religious. The Black Church was at the very center of the mass movements and served as the institutional base of power.[73] Public demonstrations were rooted and organized in Black Churches. They began with rallies that followed a pattern of song, prayer, bible reading, discussion of goals, and speeches that often resembled sermons. These rallies were "churchly" in most every aspect. The hymnody was especially and profoundly religious. The central voices of the Movement motivated the cause by appeal to a religious conviction—that God had created all with dignity and purpose and no human

---

70 The extensive literature wrestling with the relationship of African culture and religion to African-American culture and religion points in this direction. Whether the intuition about the sacredness of all of life arises from African roots or American influences the conclusion is similar, in that there is an enduring sacredness to life in the black community well past the mid-twentieth century. For contrasting arguments see C. Eric Lincoln and Lawrence H. Mamiya, "The Religious Dimension: The Black Sacred Cosmos" in Larry Murphy, *Down by the Riverside: Readings in African American Religion* (New York: New York University Press, 2000) and Albert Raboteau, *Canaan Land*. Eugene Genovese's work, *Roll Jordan Roll*, remains controversial for its argument that slave culture was a function of the interaction of white and black in the antebellum South, neither primarily a reflection of the African world view nor a repudiation of the European world view. Conflict was central in Genovese's claim, but it was a complex conflict that often transmuted into remarkable convergence at points.

71 Baer and Singer, *African American Religion*, Ch. 2.

72 It is significant that most of the southern white churches initially gave strong support to the "Brown vs. Board of Education" decision of 1954. Southern Baptists, Methodists, Presbyterians and Episcopalians all urged compliance with the decision. There appeared to be an attempt to speak prophetically to the wider social context of the segregated South. See David W Wills, "An Enduring Distance: Black Americans and the Establishment," in William R. Hutchison, ed. *Between the Times: The Travail of the Protestant Establishment in America, 1900–1960* (New York: Cambridge University Press, 1989).

73 Aldon Morris, *The Origins of the Civil Rights Movement* and Raboteau, *Canaan Land*.

could steal that away. Martin Luther King may have been adroit in recognizing and exploiting the opportunities afforded by the national media, but King cannot be understood as simply a media creation. As Taylor Branch's magisterial biography compellingly argues, King's vision of a just social order and that of the Southern Christian Leadership Conference were rooted and their leadership justified in and by the Black Church.[74] It is first and foremost a theological narrative that bound King together with his followers. The vitality of King's voice in the Civil Rights Movement was itself a strong religious protest against the dehumanizing and alienating character of modernity.

King's protest against the idols of the age was also a protest against the core values of modernity. His commitment to non-violence and his objections to the Vietnam War were protests against the triumphalism of the West aided by its military might. King affirmed a just war theory, but disapproved of the spirit of the age that could not look critically at its own discriminations. He successfully organized economic boycotts throughout the South and railed against the commodification of individuals in the modern market economy. Too often the "business" of culture determined people's destiny rather than supporting their intrinsic dignity. In his sermons he continually protested the institutionalization of ordinary life which undermined the worth of ordinary people.[75] People were not simply objects in the world. He strove to remind the African-American community that they could make a difference in the world while also soberly realistic about the forces of evil arrayed against a just and caring society.

The transcendent religious claim provided the internal authorization for the Movement while the belief in the immediacy of God's presence in the African-American experience compelled action outside of itself.[76] The churches' prophetic edge was to a great extent bound up with their ability to retrieve the past in confrontational manner and thereby isolate the alienating and dehumanizing characteristics of modern experience. It is this religion of retrieval and of suspicion by Black Churches during the era of Civil Rights which is yet another indicator of its overlap with the advent of a postmodern pattern.

The pattern is made more complex with the realization that the underlying socio-economic structures of modernity persist in and through the postmodern era. The alienating character of secular modernity was often resisted but not finally eradicated. The false triumphalism of the modern period was not replaced with a new utopian reality. Deep within the character of the present age, is the

---

[74] Taylor Branch, *Parting the Waters and Pillar of Fire.*

[75] Cornel West, *Prophetic Thought in Postmodern Times* interprets the work of King against this backdrop of protest in the face of the hubris of modernity.

[76] David Daniels, "God's All in this Place: God and Historical Writing in the Postmodern Era," in Cornel West and Quinton H. Dixie, eds, *The Courage to Hope: From Black Suffering to Human Redemption* (Boston: Beacon Press, 1999) writes, "The (Civil Rights) activists believed in God as a sustaining cause to the Movement. Historians of the movement have largely erased God as a subject," p. 7.

realization that evil is both persistent and pervasive. In this regard, the deeply religious character of the Civil Rights Movement provided a prophetic edge in the face of the hostile forces of modernity and yet served as a predictor of its eventual frustration in the face of a persistent secularized culture.

The spirituality of Black Churches resembled the ethos of a closely-knit family who had learned to enjoy the celebration of life together while not altogether having lost the bittersweet taste of having endured horrific family tragedies. When this "family" bumped up against the bureaucratization of modern life, inevitably the very ethos of the family was transformed. The implicit social bargaining which permitted the voices of the Movement to be heard on the national stage eventually drained the Movement of its prophetic edge and foreshadowed immense social progress. The very mediums which brought national awareness also undermined the close knit ethos of the black community. The outsider status was originally a badge of honor for the Movement, but increasingly others viewed it as another establishment in which outsiders had become insiders.

A Postscript to the Civil Rights Movement: Black Theology

A testimony to the prophetic character of the Civil Rights Movement was the Black Theology Movement. Black Theology grew in the period after King's death when there was increasing discontent with the pace of change in America. Non-violent resistance seemed to lack any further "bite" against the injustices still present within the system. A conceptual fork in the road was reached in the middle of the 1960s regarding the nature of protest itself within the African-American community. Should it continue in the tradition of King or should it be more militant in the tradition of Malcolm X?[77] The riots in the summers of 1964 and most especially in 1967 and 1968 caught establishment power brokers by surprise. They had supposed that the legislative gains of the Civil Rights Movement presaged a new era of peace and equality.[78] The persistent poverty of the African-American community suggested otherwise.

With the advent of Black Theology, there emerged another confounding issue for establishment religious leaders. God, according to the early black theologians of the 1960s, was unequivocally on the side of blacks in their oppression by "white" America. The rhetoric of James Cone, the most influential of the black theologians, was strongly condemnatory of white liberal religion, arguing that it

[77] Malcolm X was murdered on 21 February 1965. His autobiography was published later that year and through it, his voice reverberated throughout the post-Civil Rights era.

[78] The first clear statement of a change in strategy and emphasis among Black leaders was the "Black Power Statement" published in the *New York Times* by the National Council of Black Churchmen in 1965. It argued for reparations and a renewed black nationalism. Its strident tone presumed the age of innocence was over. A different interpretation of America's past empowered black intellectuals to think outside the canons of modernity.

had legitimated a religious sub-culture which not only tolerated segregation but which actively promoted it. This tradition of "white" theology had been far too apolitical and seemed unconcerned with the plight of blacks in America. It had stood on the side of the oppressors against the oppressed.

The term "Black Theology" itself emerged in this period of the 1960s among various African-American clerics involved in the Civil Rights Movement and then the Black Power Movements.[79] Black Theology sought to institutionalize social protest against oppression as the heart of the African-American community's identity. Social protest and solidarity with those who suffer were not simply aspects of African-American identity, but the very center of it. The black Christian's calling was revolutionary and unapologetically biased towards those who suffer. These themes echoed those heard often on the lips of black preachers at the height of the Civil Rights Movement, but the tone was far more strident and intentionally divisive. Patience was no longer a virtue according to Cone. Black Theology repudiated core values of the economics of modernity as had many in the Civil Rights protests. However in sharp contrast to the major leaders of the Civil Rights Movement, Black Theology was strongly critical of the Black Church for being too passive and lacking the internal religious resources to sustain a militancy in the face of oppression.

Theologians working out of this paradigm identified theology as peculiarly "black" when it was able to retrieve an image of Jesus Christ as a liberator of black people against human oppression.[80] The liberation of the black community became the essence of the Christian message. Salvation was transmuted into liberation, not simply as one important result of being reconciled to God but as the sum and substance of that reconciliation. Theology in this sense was driven not by the norm of a religious text but by a religious experience—the oppression of the black community and the continuing exploitation of the black community.[81] In contrast to classic liberal theology, religious experience was not a unifying factor among

[79] By most accounts, Black Theology as a distinct movement never found a majority audience in the Black Churches. Its academic jargon, its roots in the liberal/neo-orthodox tensions of the European theological academy, and its prestige in white liberal seminaries all undermined its acceptance by the wider African-American community.

[80] The differences between the earliest proponents of Black Theology, James Cone and J. Deotis Roberts were largely differences of tone. Cone saw the theological center of the paradigm as "liberation." J. Deotis Roberts saw the center as "reconciliation." Both were in firm agreement as to the nature of the "problem" which gave rise to black theology in the first place, the suffering of the African American community. See Cone, *A Black Theology of Liberation* (Philadelphia: Lippincott, 1970) and Roberts, *Liberation and Reconciliation: A Black Theology* (Philadelphia: Westminster, 1971).

[81] Religious experience was a norm in most liberal theologies of the twentieth century. What was unique about Cone's framework was the foundational assumption that religiously significant experience was communal by nature, and identifiable by its character as suffering. See his, *Black Theology and Black Power* (New York: Seabury Press, 1969).

humans but a deeply alienating one. In this regard the black theologians were neither liberal nor conservative, presaging the birth of other post-theologies.

Black theologians sought to justify the struggle for civil rights as an inherently Christian struggle. They sought to interpret the Movement theologically. There was no intention to be objective or simply rational in their conclusions. Modern theology's love affair with science had for too long left the oppressed in oppression. It was time to take sides. It was time to assume a peculiar perspective. Black Theology offered an explicit criticism of modern theology's commitment to the virtues of objectivity and dispassionate analysis. Historical criticism had vitiated the ability to protest with distinctively religious resources. Black Theology assumed a perspective rather than rationally arguing for it.

The earliest proponents of Black Theology, James Cone and J. Deotis Roberts seemed acutely aware of the class structure of American society and urged the black community to resist the dehumanizing dimensions of that class structure. James Cone's first major work, *Black Theology and Black Power*, appeared in 1969 and repudiated this dehumanization against which the Civil Rights Movement had defined itself. Cone and Roberts drew attention not to the American narrative of progress, but to a black narrative of suffering. Suffering became a major key in the symphony of Black Theology. It was the awareness of a narrative of suffering in the midst of the older narrative of progress which brought a newfound cynicism about progress. The cultural suspicion of the American myth of progress became a core value to black theologians. In this they foreshadowed other postmodern thinkers who sought to capture the prophetic voice of social protest.

Theology as a discipline after Cone and Roberts, found itself unquestionably on the side of those who struggled. Black Theology foreshadowed a peculiar (and postmodern) commitment to the situational character of rationality. The overriding situation of oppression for Black Theology trumped any other truth claims offered from situations of power or prestige. No longer was it possible to believe in the canons of rationality as universal and uniform. Prophetic protest could be sustained only by recognizing the racial character of oppression. What divided America was more important than what unified America. The recognition of division would eventually give way to the realization of genuine diversity. Only when that diversity came to be celebrated rather than lamented would the rights of all be secured, or so thought the early theologians of a black (postmodern) perspective.

Chapter 4
The Critique of Mass Culture and the End of Ideology

> If mass culture as portrayed [by the left] in the 1950s, was not the cold dark dungeon of Stalinist-style totalitarianism, it offered only the dubious advantages of being stuck between floors in a brightly lit elevator with piped-in muzak. Americans were being psychologically manipulated in ways they could not understand, their deepest anxieties deliberately exploited by politicians, propagandists, and advertisers.
>
> Maurice Isserman[1]

Karl Marx cast a long shadow over the intellectual world in America through the first half of the twentieth century. Marx's concrete political influence reached its zenith in the U.S. during the period 1930–1950, though the actual influence was but a small blip on the American political radar screen.[2] Marx's disputed critique of Western capitalist culture did, however, set the stage for much hand-wringing in American universities during the 1960s. Long considered conceptually naïve in comparison to the great European universities, the American intellectual community struggled not only with a grave sense of inferiority by comparison but also with a complex and often ambiguous relationship to the great intellectual movements of Europe, especially as the nineteenth century closed and the twentieth century dawned. This was manifest in no clearer context than with respect to its appropriation of Marxist philosophy as a bulwark against the establishment political pragmatism of mid-century America.[3]

In an ironic twist, Marxist-leaning intellectuals were clumped together with religious and political fundamentalists by establishment liberals in this period. The regnant mythology of pragmatic liberalism was that the Left and the Right had been discredited by the sheer material success of modern secularity. Affluence brought an end to extremist ideologies of all varieties. There were no longer any "causes" worth believing in, or so many establishment liberals supposed as the

---

[1] Maurice Isserman, If I had a Hammer. The Death of the Old Left and the Birth of the New Left (New York: Basic Books, 1987), p. 100.

[2] At its height, the American Communist Party numbered only in the thousands, hardly a dominant political force in a country of nearly 150 million people.

[3] It is a minor matter of note, but in American intellectual circles of the 1950s, Marx's thought was referred to universally as "Marxian philosophy" but by the 1970s, usage had mutated to "Marxist thought." How or why the 1960s occasioned this linguistic change is unknown.

1950s dawned. The narrative of protest in the 1960s emphasized the Left as the primary reaction to the pragmatic center but as the chapter will argue, the intuitions of conservatives mirrored many of those on the Left and thus may illuminate the complicated nature of the protest.

Having been seared by the wrenching world transforming events of the first half of the twentieth century,[4] American intellectuals struggled to come to grips with the new found leadership vested in America by the non-communist nations at the mid-century point. No sharper discussion emerged among these intellectuals than the place of the Marxist critique of capitalism, nor was any discussion more charged on the political landscape than this one. The larger political realities during the 1950s had precious little place for any official communist structure, but it was the intellectual Left's unflinching criticism of American "mass culture" in the 1950s which clearly manifested the growing chasm between ideologically minded academics and the liberal political establishment. It was this divide that so sharply and clearly foreshadowed the massive cultural upheavals of the 1960s. Strangely though, the sharp divisions between the Left and the establishment were mirrored in the increasing antagonism between many conservative cultural movements and that very same establishment.

The widespread "cultural dissent" of the 1960s often focused on the shallowness of consumer life in America. This dissent required an ideological framework to justify its enduring power and hold on the conscience. There had to be a "story" which warranted its intuitions about the "way life really was." The "story" may not have been the prime motivation behind the intuitions, but without the "story" the intuitions would not have taken hold collectively in the wider culture. The story as narrated by Marxist leaning intellectuals provided an intellectual grid map, which marked out the terrain by which many young Americans questioned the pervasive commercialism of American culture.

It is the story of intellectual Marxist dissent at the end of the 1950s that I want to focus on in this chapter. It is important to consider the possibility that the ideological frameworks conceptually supported the cultural revolutions of the 1960s without supposing that there was a direct correspondence between the intellectual revolutions and the much more manifest cultural upheavals. The cynical response to a career in plastics by Dustin Hoffman's character in the classic 1967 film, *The Graduate* was not directly owing to the New Left's trenchant criticism of American capitalism. However, the film gained a hold on the conscience of many young adults precisely because the New Left had provided the intellectual supports for an attitude of cultural suspicion about affluence. There was manifest an increasing and surprising suspicion regarding the superficiality of the post-War economic boom among young adults and Hoffman's character gave ready evidence

---

[4] World wide economic depression, deepening ethnic and immigration struggles, the rise of fascism and racial imperialism as dominant global forces, two destructive wars of a breadth and scale hitherto unknown including the bureaucratized murder of millions in concentration camps and death chambers.

of this. The very ones who appeared to benefit the most from great material well being were the ones often most cynical about it. The debates about mass culture by the New Left in the late 1950s help provide perspective to this surprising reaction to the fruits of capitalist modernity in America in the 1960s.

A History of the Left

Historians sharply distinguish between the Old and the New Left in American politics. The Old Left was constituted by those structures and organizations whose identity was closely allied to the Marxist revolution in Russia. The central organization of the Old Left was the American Communist Party (ACP) and its central tenets were the defense of a proletarian revolution and the attack upon American democracy as a thinly veiled aristocracy run by political elites. The ethos of the ACP was notoriously "radical" in the countercultural sense of the term, while also being rigidly authoritarian in its organizational structures. Its period of influence lasted roughly from 1930 to the middle of the 1950s.

The New Left, on the other hand, consisted of countless countercultural groups that emerged most clearly in the 1960s.[5] The central elements in the New Left were the Civil Rights Movement, the anti-war movement and campus radicalism.[6] The identity of these groups was much more eclectic than the Old Left and much more cautious regarding any endorsement of the "Russian solution." These groups were equally "radical" though much more clearly committed to a notion of participatory democracy not simply as a solution to political questions, but also in their own internal organizations. They also tended to be much more naïvely optimistic about the potential for a peaceful human community in the midst of the great world conflicts.[7]

---

[5] The beginnings of a list would include: Students for a Democratic Society (SDS), Student Non-violent Coordinating Committee (SNCC), Students for Sane Nuclear Policy (SANE), Student Peace Union and Berkeley Free Speech Movement. There is little doubt, however, that SDS was the dominant group within the New Left. In 1962 SDS had merely 300 members but by 1968 it had 300 chapters. In that period SDS becomes almost synonymous with the New Left. At its height SDS had three or four times as many members as all the student left of the 1930s combined.

[6] It is imperative to note that the Civil Rights Movement was the training ground for many in the New Left, though the Civil Rights Movement was not early on motivated by the Old Left nor any connections to Marxist thought. The complexities of the ideology of the Civil Rights Movement are treated in the succeeding chapter.

[7] A representative statement from a member of the New Left: "If you want to know what we mean by the good society, it is this; we would like to live in a world in which each person in the community of humankind would have the deep and powerful experience of being in a touch with his feelings and with himself, a community in which each individual could say: 'I am in love in a society of friends.'" From Greg Calvert and Carol Neiman Calvert, *A Disrupted History: The New Left and the New Capitalism* (New York: Random House, 1971), p. xii.

The concern of this chapter is less the relationship of the Left to the Russian Revolution than to the American Revolution of the 1960s. And on this point, the New Left is absolutely front and central, therefore the question of the relationship of the New Left and the Old Left takes on great significance for any analysis of the 1960s.

It is quite clear that there is a great overlap between the Old and the New Left. Central figures and ideas migrate from the Old to the New Left and in both movements the radical subculture was maintained.[8] But the New Left was profoundly different from the Old Left in its understanding of democracy. The fundamental critique of the Old Left by the New Left was its commitment to "bureaucratic collectivism," therefore that the Old Left had substituted genuine participatory democracy (the hope of the 1917 revolution) for a bureaucratic revolution. This was the point around which many of the small sectarian socialist groups in the 1950s joined hands. Both Old and New Left had in common a declared passion for social justice, but New Leftists believed they were more concerned to use democratic means to achieve political consensus than by manipulating those whom they were trying to organize.

The traditional Left looked to industrial workers as the primary agents of social change, while the New Left, at one time or another, thought of everyone except industrial workers (and power elites) as potential rebels. The Old Left was ideologically influenced primarily by Marx, Engels, and Lenin. By contrast the new radicals discovered wisdom in a highly eclectic assortment of personalities including Albert Camus, Gandhi, Fidel Castro, Bob Dylan, Mao Tse Tung, Che Guevara, Emma Goldman, and the Beatles.[9]

The cultural reasons why the New Left appeared at the outset of the 1960s were the complex interplay of the nascent baby boom generation, the post-War expansion of education, and the redistribution of the black population to urban centers in the North as well as the South. All of these factors prompted a genuine soul searching about the "other America," that part of the American population which did not share in the general prosperity of the post-War boom and which had little access to the corridors of power. It is also significant that the Old Left lost important constituencies with the dispersal of many ethnic working-class neighborhoods brought about by the rapid suburbanization of the post-War period. There was as well, the dilution of class consciousness as a result of the "leveling" influences of television and the advertising industry.

Global conflicts also raised the specter of East vs. West comparisons in the minds of many. There might have been the lessening of immediate prospects of nuclear war but there was an increase in the reporting of significant "international

---

[8] The general outline of the following material comes from Maurice Isserman, *If I had a Hammer: The Death of the Old Left and the Birth of the New Left*, which is the best (and fairest) historical treatment of the relationship of the Old and New Left in American politics.

[9] On this, see the helpful introduction of Judith and Stewart Albert., eds, The *Sixties Papers: Documents of a Rebellious Decade* (New York: Prager, 1984).

incidents" which continually reminded Americans of the significance of foreign policy in a nuclear age. The global and political consciousness raised by this media attention to international affairs undoubtedly was exploited by the New Left with ideological purposes in mind.[10]

The Old Left's reliance on the "Russian solution" was dealt a death blow when Stalin's reputation was torn apart shortly after the death of Nikita Krushchev. Once having so dogmatically defended every last action of Russian communism under Stalin, the American Communist Party faced a withering attack in the face of the "deStalinization" crisis of 1956–57. How could it have so slavishly followed the party line of Stalin, especially when the evidence pointed so clearly to the mass murders of the gulag under Stalin's direct orders? Ironically, when the "red-scare" trials of Senator Joseph McCarthy ended in the mid-50s, the House Un-American Committee (HUAC) lost its forum for fighting communism and the American Communist Party effectively lost its platform for defending communism. The ACP had lost its "radical" reason for existence. By the end of the 1950s any homegrown American brand of communism seemed hopelessly doomed to failure.[11]

The seeds of failure however, provided the very opportunity for radicals on the left to create a new working coalition promoting the ideological concerns of the older Marxist critique of capitalism without its overt commitments to Stalinism.[12]

---

[10] This point cannot be emphasized enough. The New Left cannot be explained solely in cultural terms—nor simply as a disembodied ideology. It was the complex interplay of factors which produced the New Left. Todd Gitlin, himself an influential player in SDS in the early 1960s writes in retrospect:

> The American youth upheaval was but part of a worldwide surge which cannot be explained simply by the baby boom, the economic boom, the growth and bureaucratization of universities, civil rights, the Vietnam War, Dr. Spock, the Democratic Party's defaults, the mass media, or any other single factor. It was partly a product of social structure—there had to be a critical mass of students, and enough economic fat to cushion them, but more the upsurge was made from the living elements of a unique, unrepeatable history under the spreading wings of the zeitgeist. Gitlin, *The Sixties: Year of Hope, Days of Rage* (New York: Bantam, 1987), p. 4.

[11] There was a massive fallout of the American Communist Party during these years. The ACP lost over 3/4 of their national membership and by 1957 they had only 5,000 members nationwide. Isserman suggestively notes, "It probably would not be going too far to say that the most influential adult radical group in the 1960s was this 'party' of ex-Communists. It was a party that could do almost everything that a more formally organized radical group could do in the same situation: everything that is, except recruit new members." Ibid., p. 47.

[12] Of particular significance in this respect is Max Schactman. Born in 1904 in Warsaw, he was the son of a proletariat father and developed intellectual tastes that left him at odds with the Workers side of the Old Left. He would become the unlikely inspiration for the New Left. Unlikely because his earlier organizations (the Worker's Party in the 1940s and the Independent Socialist League in the 1950s) never attracted more than 500 people,

It was the vigorous intellectual exchange of ideas during the dying phase of the Old Left which prompted Michael Harrington, a later luminary of the New Left to write:

> The Marxist sophistication [of the Independent Socialist League, a strident organization of the Old Left in the 1950s] stood in inverse ratio to any possibility of changing the world. But the futility of such debates obscures the real, and rather astounding truth: that theories of considerable importance were being conserved and even deepened in apparently silly little debates; and that the ideas generated there would influence the mass movements of the 1960s.[13]

What were those "silly little debates" all about? They were about the unsatisfying character of modern mass culture and its related cousin, consumer capitalism. To the waning Old Left, it was the commitment of America to the structures of mass culture, more than any other single commitment which made establishment politicians so pragmatic and which left the status quo as the only viable political option in the populace's mind. There was no other realistic alternative because the establishment had economically eliminated the possibilities. Mass consumer culture spelled an end to class struggle, leveling all political convictions by means of apathy. At mid-century, religion was no longer the opiate of the people. That role had been usurped by the "aggregate collection of consumer goods easily available to the masses."[14]

Against this backdrop, left leaning intellectuals like Paul Goodman, Irving Howe, Dwight MacDonald and C. Wright Mills began to explore alternatives to the Old Left and its commitment to mass collective action of a highly authoritarian kind. The new alternatives pointed in the way of small groups of like-minded people. The struggle was no longer simply defined in "class" terms but in "human" terms—as an attack upon the human soul.[15] A later commentator would put it this way:

> Where the search for community had captured the imagination of the Left in the 1930s, the search for identity inspired the writers and artists of the 1950s.

---

but he always allowed internal dissent. Schactman trained such luminaries of the New Left as Irving Howe and Michael Harrington. His attraction to a radical Bohemian milieu also brought him into significant contact with the progenitors of the Beat Culture, Lawrence Ferlinghetti and Allen Ginsberg.

[13] Michael Harrington, *Fragments of a Century* (New York: Simon and Shuster, 1973), p. 62.

[14] Irving Howe wrote, "Modern existence had been reduced to a simple moral choice; to be a 'cop' or to be 'victim.'" One was either protecting the status quo or repudiating it. He feared that most weren't even aware that they had been lulled into apathy by the status quo. Cited in Isserman, *If I had a Hammer*, p. 51.

[15] See Dwight MacDonald, "The Root is Man" in *Politics* 3 (Dec. 1946) for a very early statement to this effect: 191–211.

> Where social critics had once insisted on the need for collective action, they now urged individuals to resist the pressures of conformity[16]

Mills suggested that it was as much a change of mood as it was a change of political strategy.[17] And here lay the genesis for the eclectic and humanistic movements of the 1960s, all categorized under the heading "New Left," and all committed in their own idiosyncratic ways to reviving the soul of Americans.[18]

The Critique of Mass Culture

By the end of World War II the discussion of mass culture already had more than a decade of history behind it. The debate took place on a popular stage (under the rubrics of "the man in the gray flannel suit," "the organization man," and "the hidden persuaders") as well as in much more rarefied intellectual atmosphere where it had an especially radical edge. The language of "mass culture" become a code phrase in the Left intellectual circles of the 1950s to explain why socialism had failed to take root in America and therefore why mass culture ought to be repudiated at all costs. Dwight MacDonald, one of the intellectual forerunners of the New Left, wrote:

> The masses are exploited culturally as well as economically, and we must look to Popular Culture for some clue as to the kind of response we may expect from socialist ideas. The deadening and warping effect of long exposure, to movies, to pulp magazines and radio can hardly be overestimated.[19]

This assertion of the unshakable dominance of culture over politics was a widely held view in radical circles throughout the 1950s. The discussion was played out with two central dangers in mind: the tyranny of the power elites in American society and a reductionistic view of the human person prized by mass culture.

The critique of the power elite found its classic (and enduring) expression in C. Wright Mills, work *The Power Elite*.[20] The great illusion of modern politics, in Mills' view, was the notion that there was no greater force than the Great American Public. More than merely another check and balance, this public was widely thought to be the seat of all legitimate power in the modern American democracy. In official life as in popular folklore, it was held to be the very balance wheel of democratic power.

---

16 Richard Pells, The Liberal Mind in a Conservative Age: American Intellectuals in the 1940s and 1950s (New York: Harper and Row, 1985), p. 187.

17 See C. Wright Mills, "Letter to the Editor" in *Commentary*, 17 (April 1954): 404.

18 The irony is that the very diversity of the New Left was as often not simply a means to protect individual identities, but a cause of immense internal conflicts—which would eventually result in their downfall.

19 As cited in Isserman, *Hammer*, p. 98, from the journal, *Politics* (1944).

20 (New York: Oxford University Press, 1956.)

This notion of the noble public life was sustainable only as long as the corresponding notion of a noble intellect was held. Many nineteenth century thinkers thought education could solve what remained of ignorance and bias while twentieth century politicians knew that too much ignorant prejudice still remained. Siding with Freud, most of these power elites believed that the average person on the street must be viewed as having a significant irrational side, curbed only by the rational decision-making processes of the elites. Whereas earlier it may have been assumed (and still was assumed by most of the masses) that after determining what was true and right and just, the public would act accordingly or see that its representatives did so. This assumption, so Mills argued, had been upset by the great gap created between the underlying population and those who made decisions in its name, decisions of enormous consequences which the public often did not even know were being made until well after the fact.[21] Increasingly, rational public discussion was undermined by expert decisions on complicated (and ambiguous) issues and by the need to keep the public uninformed of those complexities and the consequent decisions.[22]

The decisions of experts were surely influenced by public opinion but it also had become increasingly clear to many in the New Left that the medium of mass communication available to the experts, could just as equally shape public opinion as be shaped by them. The reasoning Mills offered was simple enough. In a culture permeated by the mass media, there were far fewer people who expressed opinions than received opinions from others. And further, any opinions the masses did express could not be expressed directly in response to the opinions of the media-shaped messages. The masses received intrusive images and dominant impressions from the mass media but were unable to respond in kind. The public became a mere "media market."

Mills argued further that it was not just the formal channels of communication that had changed American culture but rather the wider realities of a culture committed to mass communication:

> The small shop serving the neighborhood is replaced by the anonymity of the national corporation; mass advertisement replaces the personal influence of opinion between merchant and customer. The political leader hooks up his

---

[21] As noted in the introductory chapter, much of the protest against Vietnam by the New Left ought to be interpreted as a protest against the secrecy of military operations. This professed "right to know" was central to the undermining of the power of the power elites. On this point see Walter Capps, *The Unfinished War: Vietnam and the American Conscience* (Boston: Beacon, 1982).

[22] For interesting parallels to Mills argument, though from a later neoconservative perspective, see Neil Postman, *Amusing Ourselves to Death: Public Discourse in the Age of Show Business* (New York: Penguin, 1986) who traces the devolution of public political discourse over the twentieth century and argues, like Mills, that it has been greatly diluted by the mass media and in particular by the entertainment concerns of the mass media.

> speech to a national network and speaks, with appropriate personal touches, to a million people he never saw and never will see.[23]

At the heart of the critique Mills was framing (on behalf of the nascent New Left) was the claim that a mass culture was not democratic. It did not permit its citizens a full range of participation in the political process. It actually masked an underlying tendency towards authoritarianism. And in this, though Mills may have not stated it this way, it was downright un-American.[24] This was a significant turn in the social critique of the Left, now trying to place the label of "tyranny" on the establishment, at the very moment the establishment wanted to bask in the claim of being defenders of freedom in a communist threatened world.

If mass culture led only to the political quiescence of the working class it would be cause enough for concern, but the debate took added gravity within the intellectual left once the full horror of the consequences of Nazism was revealed at places like Auschwitz and Dachau. Barbarism rather than reason, totalitarianism rather than socialism, had benefited from the collapse of traditional folk and elite cultures. Not only did culture dominate politics, but irrational psychological impulses appeared to decisively shape the culture of modern consumer societies.[25] Mills added cautiously:

> At the end of the road to mass society there is totalitarianism, as in Nazi Germany or in Communist Russia. We are not yet at that end. In the United States today media markets are not entirely ascendant over primary publics. But surely we can see that many aspects of the public life of our times are more the features of a mass society than of a community of publics.[26]

The very political identity of America was at stake for Mills. And yet it was this disagreement over political identity which could not be effectively "aired" in a mass culture. The public discourse could not carry on effective reflection about the discourse itself. And herein lay then the seeds of deep distrust towards public officials *qua* public officials in a mass culture. By virtue of their role in society, they could not be trusted with major decisions, for they were intrinsically driven to hide information to achieve their political goals.[27] This distrust of public institutions in American culture would profoundly reshape the political discourse in the 1960s and thereafter as well.

---

23 Mills, *Power Elite*, p. 304.

24 This brings out the irony of the critique of Mass Culture against the backdrop of the communist witch-hunting of the House Un-American Committee whose primary target was the Old Left.

25 See Isserman, *Hammer*, pp. 98–101.

26 Mills, *Power Elite*, p. 304.

27 This distrust became nowhere more powerful than in the protest against Vietnam in the 1960s.

The critique of mass culture also had a second side to it; the charge that mass culture was fundamentally dehumanizing. The structures of modern existence undermined the full flowering of human potential, stultifying it in favor of the goals of the dominant economic and military bureaucracies of the day. And the mass media served as the communicators of this radically new vision of life. Mills wrote:

> 1. The media tell the man in the mass who he is—they give him identity.
> 2. They tell him what he wants to be—they give him aspirations.
> 3. They tell him how to get that way—they give him technique.
> 4. They tell him how to feel that he is that way even when he is not—they give him escape. As a formula it is not attuned to the development of the human being. It is the formula of a pseudo-world which the media invent and sustain.[28]

This may not have been a grand conspiracy, though it was surely the way the "system" naturally worked.[29] It was as if organizations and bureaucracies ran by their own set of natural (and inviolable) laws, far more prominent than the laws of the natural environmental order.

These "laws" of mass culture were trumpeted by the mediums of mass communication, explicitly in terms of the abundance of products made available, and implicitly in terms of the efficiency of the processes without which such abundance would not be produced. The structures of mass communication heralded the advances of modern life, achieved with the new found efficiencies of large economic and military organizations.

In 1956 when the number of white collar workers finally outnumbered blue collar workers, it signaled the shift from a manufacturing to a service economy. But more radically, it symbolized the increasing bureaucratization of the economy, when work itself was oriented less towards a final product and more towards an efficient process.[30] This was equally important to the seminarian headed off to a church hierarchy, as to the doctor headed for the corporate clinic, as to the physics Ph.D. in a government laboratory, as to the intellectual on a foundation sponsored project, as to the engineering graduate in the huge drafting room at Lockheed.

Much of this "new economy" was structured in ways remarkably similar to the older "assembly line economy" of the manufacturing industries. Tasks were divided into a collection of component parts, they were sequenced according to the

---

[28] Ibid., p. 314.

[29] The issue of "conspiracy" permeates many public discussions in the 1950s and 1960s. In the era of the Cold War, this is not surprising, but the instruments of public communication also tended to push theories of conspiracy to the forefront of the public mind.

[30] The influential New Left thinker, Paul Goodman, expressed it this way, "We live increasingly, then in a system in which little direct attention is paid to the object, or the real the need; but immense attention to the role, procedure, prestige, and profit." *Growing Up Absurd* (New York: Vintage Books, 1956), p. xiii.

most efficient processes, and all of it was held together by a group of managers at various levels in the process.[31] Emphasis was inevitably laid upon technique and its intended result, predictability.

But predictability was not possible without some attempt at removing the dominance of the "human element" in the process, which in its unpredictability, made for great inefficiencies. By removing the human element, bureaucracies attempted to rid the process of these inefficiencies. And yet the Left believed passionately, people would not finally succumb to becoming machine-like at the core of their work and their being. At some point there would be widespread rebellion against the dehumanizing effects of modern bureaucracies.[32]

The mythology of the "success" of new bureaucracies was carried by attaching it to the notion of "modernization," which carried a (relatively) new social ethic.[33] The group (as opposed to the individual) was seen as the source of human creativity. And belonging to a "significant group" was viewed as the ultimate need of the individual. This "belongingness" could be most effectively achieved by the application of science to human organizations.[34]

This new social ethic was replacing the older Protestant Work Ethic by which workers believed the pursuit of salvation was reflected in individual hard work, thrift and competitive struggle. Only by continuing to use the language of individualism, could the "organization man" stave off the thought that he was in a collective as pervasive as any ever dreamed of by the Russian utopians, a group against which he was so regularly warned.[35]

Ironically, it was the apparent need to guard against authoritarianism at the top that fostered a greater sense of "group loyalties" in the new social

---

31 The categories of bureaucratization are given classic expression in Max Weber and summarized nicely in George Ritzer, *The MacDonaldization of Society* (Newbury Park, CA: Pine Tree Press, 1993).

32 The dehumanization of modern technocracies are powerfully and depressingly depicted in the early work of Jacques Ellul *The Technological Society*, trans. John W. Wilskinson (New York: A.A. Knopf, 1964). Its unremitting pessimism may well explain why Ellul was rarely mentioned by the New Left, which had a naïve and optimistic understanding of human nature.

33 So William Whyte argued in *The Organization Man* (New York: Simon and Schuster, 1956).

34 Whyte cited the evidence of the dominance of this mythology as follows: each year the number of business administration majors increased over the previous year. By 1954 they made up the largest single field of undergraduate instruction. Each year the number of majors in the humanities decreases. Each year the number of people being given personality tests in organizations increases. See Ibid., p. 7.

35 In the 1950s women were still a significantly small percentage of the new economy as to be barely noticed by social critics. The feminization of the work place had already begun to shift but its widespread impact was not widely recognized until late in the 1960s. An early bellwether of this reality is Betty Friedan, *The Feminine Mystique* (New York: Norton, 1963).

ethic of bureaucracies. Group loyalty within the bureaucracy produced a fear of any individual high up in the organization asserting too much of their own individualism. The safeguard for economic democracy was the very denial of individualism, which alleged democracies were to protect. This, in the end, was the critique gaining ascendancy in the Left.

If "group belongingness" under girded the new organizational social ethic, it also produced a widening distance from structures of permanence. No longer was one bound to the extended family or village for a definition of one's vocation and economic status. This new found freedom from the past, also brought a new rootlessness. One no longer "belonged" to the family or the village, but primarily to the organization, which one most likely moved significant distances to accommodate. This new found mobility could be intoxicating at first, but many social critics of the 1950s argued that it was finally alienating. It alienated men from that which was satisfying to their souls, the honesty of work which produced a product of significance. An influential New Left social critic, Paul Goodman wrote:

> American society has tried so hard and so ably to defend the practice and theory of production for profit and not primarily for use that now it has succeeded in making its jobs and products profitable and useless.[36]

Work became a means to another end—the end often being defined by the size of paycheck, or the relative prestige it granted one in the community. The job was the means to the good life and not a "good" in itself.

In defining the good life, organization men intuitively thought in terms of material well being and the need to continually upgrade themselves. But they also had a strong impulse towards egalitarianism, sensing that no one ought to have too much. These two impulses did not easily match up. "Getting ahead" was the goal of a consumer culture, but "getting ahead" also meant leaving someone else behind. Somewhere in the middle lay the good life, but like that elusive plateau they sought in the Organization, it seemed to vanish as quickly as one found it. Lost was the objective character of the goodness of work and in its place were the ever changing standards of affluence.[37] The problem arose because of the move from a human centered community to a modern organization where a person's worth was defined by his place in the system. This instrumentalist view of human

---

[36] *Growing Up Absurd*, p. 19.

[37] Paul Goodman writes, with his characteristic edge:

Our abundant society is at present simply deficient in many of the most elementary objective opportunities and worth-while goals that could make growing up possible. It is lacking in enough man's work. It is lacking in honest public speech, and people are not taken seriously. It thwarts aptitude and creates stupidity. It corrupts the fine arts. It shackles science. It discourages the religion convictions of Justification and Vocation and it dims the sense that there is a Creation. It has no Honor," *Growing Up Absurd*, p. 12.

dignity could not satisfy the deepest human longings. But with the newly created affluence, these deep longings could be kept at bay, at least for awhile.

The effective strategy for submerging the deep human longings for satisfaction in modern mass culture was to portray the need for peer acceptance as primary. The currency into which all values tended to be translated was the appraisal by the peer group.[38] Money still made a difference in one's sense of importance (or lack thereof) but in the final analysis the peer group did most of the "talking." And when the peer group did the "talking," inevitably conformity became the highest of values. It created a "mass culture" which thought remarkably alike despite of all the extrinsic differences in the population. The pressure to conform prompted a New Left writer to quip, "We are more alike than ever and feel a deeper sense of entrapment and loneliness."[39]

According to the New Left the fundamental culprits of this socio-psychologically depressing conformism were not individuals but the "system," the structures of modern life under the pressures of market capitalism and bureaucratization. The alleged values of this way of life were trumpeted by an ever pervasive mass media. Mills wrote, representatively of the New Left:

> Very little of what we think we know of the social realities of the world have we found out first hand. The media not only give us information; they guide our very experiences. Our standards of credulity, our standards of reality, tend to be set by these media rather than by our own fragmentary experience.[40]

Daniel Bell and the End of Ideology

The discussion on mass culture surprisingly lost some of its steam by the end of the 1950s and early 1960s in wider intellectual circles. It was not an uncommon response to the critics of mass culture to suggest that it was time to leave that debate and stop blaming the malaise of America on the notion that Americans are nothing but a mass of automatons.[41] The most significant blow to the argument had been the work of Daniel Bell, who elaborated a framework of modern social

---

38 The most influential study of "conformism" in the 1950s was David Riesman's, *The Lonely Crowd: A Study of the Changing American Character* (New Haven: Yale University Press, 1950). This work went through eight printings in eight years, astounding given that it was published by a university press and not a major commercial publishing house. Riesman was not a prophet of the New Left though his argument relating population shifts, consumption and character, was more than ably exploited by the New Left.

39 Bernard Rosenberg, *Dissent* 3 (Winter 1956): 27–8 as cited in Isserman, *Hammer*, p. 100.

40 Ibid., p. 309.

41 Isserman cites even the influential New Left thinker, Irving Howe as sympathetic with this response in the late 1950s. *Hammer*, p. 103.

life without the negative generalizations of mass culture.[42] The grand ideology of Marxism had died, but this did not entail the essentially pragmatic character of modern life should be shunned. This so-called "end of ideology" thesis was first proposed by Edward Shils at a Congress of Cultural Freedom in 1954 and later picked up by Bell and Martin Lipset.[43]

These mainstream sociologists kept hammering home the point that any theory about American society and politics has to begin from a close empirical level before making grand theoretical generalizations that some of the simplifiers (for example, C. Wright Mills, Paul Goodman, Herbert Marcuse and Norman Brown) had made. There can be no "big picture" without many "small pictures" of empirical facts.[44] Though the theory of "mass culture" may have worked at the level of large social generalizations, it had very little substance in actual analytical empirical research. The theory didn't fit anybody in particular, just everyone in general.

Bell claimed that the older humanistic ideologies derived from the nineteenth and early twentieth centuries (most notably Marxism) were exhausted as intellectual systems. They could no longer purport to be satisfying world views. Social theory was at best descriptive of modern life rather than prescriptive about sustaining core human values. If this was so, then social theorists were left without any ideological commitments, other than the commitment to no commitments. This was simply their lot in life.[45] The consequence according to Bell was the pragmatic alienation of the social critic from any and all causes which postulated a grand theory of human identity.

The post-War culture was marked by extraordinary changes in class structure, particularly in the growth of the white collar class and the spread of suburbia; by the "forced expansion" of the economy which belied earlier predictions of

---

[42] Bell's most influential (and widely discussed) work was subtitled provocatively as "On the Exhaustion of Political Ideas in the Fifties." The work was titled, *The End of Ideology* (Cambridge, MA: Harvard University Press, 1960). Also of interest in this regard is Bell's collaborative work detailing the ideological underpinnings of the radical right in the 1950s. This mirrored Bell's discussion of the ideological underpinnings of the Old Left. See Daniel Bell, ed., *The Radical Right* [formerly *The New American Right*] (New York: Doubleday, 1963—originally published 1955).

[43] Published as "Daydreams and Nightmares: Reflections on the Criticism of Mass Culture" in *Sewanee Review*: LXV, 1957. Lipset's primary work in this area was, *Political Man: The Social Bases of Politics* (Garden City, NJ: Doubleday, 1960).

[44] Though Bell does note that:

> Many social scientists, trained largely in technique, scorn ideas—and history—as vague and imprecise, while the humanist mocks the jargon and the often minute conclusions of the social scientists. Both are talking past each other. No one can quarrel with language or procedures, however technical that aim for precision rather than obfuscation. But even at best such procedures, by the modes of abstraction employed, narrow the range of one's vision. (*End of Ideology*, p. 15.)

[45] Bell wrote openly autobiographically of his own sense of intellectual alienation in the introduction to *The End of Ideology*.

stagnation; by the creation of a permanent military establishment and a bedrock defense economy; and by the heightening tensions of the Cold War. Politics could no longer be thought of simply as a reflex of internal class divisions nor as a dispute about the nature of the human person. Larger global realities mandated that politics be much more cautious, much more pragmatic and much less adventuresome.[46] Citing Morris Janowitz, Bell wrote:

> If society were as impersonal, as self-centered and as barren as described by [the mass culture critics], who are preoccupied with the one-way trend from "Gemeinshcaft" (traditional organic communities) to "Gesellschaft" (mass society), the levels of criminality, social disorganization and psychopathology which social science seeks to account for would have to be viewed as very low rather than (as viewed now) alarmingly high.[47]

The charge of "conformism" by the critics of "mass culture" particularly irked Bell. The critics had argued that American mass society imposed an excessive conformity upon its members. But it was hard to discern who was conforming to what. Bell suggested, in historical perspective, there was probably less conformity to an over-all mode of conduct than at any time within the last half century in America. With rising educational levels, more individuals were able to pursue a wider variety of interests. According to the critics, regional and local newspapers providing news and gossip about neighbors ought to have been on the decline because of the overt pressures to conform to a national standard of news, but the reverse was true. Importantly, very little concrete sociological data pointed towards individuals experiencing modern life as driven by conformist pressures. Individuals still experienced themselves as unique.[48]

There was no disagreement between the New Left and Bell as to the character and scope of many of the larger social shifts that had taken place. There had been revolutions in transportation and communications, bringing people into closer contact and binding them together. The divisions of labor had made the economic activities of the diverse sectors of the American population interdependent. Older ties of family and neighborhood had decreased as a result. Ancient faiths were increasingly questioned as the secular spirit grew. For many that had held fervently onto the conservative and to a lesser extent, liberal ideologies of the past

---

46 Bell cited the old (mythic) Polish proverb. When asked the difference between capitalism and communism, the Polish wise man responded, "Capitalism is a system wherein man exploits man. And communism—is vice versa." Bell intended this to infer that politics ought not be driven by large ideological frameworks, but rather by careful and pragmatic considerations. See his *The End of Ideology*, p. 18.

47 Ibid., p. 33.

48 Bell quipped, "The new non-conformism of the Beats has no genuine enemy. The new rebel bears a great deal of resemblance to a prize fighter trying to knock out an antagonist who is not in the ring with him," Ibid., p. 37.

there appeared to be no values which any longer unified American culture. Each person assumed a multiplicity of roles and constantly had to prove themselves in a succession of new situations. Because of all this the individual appeared to be losing a coherent sense of self. Bell readily admitted all of this.

At the root of the Bell's critique was the ambiguous manner in which "mass culture" was used, and which thereby allowed it an ideological flexibility which may have had some theoretical justification but which did not describe the actual actions of any particular person. It was the ability of the critics of mass culture to use the term equivocally across diverse contexts, which permitted the critique to gain an ascendancy in certain intellectual circles.

"Mass culture" could refer to an undifferentiated number whereby everyone was treated as the same. This happened in the case of the mass media. But no one in particular experienced television (or other forms of the mass media) as a member of an undifferentiated mass. Every particular person had particular experiences in their interactions with the mass media and which grew out of a host of factors, including their own unique sociological characteristics.

"Mass culture" could also be used as a kind of indictment upon the judgment of the masses, all of whom appeared to vote in conformist ways. Over the prior two centuries there had been a loss of a ruling aristocratic elite and in its wake, the masses were increasingly given political voice. That political voice however was muted when individuals voted in conformity with the will of new power elites. The evidence of this conformity was simply very large statistical sampling performed by pollsters. However, the ability to take surveys was no indictment upon any particular person's judgment as to what counted as most important for them in making political decisions. Individuals when interviewed separately voted in accord with their conscience, not in accord with a preconceived agenda of the power elites. Individuals only "appeared" to conform to the wills of others if a large enough sample was surveyed. In this sense then mass culture was not an inveterate form of conformism, but simply a very large statistical form of sampling. If the tools of sociology allowed the masses to be "surveyed" according to their political desires, it still remained true that individuals experienced the politics of American democracy individually.

In the hands of the Left, "mass culture" was also used to describe the mechanization of culture with its advanced and dehumanizing technology. Inevitably "work" had been restructured by this reality, but the empirical analysis was not there to support the notion that individuals experienced the new technologies as automatons. And Bell made much of the point that the removal of poverty from the lives of many as a result of the new technologies was experienced as a great blessing. People experienced this new found prosperity as enriching and rewarding, not demeaning and dehumanizing.

It was precisely the "material abundance" of life that underlay most people's experience of modern life. John Kenneth Galbraith may have been right to argue that the modern free-market economy was the first in history not to be absorbed intellectually and conceptually by widespread and entrenched poverty. Galbraith thereby reasoned that the abundance of modern life too often left the political powers apathetic towards poverty. By contrast Bell argued that political pragmatism ought not be confused with apathy. The concern to find specific solutions to specific problems was not a fundamental critique against modern politics. Rather it ought to lead to the recognition that poverty, *per se*, is no longer the central economic reality of modern experience. Poverty, as well as affluence, may induce a political apathy on the part of the populace when life was simply accepted at face value. Bell argued the radical intellectual left could only gain a foothold when expectations of social advancement outstripped possibilities of advancement and resulted in social tensions. That was patently not the case in the upwardly mobile affluent society of modern America.

Cultures dominated by poverty tended towards fatalism and despair. The only remedy in these traditional cultures was a reliance upon superstitious pleadings of supernatural help. The material affluence of modern life served as the primary check against such superstitions, though it yielded no safeguards against people accepting life at face value, nor should it.

In his critique of the critique of mass culture, Bell supposed that:

> the most salient (and empirically proven) fact about modern life was the ideological commitment to social change. And by change was meant the striving for material, economic betterment, greater opportunity for individuals to exercise their talents and an appreciation of culture by wider masses of people.[49]

"Mass culture" had variously been attached to the "bureaucratization" of the emerging white collar economy. Workers in large organizations may have felt a powerlessness over major decisions effecting the organization, but Bell argued, there was no evidence that they experienced this organization as a denial of their dignity and purpose. Purpose was simply experienced in different categories in a bureaucratized economy.

A final alternative depiction of mass culture, which came closest to Bell's own characterizations, "mass culture" was one of widespread political apathy, owing in large measure to the severing of significant traditional social bonds and the consequent political "numbing" produced by mass propaganda programs. If this was true, it was also true according to Bell that modern (Cold War) politics was necessarily more pragmatic and cautious. This may have appeared to produce apathy on the part of the populace, but in fact it was experienced as a partitioning of local personal concerns over against the national and international political concerns. This was not fundamental apathy, but rather widespread recognition of the difference between the concreteness of local concerns and the increasingly pragmatic character of national and international politics.

Bell denied that the critique of "mass culture" was a scientific statement with any hard data detailing the disintegration of society nor the demise of democratic

49 Ibid., p. 30.

processes. Rather it was an essentially flawed defense by the New Left of socialist policies and ideologies, intended to protect their radical prophetic role in modern culture. It failed to account for the differences between sociological generalizations and individual human experiences.

The great challenge posed to American society in the last 200 hundred years had always been; how, within the framework of freedom, to increase the living standards of the majority of people and at the same time maintain or raise cultural levels. By contrast the critics of "mass culture" supposed that America had lost its democratic heritage and therefore risked losing the vision which ought to have animated all public discussion of economics and politics. Bell said nothing could be further from the truth. He claimed: "the critique is too often simply a romantic protest against contemporary life."[50] Modern life was the product of change and was experienced as change. It held out the hope of bringing the "masses" into an experience of high culture from which they were once excluded and granting to each of them the right to experience that culture individually. This was the strength of contemporary culture not its fundamental weakness according to Bell.

There was little doubt that the Left at mid-century was deeply suspicious of the benefits of contemporary life. Bell had also supposed there was an equally deep suspicion of modernity on the right hand side of the political spectrum. The "radical" right had its roots in the "fundamentalist" attacks on science and the patriotic vigilantism of the 1920s. The radical right's constituency did not understand social change and appeared to hold fast to certitudes that no longer existed. Technological progress had undermined the older religious verities of God's creation of the world and of God's providence over history. The radical right claimed that a godless secular humanism was being foisted on America and would eventually undermine the fabric of American life. The public rhetoric often suggested the real enemy of the Right was the Left. Bell surmised however, the extreme right's central enemy was not godless communism but modernity, and in particular the manner in which modernity had made God irrelevant.

From Bell's vantage point the left and the right had a greater uneasiness with modernity than with each other. The right was uneasy because God and country were no longer intertwined in contemporary life. The left had long ago abandoned religion, but was now uneasy because there was no room for social passion and ideology in modern life. Ideals of social justice and equity were as irrelevant as the ideals of God and church. Godless communism and religious fundamentalism were both undermined by modern life.

According to Bell, both the Radical Right and the Old Left presented the dangers of totalitarianism, the former in religious guise, the latter in economic guise. But both threats had safely been deposed of by the events of the twentieth century. The empirical realities of the Moscow Trials, the Nazi-Soviet Pact, the concentration camps of the Russian gulag and the suppression of the Hungarian workers ultimately brought the ideologies of the Left down and its attendant

[50] Ibid., p. 38.

dangers of totalitarianism. Religious Fundamentalism had been historically discredited by modern scholarship and no respectable universities any longer tolerated fundamentalism as a viable set of convictions. Bell was convinced that few serious minds any longer could simply discount these "facts," pretending that the ideologies of the Left or the Right had any real life left in them. Modernity had brought an end to ideology of all varieties both right and left, and thereby accomplished a great good for humankind.

In America, Bell argued circumstances had created a new yearning for a "cause" on the part of the Radical Left and the Radical Right. The demise of the old causes had left an ideological vacuum that must be filled. But the reality was, according to Bell, there were precious few such causes in modern life and surely none for which the comforts of modern life would be sacrificed. Modernity had appeared to "flatten" all such causes by inducing a contentment with the prosperity of modern life. The intellectual ideologues may have yearned for a new cause, but the population was perfectly content without them.

The lesson to be learned? Bell warned the intellectual community that ideologues are "terrible simplifiers" whether on the Right or the Left.[51] For them, one simply had to turn to the ideological vending machine and out came the prepared formulae. When the formulae were suffused with apocalyptic fervor, ideas would become weapons with dreadful results. The future hope of a more just and equitable society must still be meaningful in political discourse, but no longer can it be achieved through ideology. The hope must be an empirical one, specifying where one wants to go, how to get there, the costs of the enterprise and some realization of and justification for the determination of who is to pay. If the last 100 years had taught society anything, it was that the "pragmatic means of democracy" ought to be respected. Ideologies that suppress the verities of free speech, free press, free inquiry, and the right of opposition ought to be resisted at all costs.

A Surprising Disestablishment

Bell's recognition that the critique of mass culture had two opposing sides to it, implicitly supposed that there was a "middle." And in American politics the coalition that held the middle together was always notoriously fragile, if for no other reason than the disestablishment of the middle was an enduring American cycle. The 1960s would bear out this long established tendency. Initially intended as a shot across the bow of the Radical Right, Bell's argument in fact served to galvanize the New Left while also planting the conceptual seeds for the rebirth of the neoconservative movement at the end of the 1960s. Though writing from the vantage point of a chastened establishment liberalism in the aftermath of World War II and the height of the Cold War, Bell's argument served as a platform that sought to justify the cautious intellectual spirit of mid-century America. Bell and

[51] Ibid., p. 405.

his colleagues little realized however, that the unleashing of forces (intellectual as well as social) on the Left and to a lesser extent on the Right, would soon engulf the country. The end of ideology theorists did not see the need for a larger moral vision to sustain a liberal society. As the 1960s proceeded it became painfully clear that human beings needed a moral vision as much as they needed air to breathe.

As the decade of the 1960s opened, the dry pragmatic and behavioral language both of academic and of public liberalism left a vacuum in the nation's spiritual life.[52] Students felt mute and frustrated, experiencing fears and aspirations, moral disappointments and inarticulate longings for whose expression they had no adequate moral vision, social theory or practical method.[53] That this eruption could not be predicted may fairly be granted, without supposing that there is no important link between Bell's defense and the ensuing revolutionary protest. There may have been no causal correspondence between Bell's defense of the spirit of chastened liberalism and the flowering of the New Left, but there can be little doubt that Bell's argument prepared the way for the very conceptual moves that he had sought to undermine.

The critique of mass culture began by focusing attention around the central claims of progress of the new social order. These were the popularly received opinions of society that were perceived as "scientific" and which extended beyond the so-called hard sciences to the soft sciences. Increasingly it was widely trumpeted that human nature could be harnessed for organizational efficiencies that would forever remove the drudgery of work. This was not the claim of Bell and company, but it was the culture that Bell and company had inadvertently defended.

Edward Shils made the claim early on that the critique of mass culture by the Left had been severely mistaken in uncritically endorsing the aristocratic view that the past was dominated by a high culture that was now being debauched.[54] In fact, so Shils argued, the lives of most people in previous times had been brutalized by long hours of work at arduous labor while the entry of the "mass" in society had resulted in the extension of culture—of art, music, and literature—to a degree hitherto undreamed of. But lost on Shils was the fact that the argument was never finally about "high culture" but rather about the lack of participatory democracy at every level of major cultural trends. The critique did not yearn for

---

52 The establishment politics of J.F. Kennedy was belied by the revolutionary rhetoric of his inaugural address appealing to a deeper moral vision for a "new generation" than Richard Nixon's predecessor and therefore Nixon himself. On this point see Theodore White, *America In Search of Itself: The Making of the President 1956–1980* (New York: Harper and Row, 1982).

53 The neoconservative thinker, Michael Novak, who underwent a conversion of ideological convictions during the decade of the 1960s and defended the economics of advanced capitalism could nonetheless lament in retrospect the pragmatism with which capitalism had been defended as the decade of the 1960s began. See his, "A Changed View of 'the Movement,'" *Christian Century*, 13 September 1978: 830–32.

54 In his 1954 address to the Congress on Cultural Freedom.

a lost aristocratic elite, but rather for the wider dissemination of genuine cultural authority. And ironically the critique of the critique ended up appearing to defend the very aristocratic (therefore establishment) elite, that Bell and especially Shils had hoped to undermine.

At mid-century it was a matter of some controversy whether the study of the soft sciences were value-laden in a way that prohibited any "ideologically-free" perspective.[55] The description and critique of mass culture by the Left may well have served larger ideological purposes, but the critique of the critique likewise involved a bias (though not openly and probably not maliciously so) in shaping public opinion.[56] The notion of an ideologically-free ideology seemed somewhat obvious to Bell, but it was ever more precarious as the 1960s progressed. The establishment wrote as if careful and cautious sociological and political analyses had achieved the end of objectivity and neutrality, if not entirely then at least in large part. Cautious empirical studies would protect the wider population from being duped by large ideologically driven projects.

But as the 60s came into full swing the very notion of ideological neutrality came under blistering attack by the New Left and then later by the nascent neo-conservative movement. Even as the self-styled radical intellectuals proposed a far-ranging critique of American culture, the response all too often appeared as an establishment attempt at quieting dissent. Bell was quite conscious in his concern not to carry on the critique of the critique in this fashion, but conceptually it fell there anyway.[57] The defense of the status-quo was not intended as such, but the New Left was able to effectively paint it as such, following centuries old tradition within American anti-establishmentarianism. Those defending those in power were the most to be feared. And from the beginning, the New Left understood this tradition in a way the Old Left never did.

In the decade of the 1950s there was a widespread sense that political apathy had set in due to the conditions of advanced industrialism in the West. The end of ideology theorists had supposed that there were no longer any social roots for a politics which proposed a revolutionary transformation of the social order. But this also appeared as a defense of the political apathy of the decade and inevitably this

---

55 Riesman is one of the few critics of mass culture to affirm his own standpoint-dependent observations. He wrote, "inevitably, our own character, our own geography, our own illusions, limit our view. I must again remind the reader of the limitations of social class and region, and of observational standpoint, which frame the picture of America presented here," *The Lonely Crowd*, p. 373.

56 William Whyte, *Organization Man*, in particular notes this methodological conundrum in the introduction to his work.

57 Alisdair MacIntyre would later remark in regard to Bell's work, "The 1950s were a decade of immoderate claims made on behalf of what its defenders took to be moderation." in "The End of Ideology and the End of the End of Ideology," in MacIntyre, *Against the Self Images of the Age: Essays on Ideology and Philosophy* (London: Gerald Duckworth and Co., 1971), p. 3.

proved to be the soft underbelly of the end of ideology thesis. The very description of the political landscape served as the strongest argument for the legitimacy of ideological debate and even larger ideological claims. If there was little room for a revolutionary transformation of the social order, the 1960s would prove that there was nonetheless plenty of room for a revolutionary protest against the social order. The proclamation of ideology and worldviews, which guided and informed a politics of passionate conflict would in fact be the order of the day, in contrast to the expectations of Bell and company.

Martin Lipset had made the (dubious) historical observation that ideological theorizing in one century had inevitably led to totalitarianism in the next.[58] Bell, Shills and Lipset all believed the twentieth century had borne out this pattern distinctively well. With the demise of the ideologies of totalitarianism at mid-century they believed that empirical evidence could finally be mounted that showed that the age of ideologies was over, hopefully once and for all. But the end of Communist or Nazi ideologies was not the end of ideology as the 1960s would amply prove.

The deeper and more profound point however, was that the end of ideology thesis, by criticizing the deterministic relationship between social structure and ideology found in Marxism, were themselves now open to the charge that their anti-ideology ideology had itself been determined by the social structures of advanced industrialism. That is to say, if social structure determined ideology (or the lack thereof) then something like the old Marxist understanding of ideological formation was in fact not dead, but alive and well in the end of ideology thesis.

Ideology itself was a slippery term, which never quite appeared to be nailed down in the controversy. Generally, an ideology was viewed as an attempt to describe a set of general characteristics about the nature of reality, characteristics which were not themselves characteristics of empirical enquiry, but rather the means by which empirical enquiry itself was illuminated. Defenders of ideology began to argue that empirical evidence was evidence only within an ideological framework. Rules of evidence meant something only when the rules were a part of a larger conceptual paradigm with an established set of presuppositions. But it was precisely this larger paradigm that was disputed. And here a central institution of the Postmodern revolution lay, though it would not be "noticed" for several decades.

The intellectual project of modernity was itself profoundly ideological and perspectival. In the work of Willard Van Orman Quine, Thomas Kuhn and Wilfred Sellars, the philosophical death blow to a biased-free empirical enquiry would be launched among philosophers at the outset of the 1960s. To that episode we turn in a succeeding chapter. Prior to that, the point of this chapter may be summarized briefly.

The end of ideology debate in the late 1950s and early 1960s may well have signaled the end of the age of totalitarian Marxism in the West as a viable

58 See his *Political Man: The Social Bases of Politics* (Garden City, New York: Doubleday, 1960).

ideological framework. And further the end of ideology thesis also brought forth ample evidence to suggest that the conditions of advanced industrialism argued for a present political reality without deep social conflict. But the critics of mass culture understood far better than Bell and company that the end of ideology thesis expressed a peculiar ideology itself, an ideology deeply rooted in the social conditions of modernity. Both sides of the end of the ideology debate would experience the revolt against the establishment (non)ideology in the social protests of the 1960s.[59]

The end of totalitarian ideology was not the end of ideology. The end of the end of ideology would come as the 1960s wore on. Most especially the ideology of the "establishment" would itself prove precarious in the revolutionary decade. Alasdair MacIntyre was correct in writing a decade after the controversy:

> The children of those who define social reality in technocratic, bureaucratic, and academic terms aspire to a definition of human reality that will escape all institutional constraints. The implicit nihilism of so much student attack on institutions was the natural outcome of the defense of the institutions of the status quo as the only possible ones.[60]

Marxist ideology may have appeared "objective" to classical Marxism, only to be exposed as "biased" by mainstream western sociology. But the reverse claim was a "revolutionary discovery" of the 1960s—that mainstream sociology appeared "objective" only to mainstream sociologists. It would be exposed as "biased" by the New Left. This conceptual conundrum was one of the dominant conundrums that reverberated throughout the remainder of the century.

---

[59] Reisman prophetically asked, "We might ask, is it conceivable that these economically privileged Americans will some day wake up to the fact that they overconform? Wake up to the discovery that a host of behavioral rituals are the result, not of an inescapable social imperative, but of an image of society that, though false, provides certain 'secondary gains' for the people who believe it?" *The Lonely Crowd*, p. 371.

[60] MacIntyre, "The End of the End of Ideology," p. 11.

Chapter 5
The Ideology of Gender and the Rebirthing of Feminism

It is a well known fact that theology has been written almost exclusively by men. This alone should put us on guard, especially since contemporary theologians constantly remind us that one of man's strongest temptations is to identify his own limited perspective with universal truth.

Valerie Saving (1960)[1]

Introduction

The Movement for Women's Liberation (as it was called at the end of the 1960s) has not normally been viewed as central to the narrative of the 1960s.[2] Its public phase was relatively late in the decade and its intellectual energy found its primary expression in the 1970s and 1980s. Most histories suppose that feminism was a later derivative of the other protest movements of the 1960s.[3] There is surely some truth in this as regards the public recognition and awareness of the Movement. This standard treatment however can mask the unique contribution of feminism to the revolutionary turn and may fail to see the initial conceptual groundwork laid in the late 1950s and 1960s somewhat distinct from the other protest movements. This is to claim that the seeds of feminism can be found early in the 1960s and thus may be fruitfully mapped onto the wider grid of this era.

The Movement for Women's Liberation capitalized on the unleashing of the democratic impulse characteristic of post-War America. "Equal Rights" was a rallying cry of the Movement and at times the Movement appeared to be content with public policy changes eliminating discrimination against women. However, it had a deeply embedded radical strain which refused the standard readings of the public/private dichotomies so characteristic of post-War America. The personal was political to 1960s feminists. There were no hard and fast boundaries between

1 "The Human Situation: A Feminine View," *The Journal of Religion* 40/2 (1960): 100.

2 Alice Echols is one of the few who have argued for the centrality of feminism to the narrative of the 1960s. See her *Shaky Ground: The 60s and Its Aftershocks* (New York: Columbia University Press, 2002).

3 The standard history of the movement is Sarah M. Evans, *Personal Politics* (New York: Vintage Books, 1980) whose subtitle, *The Roots of the Women's Liberation in the Civil Rights Movement and the New Left*, underscores this point.

the public life of society (politics and economics primarily) and the private lives of its citizens (home, neighborhood and religion). It was the feminist challenge to the privatization of women's lives in particular which served as the catalyst to the much wider conceptual critique not merely to the social status quo, but to the grounds on which that social identity had been established.

The Feminist Movement of this era was less enamored with a hermeneutics of retrieval than a hermeneutics of suspicion. It was far more interested in jettisoning American traditions especially as regards gender than it was in recovering lost ideals of the past which had inadvertently been submerged in the prior century. It viewed the Western tradition as mostly patriarchal at its core and thus its critique tended to sound more persistently radical than the Civil Rights Movement. The feminists tended to engage in social projects of deconstruction both more surprising and more universal in scope than other characteristic movements of the era. The feminist critiques were surprising because they suggested that unbeknown to affluent and middle class white women, their lives manifested a deep and persistent oppression. It appeared as if one had to convince the oppressed they were indeed truly oppressed. This was not altogether unusual as the Civil Rights Movement had faced this issue as well. But especially surprising was their claim that the economically advantaged were in reality socially disadvantaged. Making good on this claim required a more expansive critique leading to the abandonment of fixed notions of human identity. The calls for gender equality were accompanied by a calling into question the very nature of gender and therefore to stable (or what appeared to be stable) notions of human identity. In this fashion, oppression was far more extensive than merely economic or legal discrimination. It was a discrimination of identity whose dimensions included the economic and legal spheres, but could also be extended to include the psychological, the religious, and almost any other socially significant sphere. In making the claim that gender was a socially constructed identity, the Movement for Women's Liberation signaled the demise of the "manly age of modernity" and the emergence of a new era of pluralism and ambiguity. For these reasons feminism deserves inclusion in any archaeological dig for the fossils of the revolution.

First and Second Wave Feminism

The years 1920 and 1972 mark out the defining pieces of legislation associated with the two phases of modern feminism in America.[4] The first Feminist Movement

---

[4] Three useful resources on the social-political history of women in America are Nancy F. Cott, ed., *No Small Courage: A History of Women in the United States* (New York: Oxford University Press, 2000), Ellen Carol Dubois and Lynn Dumenil, *Through Women's Eyes: An American History with Documents* (Boston: Bedford/St. Martin's, 2005) and Sara M. Evans, *Born for Liberty: A History of Women in America* (New York: Free Press, 1997).

crystallized around the passage of the nineteenth Amendment in 1920 granting women the right to vote. 1972 marked the passage of the Equal Rights Amendment (ERA) in both houses of congress specifying the consequences of the Civil Rights Act of 1964 on the matter of gender discrimination. Both official acts of legislation were preceded by years of public agitation and by significant conceptual defenses of women's equality. It is not a historical accident that both were also inextricably linked to movements for racial equality.[5]

The women's rights movement, which started as early as the 1830s and became intertwined with the struggle to abolish slavery, gained early public notoriety at the Seneca Falls Convention of 1848.[6] Elizabeth Cady Stanton and Lucretia Mott, who had previously met as abolitionists working against slavery, convened a two-day meeting of 300 women and men to call for the elimination of public discrimination against women and demand the enfranchisement of American women. A Declaration of Sentiments was adopted by a significant majority, but the proposal for woman suffrage met with greater resistance. The key figure urging the suffrage issue was, quite significantly, Frederick Douglass. On that basis, the conference was historically significant for intertwining race and gender issues. But, as in the twentieth century, so through the end of the nineteenth century, the movements for racial equality would precede those for gender equality.

In 1869 a rift developed among feminists over the proposed fifteenth Amendment, which gave the vote to black men. Susan B. Anthony, Elizabeth Cady Stanton, and others refused to endorse the amendment because it did not give women the ballot. Stanton, Anthony, and Sojourner Truth forcefully sought to link the push for racial equality to that of gender equality. This strategy met with mixed results, failing to have women included in new constitutional amendments (14th and 15th) giving rights to former slaves.[7]

Other suffragists, however, including Lucy Stone and Julia Ward Howe, argued that once black men were enfranchised, women would inevitably achieve their goal. They sought to allow progress to occur incrementally rather than force it to occur simultaneously along racial and gender lines. This latter group supposed that peaceful change had a far better chance in post-Civil War America.

---

5 A thoughtful treatment of the linkage between race and gender in American history can be found in Estelle Freedman, *No Turning Back: The History of Feminism and the Future of Women* (New York: Ballantine Books, 2002). See especially Chapter 4, "Race and the Politics of Identity in U.S. Feminism."

6 See Ellen Carol Dubois, *Feminism and Suffrage: The Emergence of an Independent Women's Movement in America, 1848–1869* (Ithaca: Cornell University Press, 1999).

7 In 1872, Anthony actually went to the polls in Rochester, NY, and cast a ballot in the presidential election, citing her citizenship under the 14th Amendment. She was arrested, tried, convicted, and fined $100, which she refused to pay. In 1875, the U.S. Supreme Court in *Minor v. Happersett* said that while women may be citizens, all citizens were not necessarily voters, and states were not required to allow women to vote.

As a result of the conflict two separate organizations emerged. Stanton and Anthony formed the National Woman Suffrage Association to work for suffrage on the federal level and to press for more extensive institutional changes, such as the granting of property rights to married women. Stone created the American Woman Suffrage Association, which aimed to secure the ballot through state legislation. In 1890 the two groups finally united under the name National American Woman Suffrage Association (NAWSA). In the same year Wyoming entered the Union, it also became the first state with general women's suffrage (which it had adopted as a territory in 1869).

The first two decades of the twentieth century saw a profound change in the lives of women, as they joined the workforce in increasing numbers, led the movement for progressive social reform, and finally generated enough mass power to win the vote. Carrie Chapman Catt and the NAWSA were a mainstream lobbying force at every level of government. By contrast, Alice Paul and the National Woman's Party were a small, militant group that not only lobbied but engaged concerted acts of civil disobedience, conducting massive public marches, political boycotts, and even picketing of the White House. This reflected the now half-century old divergence of strategies within the women's movement. One side was politically connected and publicly peaceful, the other contained political dissidents and was publicly militant. Both were angered that the constitutional amendment granting women's suffrage had been introduced in Congress all the way back in 1878 but otherwise languished in the halls of Congress. This proposed amendment remained a controversial issue for over 40 years, during which the women's movements diverged over strategy but remained ardent allies for the passage of the Amendment. These diverse political actions were reinforced most profoundly by the record number of women entering industry during World War I, which served as the final social argument in favor of women's suffrage. Together it resulted in the adoption of the 19th Amendment on 26 August 1920, granting the ballot to American women.[8] The amendment affirmed that the right of citizens to vote, "shall not be denied or abridged by the United States or by any State on account of sex".

---

8 On the history of the 19th Amendment see Dorothy Schneider and Carl J. Schneider *American Women in the Progressive Era, 1900–1920* (New York: Facts on File, 1993). Profiles of significant women in the struggle can be found in Jean H. Baker, *Sisters: The Lives of America's Suffragists* (New York: Hill and Wang, 2005). The best history of the movement for women's suffrage can be found in Ellen Carol Dubois, *Harriot Stanton Blatch and the Winning of Women Suffrage* (New Haven: Yale University Press, 1997). Dubois places the suffrage movement against the backdrop of the progressive era in which the suffrage movement is not normally placed, but which Dubois argues may be the most typical of the progressive mass movements.

The second Feminist Movement is most often narrated as emerging from the New Left with not a small indebtedness to the Civil Rights Movement as well.[9] The New Left and the Civil Rights Movement unleashed powerful democratizing forces which inevitably produced a backlash against the system of gender relations as they had come to be defined in the post-War period.[10]

There were a few public hints in the early 1960s that an emerging women's movement might be forthcoming. Most notable among these was JFK's creation of a Presidential Commission on the Status of Women, naming Eleanor Roosevelt, the most venerated and admired woman in the country, as its honorary chair. The Commission issued its report in 1963 calling for equal pay for equal work. The very presence of a presidential commission on the issue suggested significant unrest about the status of women in American culture, though the report appears to have had little actual public policy consequences.[11]

The first genuine realization by the wider American public of the women's movement came relatively late in the 1960s often associated with the political push for the Equal Rights Amendment (ERA) in 1968–72.[12] This had been preceded by the formation of the National Organization of Women (NOW) in 1966 with the express intention of lobbying on behalf of the ERA. The actual passage of the ERA ironically also led to its greatest defeat, as the ERA failed to be ratified by a 3/4 majority of states in the union even though it had gained a consensus in both houses of Congress.[13]

The central figure in the founding of NOW was Betty Friedan, whose best selling book, *The Feminine Mystique* (1963) had caught the attention of a culture

---

9 Sarah Evans, *Personal Politics*. Evans traces the origins of the movement into the personal involvement of individual women in the protest movements of the Civil Rights Movement and the New Left, most particularly the Student Non-Violent Coordinating Committee (SNCC) and Students for a Democratic Society (SDS).

10 Most histories of this period draw closer links between the Feminist Movement and the New Left rather than the Civil Rights Movement, again suggesting its more narrow demographic of white middle class women. On the tension within the movement regarding this demographic see Susan Brownmiller, *In Our Time: Memoir of a Revolution* (New York: Dell, 1999). She writes: "There was a common criticism of the women's movement for being white and middles class from its inception, yet no movement agonized more, or flailed itself harder, over its failure to attract vast numbers of women of color," p. 33.

11 Evans, *Born for Liberty*, Ch. 12, "Decade of Discovery: The Personal is Political" chronicles this episode along with several other political demonstrations early in the decade.

12 See William O'Neill, *Feminism in America: A History*, Second Edition, Revised (New Brunswick: Transaction Books, 1989).

13 Out of the 38 states necessary, only 35 passed the amendment. There have been attempts to reintroduce the passage of the ERA in the last decade most notably the so called "three state strategy" arguing that only the ratification by three more states are required for final ratification of the amendment. See, "Why the ERA Remains Legally Viable and Properly Before the States," A. Held, S. Herndon and D. Stager in *William and Mary Journal of Women and the Law* (Spring 1997).

wracked by the conflicts of the Civil Rights Movement and the assassination of its youngest president ever.[14] The book seemed to capture the spirit of weariness of domestic life in the 1950s among many middle-class women. She wrote of the quiet desperation many women experienced when consigned to the vacuous life of a suburban housewife:

> a baked potato is not as big as the world, and vacuuming the living room floor—with or without makeup—is not work that takes enough thought or energy to challenge any woman's full capacity.[15]

Consigned to the trivial, women were in danger of becoming trivial themselves. Her argument did not address classical notions of gender inferiority, as much as the sheer boredom housewives had been assigned in their domesticated tasks. Household chores had been effectively mechanized in the post-War period, but this simply freed women to become enslaved to the machines and to the menial chores so many more of which could be accomplished around the house.

At this populist level, Freidan's critique was less distinctively feminist and much more a dimension of the general critique of mass culture.[16] The post-War period had witnessed an unprecedented economic boom. The Depression era gloom had been replaced by a social optimism in the 1950s. The world's greatest tyrannical powers had been defeated and the growth in the national economy appeared to dull even the psychological tension of the Cold War in that era. Well chronicled now is the entrance of women into the labor force during World War II in ever increasing numbers. With the end of the War, many women remained in the labor force owing to the great expansion of the service sectors of the economy after the war. Rising consumer aspirations required a second family income. With the introduction of the birth control pill in 1960 there was a powerful new means of family planning which in turn allowed women to plan a family around the need to work in the labor force.[17]

The consumer based economy of the post-War period was filled with industrial and technological objects of which most families heretofore had not realized they

---

14 *The Feminine Mystique* (New York: Norton, 1963).

15 Ibid., p. 67.

16 Chapter 4 of the present work explores this critique at greater length. It should be noted that there was considerable tension in the workplace when the servicemen returned home from World War II and pushed many women out of jobs they had held during the war. The tension appeared to remain below the surface during the 1950s, finding its release point in the 1960s. See Elaine Tyler May, "Pushing the limits: 1940–1961" in Nancy F. Cott, ed., *No Small Courage: A History of Women in the United States* (New York: Oxford University Press, 2000) pp. 473–528.

17 Birth control was legalized in 1930 and by 1942 there were more than 800 birth control clinics in the U.S. The pill became FDA approved in 1960. The National Council of Churches officially approved birth control in 1961, Ibid.

were in need. But now the concern to acquire social status influenced the purchase of a suburban home, a second car in the driveway, new refrigerators and washing machines, multiple televisions and radios, and significantly a college education for their children.[18] All of these made it difficult for an ordinary family to survive on the father's income alone. It required the woman of the house to leave home and head off for the office parks being built near the ever-expanding suburbs. Dad might be thinking about middle-management. Mom was left to ponder a career as a secretary. They may have been equally educated, but their job prospects were considerably different.[19]

At home in the suburbs, there had developed a radical separation of domestic life from the world at work, the origins of which date from the nineteenth century. The family unit was no longer economically significant a century after the agrarian economy had ceased to be dominant in America. There had been a radical decline in household production over the previous century and the rise of wage labor made it possible to conceive of the family as a "private retreat from a public world increasingly dominated by impersonal mechanisms of the market."[20] The image of the family as a "haven in a heartless world" helped Americans negotiate the ambivalent emotions evoked by the new work places in the concrete jungles of the urban setting. On the one hand ordinary families wanted the comforts and conveniences furnished by industrial progress; on the other hand the means of progress—the free market—appeared to foster a type of greedy individualism that left little room for moral considerations. Values such as compassion, fidelity and intimacy were pushed to the margins of significance. The result was the growing separation of the public and the private. The private sphere had been associated with the women's arena of responsibility: the home. Her role had been defined to protect the moral spaces of the traditional family from the intrusions of the modern industrial world. The inevitability of industrial progress made the split between the public and private seem almost intrinsic to the "way things are." The "traditional family" was the outcome of such a historical trajectory. The problem was the perception that the traditional family was grounded in the ontology of human beings themselves. In retrospect it may be said that the "traditional" actually meant the "traditionally modern" in the post-War period. The family had been "created" with a modern industrial culture in view. As Christopher Lasch notes:

---

18 For the general social conditions under which a women's identity was shaped in the 1950s see Eugenia Kaledin, *Mothers and More: American Women in the 1950s* (Boston: Twayne, 1984).

19 In 1940 only 15 per cent of women high school graduates went on to college. By 1965, this number was 45 per cent. Virtually overnight America had become a knowledge society. William H. Chafe, "The Road to Equality: 1962–today" in Nancy F. Cott, ed., *No Small Courage*, p. 550.

20 Christopher Lasch, *Women and the Common Life: Love, Marriage and Feminism* (New York: Norton 1997), p. 102.

> The traditional family so called, where the husband goes out to work and the wife stays home with the children, was not traditional at all. It was a mid-20th century innovation, the product of a growing impatience with external obligations and constraints, of the equation of freedom with choice, and of tumultuous world events that made the dream of a private refuge in the suburbs more and more appealing.

The older structures of family life built into agrarian dominated cultures assumed an extended clan and a persistent integration across different dimensions of society. The role differentiation so much a part of the public/private dichotomies of the twentieth century, depended on divisions of labor which only make sense in advanced industrial economies. Without the industrialization of the twentieth century the "traditional family" might not have ever existed.

Domestic life at mid-century was intended to protect the nuclear family from the immorality of the outside world. But with the ever encroaching consumer culture, domestic life became enamored with the comfortable and the convenient. A suburban housewife may have been spared the drudgery of agrarian life, but she had been freed only to find herself in the "comfortable concentration camp" to borrow Freidan's haunting phrase. She was condemned to the vacuous life of being a domestic manager whose chief responsibility was to run the household efficiently with the new fangled machines intended to free her from this very responsibility. Washing machines and vacuum cleaners were invented to allow the housewife to escape the daily drudgery of cleaning the clothes and scrubbing the floors by hand. The unintended consequence was to force her to become an industrial manager in the home, now capable of so much more because she had so many more tools at her disposal. Chores were more efficient, but no less time-consuming because so many more of them could be accomplished in the course of a day. The vicious cycle of the ever expanding power of her domestic tools led to ever expanding expectations about domestic improvements.

The problems were compounded for women who stayed in the public work force, often in low status jobs. They had the double burden of sustaining a low paying menial job alongside their domestic responsibilities at home. There was little economic justice at work where women working the same jobs as men were received less pay. And there was very little equity in sharing chores with their husbands in the home. They were doubly bound to insignificance. For a period of time, the steam in this kettle was held on by tightly capped social expectations. Those expectations came under sharp criticism during the 1960s.[21]

---

[21] Suggestive of this ferment, Sara Evans notes that in 1960 the housewife's predicament was examined the *New York Times*, *Good Housekeeping*, *Redbook*, *Time*, *Harper's Bazaar*, and on CBS Television. In Newsweek there was a Special Science Report and cover story entitled: "Young Wives with Brains: Babies, Yes—But what Else?" See Evans, *Personal Politics*, p. 17.

The post-War generation of suburban women appeared to repudiate the culturally significant life of their predecessors. They saw the family as a refuge from hostile conditions in the public world but also as a retreat from any public responsibilities which their predecessors embraced. Women who took on public commitments outside the home were less likely to move to the suburbs, but such women seemed to be a disappearing breed. These women did not regard themselves exclusively as housewives. They had other contributions to make to the well being of society. The suburban housewives had lost their identity by their implicit acceptance of the roles as managers of the trivial and inconsequential. Women of this kind even refused to take policy-making positions in community organizations, leaving the really interesting volunteer jobs to be filled by men. They justified their resistance to serious community responsibility on the grounds that their families took all their time. Since housework and child care did not absorb their "full capacities" they soon developed the symptoms described by Friedan's "problem that has no name"—chronic fatigue, boredom, loneliness and "nameless aching dissatisfaction." They may have projected an image of being protected from the harsh realities of public life. In reality they were condemned to the even harsher reality of insignificance. From the point of view of the "comfortable concentration camp of the suburbs," the masculine world of competitive achievement looked glamorous and exciting just as suburban domesticity looked warm and reassuring to those disaffected with the rat race. This was not a social balance that could be kept for very long.

Below the surface of these social criticisms of *The Feminine Mystique*, but frankly very much on the surface of Friedan's intentions, were profound challenges to the notion of gender identity and the emergence of cultural stereotypes.[22] Friedan was deeply indebted to the work of Margaret Mead and her findings that human nature expressed enormous flexibility across cultures. There was no such thing as a fixed female nature, much less one as defined by America in the twentieth century. There were no enduring principles which frame a feminine identity in any and every age. There may be a fixed anatomy of the female, but Friedan supposed there was a significant plasticity to the feminine identity manifest in the sheer diversity of sex roles in the different primitive cultures of Mead's studies.[23]

Neither level of Friedan's argument (populist or conceptual) made a central appeal to natural rights, which was so much a part of the Civil Rights Movement and the New Left. Egalitarianism seemed to unite the three movements, but the Second Feminist Movement was not content with the mere expansion of the democratizing

---

22 Friedan's work was much more intellectually nuanced than popular reception suggested. This is to say its conceptual subtleties belie its popular best seller status. On the social significance of Friedan's book in the 1960s see Daniel Horowitz, *Betty Friedan and the Making of the Feminine Mystique: The American Left, the Cold War, and Modern Feminism* (Amherst: University of Massachusetts Press, 1998).

23 See especially Chapter 6, "The Functional Freeze, The Feminine Protest and Margaret Mead," in *The Feminine Mystique*.

process. The Second Feminist Movement was struggling to redefine a women's identity altogether—not only to place it on par with men. In common with the New Left, feminists had a deep suspicion about the economic and consumer impulses of modernity as they came to expression in America at mid-century. But in contrast with the New Left, feminists were intrigued by notions of a radical fluidity to human identity. The Civil Rights Movement had not been much interested in the critique of modernity since they had shared so little in its blessings, but rather had concentrated their critique straightforwardly around racial equality. Only much later did the issue of race identity emerge in the Black Power Movement. For feminism, female equality was important but it was interwoven with the issue of female identity.

The historian William Chafe frames the difficulty of feminism in drawing alliances with these other protest movements of the 1960s:

> If, as some argued, women were oppressed like minorities, they surely did not share the same material circumstances, suffer the same degree of discrimination, or live together in the same run down neighborhoods as some African Americans did on Chicago's South Side, or as Mexican Americans did in the Los Angeles barrios. What, then, did it mean to share an identity? Did a rich white, college-educated woman who ran the local Junior League have more in common with her Latina maid who had never gone to high school than with her rich, white, college-educated husband? What defined the bonds of gender? And could they be as strong as the bonds of class or ethnicity or religion?[24]

The demographic net cast by Betty Friedan in her widely provocative work, covered mostly white affluent suburban married women. Politically well connected, this group nonetheless did not appear overly oppressed on the surface by comparison to many other segments of the female population in the U.S.[25] What this manifested, by contrast to the Civil Rights Movement, was that gender was not a unifying demographic analogous to race, religion or class at mid-century. Race, religion and class were potent social identifiers, but gender appeared fragmented by too many other demographic realities.

At its most popular level, second wave feminism was primarily an affirmation of the equality of the sexes. This provided its moral clarity early in the 1960s when the democratic impulses had been so prophetically proclaimed by the Civil Rights Movement. Extending those impulses to include gender seemed morally and conceptually clear to the early feminists. Moral ambiguity arose however when the category of gender was conceptually dissected in counter-cultural ways.

---

[24] "The Road to Equality: 1962–today" in Nancy F. Cott, ed., *No Small Courage*, p. 552.

[25] Elizabeth Fox-Genovese writes in retrospect, "Who do women mistrust feminism? The short answer is that they do not see feminism as a story about their lives. For some it is a story about rich women's lives, or white women's lives or career women's lives." *Feminism is Not the Story of My Life* (New York: Doubleday, 1996), p. 8.

Were the differences between the sexes only biological? Was there a unique "feminine experience?" Were there fundamental differences between the sexes rooted in biology but whose consequences extended into differences of sexuality and relationships? Were women merely human, or was there something above and beyond being human, which was unique to women? And most poignantly, what was the relationship of gender and sexuality?

The voice of feminist protest was both more complex and more strident than the Civil Rights Movement. The suffering of women was less transparent than that of African-Americans in the age of segregation, but ironically the protest of the feminists were often more radical. They thought not only in terms of equal opportunity, but also of new notions of gender altogether. While there was not a wide consensus on the question of gender identity among the feminists, there was nonetheless an impulse in the Movement that this Pandora's Box must be opened.

The moral clarity of the Civil Rights Movement gave way to the moral ambiguities of the New Left Movements and in this surprising vortex the second feminist movement emerged. The call for racial equality seemed of a different moral order to Americans than the student rights and the sexual revolution and the anti-war movements. In surprising fashion the second wave of feminism captured both the moral clarity of the Civil Rights Movement and the moral ambiguities of the New Left. The core of the Movement consisted of white middle-class educated women, many of whom had been active in or sympathetic to the Civil Rights Movement and the variety of New Left Movements including the anti-war protests. The core issue to feminists of gender, like race after all, could be easily identified and the respective cultures of discrimination justly criticized. However unlike race, gender admitted a far wider set of distinctions beneath the surface, including that of race, class, religion and ethnicity. The moral clarity of race and religion in this era seemed of a different order than gender. And therein lay the dilemma; connect race and gender too closely and the only result would be greater democratization. Disconnect race and gender too much and the moral analogies with the Civil Rights Movement would be lost for the feminists. And one ought not forget that just below the surface for feminism in the 1960s was the socially charged issue of sexuality.[26] That issue was indeed a socially charged issue as the entrenched nature of the culture wars of the last 40 years has born witness. The divergences over gender identity and the nature of sexuality splintered the women's movement at the end of the 1960s in several conflicting directions.[27]

---

26 Martha Nussbaum places the issue of a socially constructed (rather than biologically determined) sexuality at the intersection of the Feminist movement and the work of the postmodern theorist, Michel Foucault. See her, *Sex and Social Justice* (New York: Oxford, 1999).

27 The legacy of this phase of feminism was its intractable fragmentation in several conflicting directions during the succeeding three decades. Rosemarie Tong distinguishes eight different streams in contemporary feminism (Liberal Feminism, Radical Feminism [libertarian and cultural], Marxist Feminism, Psychoanalytic Feminism, Existentialist

The forces of protest unleashed by the women's movement gained social consensus only when the similarities of males and females were emphasized. The argument was straightforward. Each individual human was bestowed with inalienable civil rights regardless of their gender. Each individual human ought to be protected from discrimination in their public roles, as worker, as voter and as consumer. In this regard, race and gender stood on par. When the differences between women and men were brought into the argument, the consensus inevitably broke down. The nature of gender was not a point of cultural consensus, at least not beyond the obvious anatomical differences. At mid-century, America was not persuaded by androgyny, and did not have conceptual or cultural resources to forge a vision of differences in the midst of similarities of women and men.

Feminist Conceptual Resources Emerge

The first significant intellectual salvo at gender stereotypes was Simone de Beauvoir's provocative tract, *The Second Sex*, published in 1949 trenchantly arguing against gender stereotypes.[28] Her work stood almost alone in the post-War world as an assertive feminist challenge to the prevailing ideology which defined the place of women in the home and their natural role as that of the care of men.[29] She steadfastly claimed that "women are made, not born," seeking to demonstrate the social processes through which women acquire those characteristics stereotypical of western femininity and which carried with them submission to male interests. For de Beauvoir, World War II brought German occupation and greatly restrained personal freedoms. In the mid-1940s, when she was composing *The Second Sex*, she had a sense of belonging to a generally defined group—women, who under Nazi occupation had no social space in which to exercise any public roles. This stood in stark contrast to her pre-War existence in which she carried significant public responsibilities. De Beauvoir overlooked the complicating role of German Nationalism in the gender stereotyping and instead considered the simple natural fact that women would always be the "victim of the species" as a result of the biological differences of the sexes:

Feminism, Postmodern Feminism, Multicultural Feminism, Ecofeminism) all of which see significant conflicts with the other streams. Rosemarie Putnam Tong, *Feminist Thought: A More Comprehensive Introduction*, second edition (Boulder, CO: Westview Press, 1998).

28 Simone de Beauvoir, *The Second Sex*, Translated and edited by H.M. Parshley (New York: Alfred Knopf, 1952, originally 1949).

29 See Mary Evans, "Simone de Beauvoir: Dilemmas of a Feminist Radical" in *Feminist Theorists: Three Centuries of Key Women Thinkers* Dale Spender, ed. (New York: Pantheon Books, 1983), pp. 348–65. Evans sets de Beauvoir in the context of contemporary feminism, both in terms of the ways de Beauvoir is ahead of her own times, and the manner in which she still reflects the very stereotypes she is attempting to overcome.

> On the average she (women) is shorter than the male and lighter, her skeleton is more delicate. ... Muscular strength is much less in women. ... she has less respiratory capacity, the lungs and trachea being smaller. The specific gravity of the blood is lower in woman and there is less hemoglobin; women are therefore less robust and more disposed to anemia than are males. .... Instability is strikingly characteristic of woman's organization in general. This lack of stability and control underlies woman's emotionalism, which is bound up with circulatory fluctuation—palpitation of the heart, blushing and so forth—and on this account women are subject to such displays of agitation as tears, hysterical laughter, and nervous crises.[30]

These biological realities led eventually to cultural stereotypes about gender and for which the Nazis simply employed one cultural variant of the universal tendency to subordinate women to men. A fixed biology was "used" to construct gender identities unfairly favoring men.

De Beauvoir argued that the human species alone among the animal kingdom did not have a fixed identity though the facts of their anatomy were indeed fixed: "I deny that [the biological facts] establish for her a fixed and inevitable identity." Humans are creatures of "becoming," not saddled with a static identity as are those of the rest of the animals on earth. The human species is forever changing, not its physiological realities, but its choices and thereby its history. Human identity lies in the underdetermined psychology of the species, not in its over-determined physiology.

It is only in a human perspective that we can compare the female and the male of the human species. But [generic] man is defined as a being who is not fixed, who makes himself what he is. As Merleau-Ponty very justly puts it, man is not a natural species: he is a historical idea. Woman is not a completed reality, but rather a becoming, and it is in her becoming that she should be compared with man; that is to say, her *possibilities* should be defined.[31]

> Humans are what they choose to become. Women are not any different in this regard than men. The cultural myth has supposed that only men were really human. Women somehow existed with an identity partially like an animal and partially like a beast.
>
> One is not born, but rather becomes a woman. No biological, psychological or economic fate determines the figure that the human female presents in society; it is civilization as a whole that produces this creature, intermediate between male and eunuch, which is describe as feminine.[32]

---

30 *Second Sex*, pp. 31–2.

31 Ibid., p. 34.

32 Ibid., p. 267.

Here de Beauvoir's indebtedness to Sartre and the existentialist movement of the 1930s is clear.[33] Though there are biological fixed points, one's social identity is a blank slate filled in either by the fully deliberate choices of the individual or by the choice to abdicate these robust human responsibilities. Women can regain their humanity by asserting the freedom of their will or they may accept the condition of passivity imposed upon them by their social expectations. Her higher calling, quite obviously was to actively participate in the culture-making responsibilities which heretofore had been the province of men alone.

The abdication of the culture-making responsibilities most often happened by accepting the stereotypes which their surrounding culture had placed upon them. In most traditional Western cultures this social identity of women has appeared as fixed as their physiology of reproduction. The biological realities of the reproduction organisms in fact served as the justification for grounding a women's identity in her status as mother. For de Beauvoir, mothering is almost always laborious and burdensome: "Mother, wife, sweetheart are the jailers."[34]

These social roles inevitably imprison a woman to the home and away from public life. They undermine her ability to speak as men speak to the great issues of the day, or to create in the way men create the great works of culture. She longed for an equality, not simply of opportunity in the public arena but also of actual cultural production. She wanted to unleash the potential of women to take on roles and responsibilities that had historically been denied them. She wanted women to become like men in this regard, exerting their wills independent of any cultural prohibitions. Removed from these limitations, she was convinced that eventually the ranks of cultural geniuses would include both women and men.

For de Beauvoir, there was not yet a deepened sense of anything peculiar to a women's way of being as there would be in later feminism. Underlying her criticism of cultural stereotypes was nonetheless still a "universal human nature" in which both women and men should strive to actualize in their own person. She could also but glimpse into a future where women would gain technological control over their reproductive capacities along with the consequent revolution in cultural attitudes towards sex and sexuality. She was enamored with taking control of one's own destiny, but did not yet grapple with the conceptual complexities of gender in a technologically affluent culture.

---

[33] It has long been a question whether Sartre exerted the more significant philosophical influence in the partnership with de Beauvoir or the other way around. There can be little doubt that de Beauvoir was a first rate intellect in her own right. It was probably nearer to the truth that their work, even when composed separately manifested a complicated and interwoven partnership of ideas. For the most recent book length review of their relationship see Hazel Rowley, *Tete-a-Tete: Simone de Beauvoir and Jean-Paul Sartre* (San Francisco: HarperCollins, 2005). De Beauvoir and Sartre's longstanding relationship is well documented by de Beauvoir in her autobiographies; *Memoirs of a Dutiful Daughter, The Prime of Life, Force of Circumstance* and *All Said and Done.*

[34] *Second Sex*, p. 717.

It is not sure that her "ideational worlds" will be different from those of men, since it will be through attaining the same situation as theirs that she will find emancipation; to say in what degree she will remain different, in what degree these differences will retain their importance—this would be to hazard bold predictions indeed. What is certain is that hitherto woman's possibilities have been suppressed and lost to humanity, and that it is high time she be permitted to take her chances in her own interest and in the interest of all.[35]

De Beauvoir chastised socially-embedded gender roles, but could not yet see the manner in which this problematized the very conceptual constructs of gender. It is that problematizing of gender, much more pronounced than even the problematizing of race, that served as a critical piece in the nascent cultural revolutions in the early 1960s.

What appears as the first serious essay engaging the conceptual questions at the heart of the later feminist controversy was a little noticed article by Valerie Saiving published in the *Journal of Religion* in 1960.[36] It predated by almost a full decade other serious work among feminists in protesting the notion of a "universal perspective" inclusive of both genders.[37] There is no more clear conceptual boundary demarcating the modern from the postmodern than the revolt against a "universal perspective." What marks Saiving's essay as uniquely significant is not its later direct influence upon the early prophets of the postmodern turn, nor her status in the intellectual community, but rather her near prescient analysis of the importance of "perspective" to the project of human knowledge.[38]

Saiving's essay is all the more striking because the religious guild was stereotypically closed to women at this time, and also because the vanguard of feminist fragmentation in the 1970s was most assuredly in the religious guild. As in the Civil Rights Movement, religion in the early years of the feminist movement was a keen but overlooked generator of conceptual change. At mid-century religion was conceived as a conserving force in American public life, but in this regard it also served to conserve the ideals of democracy and justice. Religion may have

---

35 Ibid., p. 715.

36 Valerie Saiving, "The Human Situation: A Feminine View:" 110–12.

37 Ginette Castro argues that there are three phases to the second feminist movement: the first was individual and collective consciousness-raising; the second involved exploration of women's historical legacy; third and final stage was the devotion to developing an ideological framework which legitimated the earlier phases. See her *American Feminism: A Contemporary History* (New York: New York University Press, 1990). The surprise is that Saiving's article appeared prior to the outset of the first phase, as a conceptual argument justifying the two later phases, at least in religious circles.

38 Angela Pears maps religious feminism onto the two main phases of feminism in American history. She argues that in fact one cannot separate the one from the other, and cites the essay by Saiving at such an early stage of the second feminist movement as one indication. See Pears, *Feminist Christian Encounters: The Methods and Strategies of Feminist Informed Christian Theologies* (London: Ashgate, 2004).

provided a context for the abuse of these ideals as well, but it provided a reference point outside of the social status-quo to serve as a rebuke to the very abuses it often perpetuated.

Saiving spelled out the dilemma facing the religious guild in the ambiguities of perspective in a manner characteristic of the second feminist movement and which helps to map the early conceptual grid of feminism onto the wider construct of postmodernism. The ambiguities of perspective were rooted in the differences and yet similarities of women and men. The realities which religion strove to explicate had to be filtered through different sets of lenses in the case of women and men. Saiving may have written in overly large generalizations about the "feminine experience," but she steadfastly refused to accept that a women's experience of the world was in all respects identical to a man's experience:

> It is a well known fact that theology has been written almost exclusively by men. This alone should put us on guard, especially since contemporary theologians constantly remind us that one of man's strongest temptations is to identify his own limited perspective with universal truth.[39]

What Saiving refers to as "well known" was surely not yet a part of the intuitive structures of theology and yet would become almost second nature once the postmodern theorists gained sway a decade and half later. The entrenched nature of "perspective" would require the project of deconstruction to which Saiving quite assuredly did not commit herself. But nonetheless she argued that the differences between men and women had for too long been neglected in academic inquiry. These differences would become themselves points of great controversy, but Saiving significantly rooted her perspective on "perspective" in the diverse sexual identities of women and men:

> The twentieth century has witnessed the shattering of too many of our traditional conceptions of sexual differences for us any longer to ignore the tremendous plasticity of human nature.[40]

The "shattering" of the stereotypes of gender had been accomplished by the work of cultural anthropologists in the three decades prior to Saiving's article. She referenced the work both of Ruth Benedict and Margaret Mead. Theologians of neo-orthodoxy at mid-century would have rarely appealed to cultural anthropologists such as Benedict and Mead. Yet Saiving, trained at Chicago in theology and anthropology, saw trajectories of influence little noticed at the time.

Human nature was the object of great theological interest classically and in the post-War period. Reinhold Niebuhr's *Moral Man and Immoral Society* (1932) expressed a deep and enduring interest in the fragility of human nature against the

---

[39] Saiving, "Human Situation:" 100.

[40] Ibid.: 101–102.

backdrop of the great social conflicts of the early twentieth century. Niebuhr came to embody the politics of Christian realism which took radical human sin seriously. He was constitutionally opposed to the optimism which pervaded both the social project of liberal Christianity and the anti-social evangelism of fundamentalist Christianity. Niebuhr broke decisively with the "social gospel" outlook of the Christian left and the revivalist preaching of the early Billy Graham. In contrast to both, he argued that power was the principal ingredient in negotiating the competing claims of nations, races, and social classes. Conflict and tension were permanent features of history because human sin was persistent across all civilizations and time periods. Niebuhr's overtly pessimistic account of human nature and the body politic was rooted in the theological construct of sin as a prideful exercise of power. It was based not merely on observation of the world as it is, but also on a theology which emphasized that sin is endemic to the human condition in history. From the beginning humans were centrally tempted to prideful assertions of their will granting them an illusion of control and purpose. Human reason (ala the social gospelers) nor mere faith (ala the fundamentalists) could by themselves constrain selfishness and the will to control others. The fundamental social dialectic for Niebuhr was rooted in this theological account of human nature and human sin.

Though hardly in tune with the consumer optimism of American culture at mid-century, Niebuhr argued (unwittingly) that the pervasiveness of sin was accounted for by appeal to a universal conception of sin—as the prideful exercise of power. This may have appeared prophetic well into the naively-optimistic decade of the 1950s, but to Saiving in 1960, Neibuhr's construct of human nature could not account for the cultural diversity of human nature. Benedict and Mead had shown there was a relativity of social constructs of human identity across primitive cultures. In particular cultural anthropology at mid-century, was committed to the notion that gender differences, though persistent across cultures, were spelled out in a multitude of diverse manners. Gender roles were inventions of culture rather than fixed points across all cultures. This required for Saiving the recognition that the theological construct of sin ought to be "adjusted" to account for the diverse accounts of human identity.

The concept of sin as a prideful exercise of power was rooted in a western male experience. A young boy goes through the rituals of adulthood by proving himself in distinction from the rest of his clan or family. A young girl goes through the rituals of gaining access to adulthood by becoming like her mother, "authenticated by a series of definite natural and irreversible bodily occurrences: first menstruations, defloration, child-birth, menopause." In their sexual relations, "the man takes the action, the woman largely receives the action."[41] "The man succeeds or fails by acting or not acting."

The will to power to which Niebuhr pointed as a universal condition of sinful human creatures, was in reality the peculiar temptation of men in Western

41 Saiving was again prescient of later feminism in seeing rape as a social behavior largely condoned in the West because of its "male" orientation.

culture according to Saiving. The male identity had been grounded in this cultural assertiveness and its excesses may well have been adequately described by Niebuhr. Saiving goes so far as to say:

> Every culture, as we have said, superimposes upon the necessities of sexual roles a whole structure of masculine and feminine character traits. Many of these addenda are only tenuously related to the foundation on which they rest, and they may even be completely contradictory to that foundation. When this phenomenon is carried to its extreme, so that women, for example, are educated by their society to despise the functions of childbearing and nurture, then the society is in grave danger of bringing about its own destruction. Similarly, where procreation is valued so highly that men attempt to participate directly in the processes of pregnancy, birth and the rearing of children to the exclusion of other kinds of creative activity, the social fabric again becomes dangerously weak.[42]

Western culture had tended to overvalue the traits characteristic of men. The modern era stretching roughly from the Renaissance and Reformation to the contemporary period had been a "masculine age par excellence." The rise of capitalism, the industrial revolution, the colonial era, the triumphs of science and technology emphasized and encouraged precisely those values classically and stereotypically associated with men. It placed the highest value on external achievement, on economic competition and uncertainty, and most especially on the widening of the gulf between family relationships, on the one hand, and the public life of business and politics, on the other. There can be little doubt that it increased a natural sense of insecurity and anxiety. The naïve optimism which Niebuhr was attempting to counter, was rooted in the mythology that modern "man" could eventually accomplish all these goals and conquer all these obstacles—by asserting himself more fully. His theological account of sin written in the classic tradition of the West, inevitably came to be suspicious of this stereotypical male perspective. This suspicion led to a theological universalizing about the nature of sin across all humans, as if all humans were tempted by the desire to conquer the world. Undoubtedly there may have been some women in the modern era who accepted these prevailing values of the stereotype but refused to accept its fixed gender distinctions. They sought a male identity, taking on "the challenges and opportunities, risks and insecurities of participation in the masculine world." To these women who had essentially sought to become stereotypical males, classical Western notions of sin may have been appropriate. But most women had not sought to instantiate the cultural values of the male stereotype. Most women had in fact succumbed to a different malady altogether. To the vast majority of women, therefore, Niebuhr's account of sin was not adequate:

---

42 Ibid.: 105–106. It would be left to later feminists to argue that notions of sexuality themselves were socially constructed.

> [T]he temptations of woman as woman are not the same as the temptations of man as man, and the specifically feminine forms of sin . ... have a quality which can never be encompassed by such terms as 'pride' and 'will to power'. They are better suggested by such terms as triviality, distractibility, and diffuseness; lack of an organizing center or focus; dependence on others for one's self-definition; tolerance at the expense of standards of excellence. ... in short, underdevelopment or negation of the Self.[43]

The possibility that women could actually lose a sense of significance had not been countenanced on the conceptual horizons previously. That a woman could "give too much of herself" away and thereby cease to have anything left to give, seemed counter-intuitive to male notions of pride and power. "Feminine sins have little to do with pride or will-to-power," but much to do with triviality and insignificance. The "feminine dilemma" was the acceptance of a religious notion of self-sacrifice combined with the very real cultural possibility of the sacrifice of self altogether. The cultural stereotype of the female tended to encourage women to lose themselves in activities which were merely trivial.[44] The loss of significance rather than the aggrandizing of significance was the peculiar dilemma to which theologians had blindly not addressed themselves.

Saiving ends her provocative essay with suggestive comments about the era into which the modern world was entering, or "ending" as some now muse. Technology itself had presented the possibility that "women's work" could be left to machines, presenting women with the possibility of escaping the realms which traditional stereotypes assigned them. Yet there were other forces at work in the culture exercising enormous pressures of conformity to these very stereotypes. The power of technology both to liberate and dominate presaged a day not far in the future when men and women risked losing their significance, not by the prideful exercise of power, but the self negating and passive permitting of technology to rule all of human life: "There is, it seems to me, a growing trend in contemporary life toward the feminizing of society itself including men as well as women."[45]

---

43 Ibid.: 108–109.

44 Saiving adds in somewhat dated terms, "Yet it is the same lack of creative drive which may make it possible for her to perform cheerfully the thousand-and-one routine tasks—the woman's work which is never done:" 109.

45 Ibid.: 110. It should be remembered that Saiving wrote this nearly 20 years before Ann Douglas' work, *The Feminization of American Culture* (New York: Alfred Knopf, 1977) laying out the argument at any length to which Saiving here points out. Hans Frei supposed that Saiving ought to have said what Douglas later was to argue, that the sentimentalizing themes of American culture point not to a distinctively female perspective on sin, but rather to a cultural embrace of romanticizing trends. Frei may be correct, but that Saiving still pointed to a distinct feminine perspective is suggestive of the "turn to perspective," characteristic of the later postmodern ethos. See Frei, "Comments on Elizabeth Moltmann-Wendel" at http://www.library.yale.edu/div/Freitranscripts/Frei07-Patience.htm.

America may have been a culture of dissent on the surface, but underneath there was a high degree of conformity. This very trend she suggests, "presages an era as different from what we call the 'modern age' as the modern age differs from the medieval."[46]

Feminism and The Radically Radical?

Mapping second stage Feminism (in its early 1960s phase) in this fashion illuminates why it was the most radical of the protest movements of the era precisely because it was most conceptually dissonant movement. Its paradigmatic skepticism of received opinions about gender mark the Feminist Movement very much a part of the revolutionary decade, but its protest seems more radical in retrospect than other protest movements of the era. The feminist challenge was rooted not only in an extension of the democratizing ethos of the other movements, but also in a persistent questioning of the cultural intuitions about the nature of the democratically constituted self. In other words, feminists criticized both the passive role assigned to women in American culture at mid-century, and also questioned whether there was anything stable about the feminine construct as a whole.[47]

De Beauvoir, Saiving and Friedan each expressed a disdain for the hubris of Western culture in carefully controlled gender stereotypes.[48] They were suspicious, for different reasons, of the picture of knowledge as objective and neutral, inherited from generations past. Knowledge of gender relations largely excluded a "women's perspective," even if there was no consensus about the nature of a "women's perspective."[49] There was no longer any confidence that men could speak on behalf of every human. The perspective from which one spoke deeply

---

[46] Saiving refers at this point to David Reisman's *The Lonely Crowd* (1950), Hannah Arendt's *The Human Condition* (1958), and Lionel Trilling, *Freud and the Crisis of Our Culture* (1955), each of which raised deep suspicions about the arrogance of the modern era and thereby lent a hand in the cultural revolution of the 1960s.

[47] On the intersection of later feminist developments and postmodernism, see Nancy Frazier and Linda Nicholson, "Social Criticism without Philosophy: An Encounter between Feminism and Postmodernism," in Linda Nicholson ed., *Feminism/Postmodernism* (New York: Routlege, 1990), pp. 19–38.

[48] Echols comments, "Women liberationists developed an understanding of power's capillary-like nature, which in some respect anticipated those being formulated by Michel Foucault and other poststructuralists. Power was conceptualized as occupying multiple sites, and as lodging everywhere even in those private places assumed to be the most removed from or impervious to politics—the home, and more particularly the bedroom," *Shaky Ground*, p. 90.

[49] It is not uncommon among feminists to suppose on this point de Beauvoir is still very much a modernist by virtue of her acceptance of enduring and essentialist notions of gender. See Christine Di Stefano, "Dilemmas of Difference: Feminism, Modernity and Postmodernism," *Women and Politics*, vol. 8, no. 3 (1988): 1–24.

mattered, especially when it came to matters of unique significance for women. Too often women had accepted their social roles, not because they were rooted in the feminine nature, nor because there was a persuasive argument nearby. Rather, their social roles were accepted because of the (mistaken) notion that this was "the way things are".[50]

The political and economic assumptions were masked behind the rhetoric of "traditional morality" or "traditional religion", as if the tradition of American gender relations was its own justification.[51] Especially in the work of Saiving, the tradition-specific nature of religious assumptions about gender was brought to the fore as the means to undercut the universalizing tendency of those assumptions. Religious belief and practice was rooted in particular and concrete traditions, many of which did not seem to speak to the predicament of women. The intuitive character of that claim today belies how radical it was in the early 1960s.

Friedan's broadside against American chauvinism borrowed heavily from the earlier critiques of mass culture in the 1950s. The "empty self" of mass culture manifested itself most clearly in the suburban housewife of Friedan's critique. The loss of substantive connections to the community and the body politic in the life of the suburban housewife were all too troubling to Friedan. Too many housewives had lost themselves not by their own willful choice but because of the social arrangements in which their lives were lived out. Their identity had been socially constructed without their consent and without their best interests in view.

The feminists of the early 1960s may have accepted the public/private dichotomies of modern life, but it seemed clear to them nonetheless that women ought not be privatized.[52] Public discrimination against women was the primary target of Friedan's work, for she believed that women ought to be treated no differently in the public spheres than men. "Equal pay for equal work" was the hallmark of her influence in the National Organization of Women. De Beauvoir believed women ought to be free to determine their own destiny as a function

[50] Susan Bordo draws a straight line from the feminist revolutions of the 1960s and 1970s to Richard Rorty, *Philosophy and the Mirror of Nature* (Princeton: Princeton University Press, 1979) on this point. She suggests that the challenge to the objective representation of gender of second phase feminism was an important seed to Rorty's claim "that ideas are the creation of social beings rather than the representations or mirrorings of nature." Bordo, "Feminism, Postmodernism and Gender-Scepticism" in Linda Nicholson ed., *Feminism/Postmodernism* (New York: Routlege 1990), p. 136.

[51] The project of deconstruction of later postmodern theorists is bound up with this kind of unmasking, by which allegedly "self-justifying" claims are themselves in peculiar historical and cultural contexts. On the manner in which this unmasking strategy is central to feminism, see Jane Flax, *Thinking Fragments: Psychoanalysis, Feminism and Postmodernism in the Contemporary West* (Berkeley: University of California Press, 1990).

[52] Later feminist theorists tended to resolutely reject the construct of the private/public realms as the last vestiges of a masculine social theory. Representatively see Anna Yeatman, "A Feminist Theory of Social Differentiation" in Linda Nicholson ed., *Feminism/Postmodernism* (New York: Routlege, 1990), pp. 281–99.

of their natural gifts. She was nervous about social determinisms of every kind. Saiving supposed there was still a public role for theology to play, but it had to be reshaped with a women's perspective if it was to remain prophetic.[53]

Each in turn operated with a residue of modern individualism believing that women had been deprived of many of the ordinary rights accorded to men as individuals in American society. Saiving was less enamored with the rugged individualism than other early feminists because she feared this was part of the mythology of the tradition of liberal theology at mid-century. Theologies which saw pride as the primary form of sin reflected a notion of human identity centered on the will. But she refused to accept this universal account of human identity, preferring instead a richer and in part a pluralistic account. The provocative nature of Saiving's argument lay in her plain sense rejection of a single metanarrative of sin. She thought it counter-intuitive to most women that theologians always spoke with their perspective in view.

The feminist constructs of the early 1960s had not yet grappled with the embrace of pluralism so prominent a decade later. There was still an explicit affirmation of modern individualism tending towards androgyny. Saiving wrote, by contrast of significant gender differences but still in such a fashion that the perspective of "all women" was describable in identifiable ways. The "mininarrative" historiography, so characteristic of women's studies in the succeeding decades, would be one way to capture the pluralist impulse embedded in the radical turn.[54] Recognizing gender as one strand alongside other complicating strands of human identity such as race, class, ethnicity and age would be another way to guard against a "universal women's perspective."[55] Early in the 1960s, the simple rejection of a single (male) perspective created the conceptual space for the later narrative turn in Feminism. The seeds had been planted but the harvest was still a ways off.

---

53 Some have questioned whether the move to empower women in the public sphere was yet one more phase of modernity's undermining of the private sphere. Jean Bethke Elshtain writes: "With the end of modernity, the question then is: will women simply accept the tenets of the modern by accepting the devaluation of the family in favor of the 'power of the public' sphere?" Elshtain, "The Power and Powerlessness of Women" in Gisela Bock and Susan James, eds, *Beyond Equality and Difference: Citizenship, Feminist Politics and Female Subjectivity* (New York: Routlege, 1992), p. 122.

54 The term "mininarrative" is borrowed from Fraser and Nicholson, "Social Criticism without Philosophy". Representative of this mininarrative approach is Sara M. Evans, *Journeys That Opened Up the World: Women, Student Christian Movements, and Social Justice, 1955–75* (Philadelphia: Temple University Press, 2003).

55 Cf. Seyla Benhabib, *Situating the Self: Gender, Community and Postmodernism in Contemporary Ethics* (New York: Routledge, 1992).

PART III
Hopeful Pessimists

Chapter 6
The End of Epistemology and The Death of Foundationalism

> For my part I do, qua lay physicist, believe in physical objects and not in Homer's gods; and I consider it a scientific error to believe otherwise. But in point of epistemological footing the physical objects and the gods differ only in degree and not in kind. Both sorts of entities enter our conception only as cultural posits.
>
> W.V.O. Quine (1953)[1]

The disenchantment with modernity which the 1960s trumpeted signaled the dawning of a new era in the discipline of philosophy. It was to be an era markedly different in tone than its predecessor, less prone to make exaggerated claims about the importance of philosophy and also much more circumspect about its possibilities. Philosophers had increasingly lost their public prominence during the first half of the twentieth century becoming more technical as well as openly hostile to the religious faith of the ordinary person. "Poets and novelists had taken the place of both preachers and philosophers as the moral teachers of the youth."[2] Among English speaking philosophers, many of the perennial philosophical problems appeared to have been dissolved into linguistic and logical puzzles and were apparently of little interest to the wider public any longer.[3] The crisis of identity for the discipline of philosophy which all of this signaled must surely be considered a part of the narrative of the wider crisis of modernity in which the intellectual and religious debates of the 1960s are to be situated.

Hitler's rise to prominence forced many European intellectuals of note to migrate across the Atlantic to America in the 1930s and brought with them a distinctive distaste for America pragmatism, the singular contribution of the

---

1 "Two Dogmas of Empiricism," in Quine, *From a Logical Point of View* (Cambridge: Harvard University Press, 1953), p. 44.

2 Richard Rorty, *Philosophy and the Mirror of Nature* (Princeton: Princeton University Press, 1979), p. 5.

3 The emergence of the Ordinary Language movement in Anglo-American philosophical guild in the 1950s associated with names such as Gilbert Ryle, J.L. Austin and Peter Strawson is testimony to this claim. An historical overview of the movement is Oswald Hanfling, *Philosophy and Ordinary Language: The Bent and Genius of Our Tongue* (New York: Routledge, 2000).

American academy to the discipline of philosophy.[4] The most influential of the philosophical immigrants brought a vigorous empiricism with them, hoping their alliance with the natural sciences could revive the reputation of philosophy in the English speaking world.[5] They had earlier been known as the logical positivists or the logical empiricists and were most publicly identified with the Vienna Circle, a group of hardheaded philosophical atheists led by Moritz Schlick who met regularly together in the Austrian city during the 1920s.[6] These immigrant philosophers were indeed strangers in a strange land upon their arrival in America in the 1930s and 1940s. Their influence however was far and wide and immediate in the American philosophical guild. They successfully captured the modern love affair of philosophers with science and brought with them the prestige of old Europe to the American academy.[7]

Their rise to prominence was unexpectedly accompanied by an equally quick and incisive critique of their convictions by several American thinkers leading to their eventual demise at the outset of the 1960s. Logical positivism was dealt these withering conceptual blows after the Second World War from diverse angles, most prominently by former positivists. At the end of the 1950s the supremely confident

---

4 Cornell West, *The American Evasion of Philosophy* (Madison, WI: University of Wisconsin Press, 1989) narrates the following story from the vantage point of the rise, decline and resurgence of Pragmatism. In particular he locates Quine and Rorty in the tradition of pragmatism. He sees the revolution of ideas in which they were major participants, as originating in the pragmatist distrust of epistemology. This distrust of epistemology gains traction because of the implosion of logical positivism from within (as narrated in this chapter) in addition to the long standing of Pragmatism on American soil (as narrated by West).

5 There are linkages among some of the German philosophers with that of American pragmatism. One thinks of the later Wittgenstein in particular. However, the general distaste for the pragmatic tradition among the German immigrant philosophers in the 1930s and 1940s is far more widespread than these linkages. See Barry Smith, *Austrian Philosophy: The Legacy of Franz Brentano* (Chicago: Open Court, 1994). Hans-Johann Glock, "Vorsprung durch Logik: The German Analytic Tradition" in *German Philosophy Since Kant*, edited by Anthony O'Hear (Cambridge U.K.: Cambridge University Press, 1999), pp. 137–66, argues that philosophical traditions within twentieth century German-speaking world had a much stronger interest in ordinary language than is ordinarily noticed. This is not to defend the claim that this was the dominant strand, simply that it was a significant and enduring one.

6 The group met periodically from 1923 to 1938. It included mathematician Hans Hahn, physicist Philipp Frank, the social scientist Otto Neurath, the logician Rudolph Carnap, the philosopher Viktor Kraft. Late in the group's tenure philosophers Herbert Feigl and Friedrich Waismann along with mathematicians Kurt Goedel and Karl Menger joined occasionally. See Thomas Baldwin, ed., *The Cambridge History of Philosophy 1870–1945* (Cambridge: Cambridge University Press, 2003).

7 For this reason as Michael Dummett has claimed it is a misnomer to refer to the tradition of philosophy concerned with analysis of language, "Anglo-American" philosophy. Rather it should be referred to as "Anglo-Austrian" philosophy given its primary roots in Vienna. See Dummett, *Origins of Analytical Philosophy* (Cambridge: Harvard University Press, 1993).

philosophical system of logical positivism was on its last legs. That demise was not merely the waning of influence of the logical positivists but in retrospect may be seen more broadly as the demise of the many dominant intuitions of the modern era of European philosophy from Descartes to Kant. This broader demise of the modern philosophical project was not as widely noticed until the late 1970s and 1980s though its sharpest criticisms were located in the late 1950s and early 1960s. The end of logical positivism also signaled a new era for religious belief in the philosophical guild, long the locus of atheism in the academy.

Certain philosophical dogma had been at the center of the modern philosophical tradition even as theological dogma had been at the center of medieval Christendom.[8] It would have seemed odd to speak of "dogma" with respect to the modern philosophical project as indebted as it appeared to be to doubt and skepticism.[9] Yet one could be forgiven for drawing analogies between the criticisms of foundational commitments in the 1520s and the 1960s. The former represented a religious upheaval of unprecedented proportions while the latter signaled very important shifts of philosophical paradigms. Through the first half of the twentieth century, the "dogma" of philosophers included the privileging of empirical observation, the objectivity of science and the autonomous knowing self. For reasons detailed below these dogmas all were repudiated in the late 1950s and early 1960s. During the last decades of the twentieth century these dogmas actually came to be viewed as heretical by the philosophical guild. The grand philosophical dogmaticians from Descartes through A.J. Ayer had led the discipline of philosophy down a dead end, though this was not readily apparent as the decade of the 1960s dawned. The perennial problems of modern philosophy were not so much solved in the 1960s as they were dissolved.[10] In retrospect it is not surprising that belief in God made a comeback when the dogmas of scientific philosophy were abandoned, if no longer on secured by the evidence of the classical proofs for God's existence. Foundations of all sorts were being undermined.

The metaphor of philosophy as "foundational" pushed modern philosophers to suppose their work was conceptually prior to all other intellectual endeavors. Through the first half of the twentieth century, this was understood largely in

---

[8] For the sake of clarity while masking enormous complexity, the "modern tradition" in philosophy refers to the period from Descartes (1596–1650) to Logical Positivism (1920–50). In standard philosophical historiography the classical modern period runs from Descartes to Immanuel Kant (1724–1804) while the late modern period spans the nineteenth century and the first half of the twentieth century.

[9] M. Jamie Ferreira, *Scepticism and Reasonable Doubt: The British Naturalist Tradition in Wilkens, Hume, Reid and Newman* (Oxford: Clarendon Press, 1986).

[10] See Robert Bambrough, "Fools and Heretics" in *Wittgenstein: Centenary Essays*, ed. A. Philipps Griffiths (Cambridge: Cambridge University Press, 1991) for an exposition of the intractable character of philosophical problems and the "dogmatic" tendency of philosophical decisions in Ludwig Wittgenstein's writings at the end of the modern philosophical project.

terms of locating the true and permanent beliefs upon which the natural sciences could be built safely, even though actual working scientists seemed to get along quite well without paying attention to any of the alleged foundations. The cultural dissonance between philosophers and scientists mirrored the dissonance between philosophers and popular culture at this point. Philosophers thought themselves far more important than anyone else.

The crack in the philosophical dike appeared when a small number of philosophers themselves abandoned the project of finding secure foundations. These folk were no longer confident of the assertions associated with their predecessors and began to raise provocative doubts about the discipline of philosophy itself. Some suspicions were local in scope, others more global. A critical mass of thinkers began to doubt prior certainties and abandoned the "self-evident truths" of philosophy as neither self-evident nor true. The tradition was not only rejected but appeared to implode from within. Its chief critics were some of its earliest and loudest proponents. What may have begun as a quibbling over some of the details of the empiricist project early in the twentieth century became at mid-century an all-out assault on the nature of the philosophical discipline itself in the legacy of the modern European traditions. Was it any accident that all of this happened in the 1960s?

The "Story" of Modern Philosophy

The "story" of modern philosophy is more complicated than standard histories suppose. The standard histories appeared to narrate the history of philosophy as if its thinkers and its ideas had little contact with actual concrete social realities. Knowledge and the search for it seemed strangely absent of personal and cultural influences. The "ideas" of philosophy seemed to float free in the ethereal world of professional philosophers. Historians of philosophy told the story of philosophy in a peculiar way so as to reinforce certain conclusions. Most notably that there was a conceptual line that reached from Rene Descartes in the sixteenth century, running through David Hume in the English speaking world and Immanuel Kant in the German speaking world in the eighteenth century. The standard historiography supposed the nineteenth century was a conflicted era in philosophy framed by central disagreements about the legacy of Kant's work. The story proceeded then to narrate the twentieth century as the re-emergence of the original lineage of the early modern period in the English speaking world with Bertrand Russell and G.E. Moore and in the German speaking world with the early Wittgenstein and the Vienna Circle.[11] The return to the early-modern period was a return to clarity and

[11] Rorty comments: "The proposed remedy for this situation (that is, philosophy not being scientific enough) typically consists in adopting a new method; for example, the method of 'clear and distinct ideas' outlined in Descartes' *Regulae*, Kant's 'transcendental method,' Husserl's 'bracketing,' the early Wittgenstein's attempt to exhibit the meaninglessness of

objectivity. It was a return to a time when philosophers only believed what could be proved. It was a return to the role of the philosopher as the policeman of ideas. This was the "story" of modern philosophy.[12]

According to the inherited story, the early modern period of philosophy initiated a critique of the religious foundations of knowledge by calling into question the fundamental principles of traditional religious belief. Religious beliefs were dubious because they lacked scientific evidence in their favor. The dominant religious framework of the medieval era had been committed to two central convictions: the affirmation of a normative divine authority and the affirmation of a divine teleology. God had spoken and God had infused history with divine purposes. Modern philosophy rejected these two convictions outright. The heart of the criticism was simply that the God of traditional Western (Augustinian) Christian theology, had died.[13] Belief in God was still alive among philosophers, but no longer as the foundation upon which the project of human inquiry was built. Several other dominoes soon fell as well. If God had died (or became silent) then the divine right of kings was but a chimera. Next followed a deep suspicion about the church as the protector of the common good. These institutions of king and church were replaced by a turn to the subject, and the "flight from authority" was on.[14]

For the paradigmatic figure of the eighteenth-century English Enlightenment, David Hume, every theological conclusion had to be supported by non-theological premises.[15] In other words, every religious belief had to have a secular reason supporting it. And according to Hume and many other thinkers of that era, the evidence was simply not there in sufficient amount to support the claims of traditional religious belief.[16] Hume and his philosophical successors still supposed

---

traditional philosophical theses by due attention to logical form." Rorty, "Introduction: Metaphilosophical Difficulties in Linguistic Philosophy," in *The Linguistic Turn*, ed. Richard Rorty (Chicago: University of Chicago Press, 1967), p. 1.

12 This is the "story" of the rise of modern philosophy as it was rehearsed in all the major histories of philosophy in the English (and German) speaking world through most of the twentieth century. Representatively see Frederick Copleston, *A History of Philosophy* (New York: Image Books, 1946–62). See esp. vols 4–6.

13 This is the claim made by David Ray Griffin, *God and Religion in a Post-Modern World* (New York: State University of New York Press, 1992).

14 This is Jeffrey Stout's term chronicling the turn to the subject in this era. See his, *The Flight From Authority: Religion, Morality and the Quest for Autonomy* (Notre Dame: University of Notre Dame Press, 1981).

15 Cf. Hume, David, *Dialogues on Natural Religion* (Indianapolis: Bobbs Merrill, 1980, originally 1779).

16 Nicholas Wolterstorff makes the claim that Christianity was radically affected by this challenge. Arising in this period was the attempt by theologians to ground their religious beliefs in secular evidences, a strategy he refers to as evidentialism. See his "The Migration of Theistic Arguments: From Natural Theology to Evidentialist Apologetics" in Robert Audi and William J. Wainwright eds, *Rationality, Religious Belief, and Moral Commitment* (Ithaca: Cornell University Press, 1986), pp. 38–81.

that knowledge required secure and stable foundations, but in the age of the European Enlightenment, those foundations had to be sufficiently secular to sustain the early-modern scientific project.[17] Religious assumptions could no longer serve that purpose and thus were relegated to a different realm, the realm of faith.[18]

In the empiricist tradition of David Hume and John Locke there was a reverence for the claims of science as the primary grasp upon the world. A disinterested, objective scholar was in a far superior position to knowing the world as it really was than any religious cleric of the pre-modern period. The academic centers of Europe and North America expressed a cultural suspicion of the authority of tradition and religion, accepting only the result of a rigorous empirical study. The suspicion of religion and the triumph of human reason as it was manifest in the scholarly guild, appeared to be the legacy of modern empiricism.[19]

Controversies in religion ought to be resolved by appeal to a neutral, objective analysis of universal human experience. Gone were the touchstone tests of faith where religious belief strove to be faithful to an ecclesiastical magisterium (Roman Catholic) or to the data of Scripture (Protestant). According to the Enlightenment ideal every belief needed a reason, except one— the belief in reason as a neutral decision-making procedure.[20] But what about this belief? Why does it not need evidence in its favor? Why should one believe in reason as a neutral decision-making procedure without any supporting reasons? Frederick Nietzsche posed these sorts of questions at the end of the nineteenth century planting seeds later harvested by the radical end of postmodern intellectuals. The historical irony is that these sorts of questions also appeared in the work of a group of positivist-inspired philosophers (quite independent of Nietzsche) at the end of the 1950s and early 1960s. At that point, the questions exposed the fundamentally mythological character of the dogmatic assertions of modern empiricism. Those dogmatic assertions clustered around the claim that reliable knowledge was built upon unshakeable empirical foundations. The assertion of unshakeable foundations however appeared as more akin to a fundamental act of faith than to a scientific and critical act.

---

17 Wolterstorff argues that Locke rather than Hume is the key figure in this development. The general trend remains the same however. See Wolterstorff, *John Locke and the Ethics of Belief* (Cambridge: Cambridge University Press, 1996).

18 The classic expression of this is Immanuel Kant, *Religion within the Limits of Reason Alone* (1793).

19 Buckley, Michael, *The Origins of Modern Atheism* (New Haven: Yale University Press, 1987).

20 The "decision-making procedure" was interpreted in a diversity of ways, though the implicit consensus was that the procedure ought not be prejudiced by religious commitments. See Planting Alvin, "Reason and Belief in God" in *Faith and Rationality: Reason and Belief in God*, Alvin Plantinga and Nicholas Wolterstorff, eds (Notre Dame: University of Notre Dame Press, 1987), pp. 1–87. See also Wolterstorff, *John Locke*.

Another working assumption which came under withering attack in the 1960s was the privileging of disinterested, objective scholarship. The privileging of the academic guild, though a long and cherished tradition in Europe seemed no longer tenable in the democratizing spirit of America in the middle of the twentieth century. Popular opinion might have agreed that ecclesiastical commitment prejudiced one's view of reality but scholars had vested interests as powerful as any priest or vicar. The seventeenth and eighteenth centuries were filled with calls to loosen the bonds of church and academy, and in the 1960s the hierarchies of professor and student were profoundly turned upside down as well. The result was a reverse privileging of ordinary discourse and the suspicion of the technical jargon of the academy.

The myth of intellectual progress associated with the Enlightenment had depended upon the functioning authority of science, but with the devastation of two World Wars, science and those who practiced it, were no longer viewed as merely neutral observers.[21] The era of scientific progress abounded but the era of scientific neutrality was coming to an end in the 1960s. It may have been possible at the end of the nineteenth century to believe that the certainty of progress lay with the work of objective and dispassionate modern scientists in building upon sure and certain foundations. That sense of progress was lost in the 1960s.

The End of the Enlightenment?

In an older religiously-inspired understanding of human inquiry, science was prohibited from addressing problems to which the church had already committed. Still in the shadow of the Enlightenment, philosophers in the first half of the twentieth century thought this restriction seemed hopelessly out of place. Empirical research could not simply be stuffed through the filter of religious belief. The promise of the Enlightenment held out too much hope to be shackled by religious conviction.[22]

---

[21] An extended narrative treatment of the myth of progress in the west and its apparent decline in the twentieth century can be found in Christopher Lasch, *The True and Only Heaven: Progress and Its Critics* (New York: Norton, 1991).

[22] It must be remembered that the Enlightenment was largely an intellectually-inspired movement and thus for most of its life was largely isolated among a relatively few university-related people. The implications of the Enlightenment are not felt (nor believed) on a popular level for well over a century or more. As James Turner remarks: "Despite the perils supposed to beset belief [in God], unbelief in fact remained unthinkable to all but a tiny handful [in the eighteenth century]." *Without God, Without Creed: The Origins of Unbelief in America* (Baltimore: The Johns Hopkins University Press, 1985), p. 35. Turner's work and Henry F. May's *The Enlightenment in America* (New York: Oxford University Press, 1976) are both helpful treatments of the diffusion of the Enlightenment into popular American culture over the past two centuries and in this sense are indispensable in grasping the lasting impacts of the Enlightenment upon contemporary culture.

The intellectual momentum at the beginning of the twentieth century was clearly headed in the direction of religious unbelief.[23] The major philosophical voices accepted the sacred and secular divide of Kant, but pressed the divide in a fashion unforeseen by Kant. The secular all but gobbled up the sacred. Traditional religious belief had been on trial for a century and the guilty verdict echoed throughout the work of the secular philosophical prophets.[24]

Kant had argued at the end of his first major work, *the Critique of Pure Reason*, that the objects of the noumenal world ("God" and "self" most prominently) were not objects of knowledge, but rather objects of faith. The secular prophets of the nineteenth century accepted this premise but instead of viewing the objects of faith as protected from the inroads of empirical and scientific inquiry (as Kant had hoped) they viewed these objects as irrelevant and in many instances, damaging to human progress. Radical thinkers of the nineteenth century had wondered aloud why people believed in God if there was no evidence for such a being. In the philosophical guild in the first half of the twentieth century, increasing numbers of professional philosophers were likewise inclined.

There was no purer form of the Enlightenment philosophical project in the twentieth century than logical positivism.[25] And there was no greater philosophical upheaval than that created by the demise of logical positivism shortly after mid-century.[26] The sharpest and most enduring critique of logical positivism occurred in the late 1950s in philosophical work largely done in the American academy and most by former positivists. These philosophers voiced cynicism about the conviction that reason simply followed the evidence wherever it led. "Reality" was not the bedrock upon which truth simply rested. "Reality" was rather a point of social consensus about perceptions of the "way things were." Deep philosophical

---

23 The rise of Logical Positivism in the 1920s was a major turning point in Europe in switching the burden of proof from atheism to theism. Two recent sympathetic histories are: Friedrich Stadler, *The Vienna Circle: Studies in the Origins, Development, and Influence of Logical Empiricism*, translated by Camilla Nielsen et al. (Wien: Springer, 2001) and Michael Friedman, *Reconsidering Logical Positivism* (Cambridge, UK: Cambridge University Press, 1999).

24 The tradition of secular prophets dated to the nineteenth century and included thinkers such as Ludwig Feuerbach, Karl Marx, Frederick Engels and Frederick Nietzsche. There was no "school" to which a secular prophet belonged. They were simply the most notable and influential philosophers encouraging a secular spirit and reacting to the negative influences of religion in the West. See Alistair McGrath, *The Twighlight of Atheism* (New York: Doubleday, 2004).

25 The standard summary (and able defense) of Logical Positivism at mid-century in English was, A.J. Ayer, ed., *Logical Positivism* (New York: Free Press, 1959).

26 Sahotra Sarkar has collected many of the primary documents surrounding the rise and demise of the Vienna Circle into a 6 volume series entitled, *Science and Philosophy in the 20th Century* (New York: Garland Press, 1996). In particular note vol. 2, *Logical Empiricism at Its Peak: Schlick, Carnap, and Neurath* and vol. 5, *Decline and Obsolescence of Logical Empiricism: Carnap vs. Quine and the Critics.*

disagreement could only be explained if truth wasn't something "out there" but rather a human construct built from diverse human experiences. Science was not that much different from religion in this regard.

In his flagship work signaling the dawning of a new philosophical era, Richard Rorty openly displayed his indebtedness to four philosophers, all of whom wrote their most influential works in the 1950s and early 1960s: W.V.O. Quine, Wilfred Sellars, Thomas Kuhn and Ludwig Wittgenstein.[27] These influential figures provided the plausibility structures whereby philosophers in the 1970s and 1980s could write as if the Enlightenment philosophical project had already been laid in the grave.

It is also significant that each of these earlier writers had been aligned with the positivist tradition in the early years of their writing. Wittgenstein was clearly the most dominant of the voices, though maybe also the most misunderstood (and recognized as such). Quine drank deeply at the wells of philosophical naturalism which so shaped the positivists and early on he conceived of his work as a fundamental extension of the atheistic postulate of the Positivists. Both Sellars and Kuhn appreciated the Positivists' love of the "hard sciences" and originally believed their work was engaged with nothing other than the attempt to describe the actual work of everyday scientists.[28]

The Story of Foundationalism

At the turn of the twentieth century Bertrand Russell and G.E. Moore were the dominant philosophical figures in the English speaking world. Both were resident at Cambridge in England and both seemed bent on promoting the interests of philosophy in the service of natural science as against its service to an older religious idealism and supernaturalism.[29] Neither of them showed any sympathy for the place of religious belief in public life.

Science had been separated in a variety of ways from the discipline of philosophy, the least of which was its separate space in the university curriculum over the last half of the nineteenth century. It had developed its own professional associations and journals as had philosophy. Increasingly philosophy's self-identity was wrapped up with its defense of the hard sciences, a defense little noticed by scientists but used ever so trenchantly by philosophers such as Russell and Moore against the older supernaturalism.

---

[27] Wittgenstein died in 1951 and most of his later writings were published posthumously, becoming available in the late 1950s and early 1960s.

[28] The turn by philosophers towards the actual practice of science in the latter half of the twentieth century is ably discussed by Philip Kitcher, *The Advancement of Science: Science without Legend, Objectivity without Illusions* (New York: Oxford University Press, 1993).

[29] See Peter Hylton, Russell, *Idealism and the Emergence of Analytic Philosophy* (Oxford: Clarendon Press, 1990) for a treatment of Russell and Moore in their rejection of Idealism, the regnant British philosophy at the end of the nineteenth century.

The methodological empiricism of David Hume formed the prologue to the story of the early twentieth century philosophers. It was a story narrated through the central methods of the natural sciences; observation and description. As Russell and Moore conceived of their tasks, they realized that philosophy could not make empirical discoveries in the fashion of science but philosophers could clearly describe the language and fundamental commitments of science and thereby perform a great service on behalf of science.

The service consisted largely of analyzing the language of science and the competing vocabularies of religion, art and ethics. As the Victorian Age was coming to an end during the early decades of the twentieth century, Russell and Moore were confident that the antiquated claims of religious believers could be set aside as well. A new day was dawning for philosophers and the optimism of the early twentieth century was reflected in the secular confidence of these philosophers of naturalism.

Ludwig Wittgenstein's early work, *The Tractatus Logico-Philosophicus* published in 1921 picked up the spirit of Russell and Moore and laid the intellectual groundwork for much of the Anglo/American philosophical work of the first half of the twentieth century.[30] It was in this work that Wittgenstein formalized an atomistic view of language, permitting philosophers to analyze the "atoms" of language much the same way as scientists analyzed the atomic parts of reality. For Wittgenstein, the atoms of language were nouns which somehow "hooked onto" the objects they named. The word "ball" was the atomic piece of language which referred to an actual round object in the world. Wittgenstein described the relationship between the noun and the object by means of an analogy of a picture and the landscape of which it was a copy. The picture "represented" or "corresponded" to the landscape. Wittgenstein believed this captured the essence of the relationship between nouns (sometimes described as mental pictures) and objects.[31]

This notion of a correspondence between language and the world, provided a ready-made framework for the relationship of science and philosophy as well. Science described the world and philosophy described the language of science. In particular philosophy was concerned with the claims of correspondence that lay at the heart of the project of the natural sciences. By analogy with a camera, science took the pictures and philosophy explained the way in which the pictures corresponded to the world. Any claim about reality which could not sustain this analysis of correspondence were declared meaningless—or as Wittgenstein wrote in his final aphorism of the book, "what you cannot speak you must pass over in silence."[32]

---

30 Trans. D.F. Pears and B.F. McGuinness (London: Routledge and Kegan Paul, 1961), first German edition, 1921.

31 See Donna Summerfield, "Fitting versus Tracking: Wittgenstein on Representation," in *The Cambridge Companion to Wittgenstein*, eds, Hans Sluga and David Stern (Cambridge: Cambridge University Press, 1996).

32 *Tractatus Logico-Philosophicus*, 6.54.

Logical positivism arose as a philosophical movement in the 1920s and 1930s inspired by Wittgenstein's portrayal of the formal character of philosophy and the material character of science. The movement also openly expressed a hostility towards all metaphysical claims outside the bounds of science. Claims about God, the "good" or the "beautiful" all had to be abandoned as nothing more than descriptions about someone's inner feelings. Science could never lay its hands on God and thus philosophers ought to stop speaking of God as if he were an object to which the noun "God" referred. Rather "god" was simply a meaningless term with no real reference in the world.

In the positivist conception, philosophy was a second order discipline that serviced the first order claims about the "world" as science understood it. It is science, they believed, that gives us our knowledge of the world. If science could not verify the existence of God, then philosophers had the responsibility to abandon such language. There is not, and cannot be a philosophical brand of knowledge which would compete or conflict with science. What then is the task of the philosopher if it is not to speak about the world like a scientist? One thing they could do, "of course, is to act as a sort of intellectual policeman, seeing that nobody trespasses into metaphysics."[33]

Logical positivism was most associated with a group of intellectuals that gathered as an informal society in Vienna around the figure of Moritz Schlick in the 1920s and early 1930s. Schlick had come to the University of Vienna in 1922 to occupy a chair in Philosophy. He began a discussion circle with a group of philosophers, mathematicians, and physicists around the central problems of philosophy. By 1929 they had published their first manifesto[34] and had taken over the influential journal, *Erkenntnis*.[35] They organized their first worldwide congress in Prague in 1929 and believed themselves to be the forerunners of a burgeoning global intellectual movement. Wittgenstein never formally joined the circle though he remained an influential voice in it through his ties to Schlick.[36]

---

33 A.J. Ayer, "The Vienna Circle" in *The Revolution in Philosophy*, A.J. Ayer and others (New York: St. Martin's Press 1956), p. 79.

34 Hans Hahn, Rudolph Carnap and Otto Neurath, Wissenschaftliche Weltauffassung: Der Wiener Kreis, ed. Verein Ersnt Mach (Vienna: Artur Wolf Verlag, 1929), trans. Paul Foulkes and Marie Neurath, "The Scientific Conception of the World: The Vienna Circle" in Marie Meurath and Robert S. Cohen, eds, *Empiricism and Sociology* (Boston: Reidel, 1973), pp. 299–318.

35 *The Journal of Unified Science* (Leipzig: Meiner).

36 The standard treatment of Wittgenstein's relationship to the Vienna Circle is found in Norman Malcolm, *Ludwig Wittgenstein: A Memoir*, second edition (New York: Oxford University Press, 2001). Wittgenstein refused to meet with the full Circle, but did meet with Frederick Waismann and occasionally Schlick. Wittgenstein appears to have been quite suspicious of Schlick's self-promoting tendencies. The details can be found in the definitive biography of Wittgenstein, Ray Monk, *Ludwig Wittgenstein: The Duty of Genius* (New York: Penguin Books, 1991).

The Vienna Circle had started out with noble enough aims. They had sought to come to grips with the tremendous impact that the empirical sciences had had upon the modern world. Most of them were trained in one or another of the sciences and only later in life turned to the classic problems which philosophy had sought to address.[37] Their manifesto brought both clarity and precision to the emerging movement. It was straightforwardly anti-metaphysical and it very clearly took the "linguistic turn."[38] The real subject of philosophy was language rather than reality, words rather than things. Philosophy was not another science, but rather the means to clarify the language of science.

In their manifesto, they claimed an historical trajectory reaching straight back to the Enlightenment figures of Hume and Hobbes and Rousseau, tough-minded intellectuals who were anti-metaphysical and generally skeptical about all religious and moral claims. This lineage justified rejecting out of court all claims not suited for the modern secular academy.

For the positivists the fundamental building block of knowledge was the simple term which denoted a simple object in the world. The central philosophical problem was then to determine how terms (and propositions which were just collections of terms) denoted or referred to objects in the world and thus how they got their meaning. The positivist program may be described as a kind of linguistic foundationalism in that language was thought to map onto the bedrock of the actual world in a one-to-one fashion. One term to one object. This was the legacy of the early Wittgenstein and carried on by the logical positivists. As they put it in the Manifesto, "there is knowledge only from experience, which rests on what is immediately given. This sets the limits for the content of legitimate science."[39] In the language of philosophy this was an affirmation of physicalism, that language was meaningful when it hooked onto physical objects. This in turn rested upon their linguistic foundationalism, therefore language was like a pyramid built upon the foundations of nouns which referred to empirical objects in the world. One of the important consequences of this kind of foundationalism was the distinction between synthetic and analytic statements. Synthetic statements were true in virtue of mapping one-to-one onto empirical facts. Analytic statements were true in virtue of language alone. These were statements about statements so to speak. "Bachelors are unmarried men" is not a statement about any objects in the world, married or not. It was rather a claim about the linguistic connection between words. The term "bachelor" is synonymous with "unmarried men." The statement was true simply in virtue of the meaning of its terms. It was a statement about language, rather than a statement about the world. The statements of mathematics and logic were

---

[37] This is especially so with the members of the Vienna Circle. See A.J. Ayer, ed., *Logical Positivism*.

[38] This is Richard Rorty's term. It is explicated in a collection of essays edited by Rorty, *The Linguistic Turn*. Rorty's "Introduction" to the original edition provides an important comparison for his later work.

[39] *The Scientific Conception of the World*, p. 300.

primary examples of analytic statements. The statements of mathematics and logic were true in virtue of the intrinsic meaning of their terms.[40]

The meaning of a synthetic statement was its mode of verifying whether the statement was true or not. Verification was an empirical or experiential project. One verified the statement, "there are 10 cows in the field" by going out and actually counting the cows in the field. As Wittgenstein said in the *Tractatus*, "to know a proposition is to know what the case would be for it to be true."[41] No incidentally the statements of metaphysics and theology and ethics were cast into the flames of meaningless discourse. Those were statements not true with respect to any empirical realities, nor were they true in virtue of the meaning of their terms. Unlike the statements of science, they had no cognitive significance.[42]

Apart from the formal and technical character of their arguments, the positivists were giving expression to a fundamental postulate of the Enlightenment. Objective knowledge consisted in those empirically tested statements of science removed from the prejudices of religion and tradition.[43] Religious belief was a hindrance to the free pursuit of knowledge. It was the philosophers' task to make the world safe for science freed from the shackles of religion. The Vienna Circle wrote of the "spirit of a scientific conception of the world," and going so far as to make the claim, "It became increasingly clear that a position not only free from metaphysics, but opposed to metaphysics was the common goal of all [of the Vienna Circle]."[44]

A Brief Eulogy

With the rise of the Nazi movement in Germany and especially with the *Anschluss* of Austria in 1938, many of the influential intellectuals in the Vienna Circle had to flee Europe. Rudolph Carnap departed for the University of Chicago. Hans

---

40 The primary resource in the positivist tradition for thinking about analytic statements was Bertrand Russell's Pincipia Mathematica (London: Routledge, 1992, orig. 1903).

41 *Tractatus Logico-Philosophicus*, 4.024.

42 The infamous verifiability criterion of meaning was the formal name given to this intuition. Only those statements which could be verified were meaningful. Since the statements of religion were not verifiable, they must be meaningless. The most notable attempt to defend the criterion was A.J. Ayer, *Language Truth and Logic* (New York: Oxford University Press, 1936). This book went through many printings with its last in 1952. The self-referential problems with the principle were well rehearsed in the philosophical literature of that time but what remains stunning is the sheer rapidity with which the principle was abandoned after being so loudly championed by the most prominent group of philosophers in Europe in the 1920s and 1930s.

43 David J. Peterson, *Revoking the Moral Order: The Ideology of Positivism and the Vienna Circle* (Lanham, Md.: Lexington Books, 1999) highlights the implicit and explicit irreligious components of the Vienna Circle's goals.

44 *The Scientific Conception of the World*, p. 299.

Reichenbach went to UCLA. Alfred Tarski landed at Berkeley. Gustav Bergman ended up at Iowa. Herbert Feigel relocated to Minnesota. Carl Hempel took up professorial duties at Princeton and Ernest Nagel went to Columbia. Their departure from Austria entailed the demise of the Vienna Circle as a definable movement but they took with them many of the fundamental convictions of the movement to America. Not insignificant to the demise of the movement as well was the murder of the original leader of the movement, Moritz Schlick in 1936. He was shot on the front steps of the University of Vienna by a demented student, whose thesis on ethics, Schlick had refused to pass.[45]

It was in the late 1950s and early 1960s that the movement was dealt its most incisive intellectual death blow in the work of W.V.O. Quine, Wilfred Sellars, Thomas Kuhn and most ironically in the later work of Wittgenstein himself. The outlines of the arguments are important to keep in mind at this point, but even more critical is the larger narrative which was being written in the work of these "post-positivists." The end of positivism signaled the end of foundationalism as an adequate picture of the way human knowledge is constructed. The end of foundationalism was the key philosophical development in the last half of the twentieth century. The demise of foundationalism allowed for diverse portrayals of truth and knowledge and consequently brought the social influences on human knowing to the fore. It might also be said that the intellectual hubris of logical positivism was brought to a screeching halt in the withering criticism of Quine, Sellars and Kuhn. Before long a deep suspicion grew about the positivist project altogether. The doors began to open towards an intellectually anarchy of ideas, cultivated in the soil of the tumult of the 1960s. The death of positivism did not force the tumultuous decade upon American culture, but it did provide a critical piece of the plausibility structure which permitted it to happen and it most assuredly presaged the advent of postmodern thought in its varied moods.

W.V.O. Quine and the Hegemony of Harvard

The piecemeal and building-block approach to knowledge made for great analogies and metaphors but it also opened the door to incisive criticism of the positivist project. The first devastating critique came from within the movement itself, from the pen of W.V.O. Quine in his widely influential article, "The Two Dogmas of Empiricism."[46]

---

45 See Barry R. Gross, *Analytic Philosophy: An Historical Introduction* (New York: Pegasus Books, 1970) for a helpful historical depiction of the movement in Vienna.

46 "Two Dogmas of Empiricism," in Quine, *From a Logical Point of View* (Cambridge: Harvard University Press, 1953), pp. 20–47.

Quine (1908–2000) was a logician who rose through the ranks in Harvard's philosophy department during a long and distinguished teaching career.[47] He had been trained as a graduate student at Harvard in the tradition of pragmatism and was also deeply influenced by the progress of the hard sciences in the twentieth century.[48] Harvard, from the 1700s onwards, was the one dominant institutional force in American philosophical circles. Quine was undoubtedly its most influential thinker through the 1950s and 1960s.

Quine rejected the analytic/synthetic distinction so sacred to the positivists and to the modern epistemological project. This shocked the philosophical world and most especially it shocked the nascent American positivist movement of the 1950s. Quine argued that truth and falsehood were functions of both language and extra-linguistic facts. There were no truths based strictly on the observation of facts. All of knowledge was mediated by the language in which it was expressed as well as the experiences which gave rise to it in the first place. Knowledge, in some sense, was relative to both language and facts. There may be some statements more connected to an experience of the world but no statements were entirely a function of our experience. All statements were connected to the language in which they were expressed. In this sense truth existed on a continuum somewhere between the world and the language in which those truths were expressed. Knowledge became a web-like structure.[49]

A significant dilemma which drove Quine to this conclusion concerned the character of "truth." There were two competing theories about the relationship of language and the world, phenomenalism and physicalism. Phenomenalism claimed that language about the world could be reduced in the end to language about particular bits of experience. The intuition was that there was no way to get outside of language to know whether language hooks on to the world truthfully or not. There is no independent perspective different from a person's individual perspective to gauge whether a person's unique perspective is true or not. One cannot know whether language actually pictures the world accurately. The more realistic claim would be to say rather that language hooks onto an individual's

---

47 For biographical details, see Quine, "Autobiography of W.V. Quine," *The Philosophy of W.V. Quine*, ed. Lew Edwin Hahn and Paul Arthur Schilpp, *Library of Living Philosophers* (La Salle, IL: Open Court Press, 1986), pp. 3–46.

48 The subplot in the story of American philosophy of the early twentieth century is the pragmatic tradition of James and Dewey. It remained a largely forgotten legacy because of the relative dominance of the European intellectual traditions in the post-War period of the twentieth century. See Bruce Kuklick, *A History of Philosophy in America: 1720–2000* (New York: Oxford, 2001) for a helpful institutional history of philosophy detailing the dominance of Harvard pragmatism at the turn of the twentieth century followed by its eclipse with logical empiricism in turn followed by the return of post-postivist pragmatism. See Cornel West, *The American Evasion of Philosophy*, for a sympathetic geneology of American pragmatism.

49 This is amplified well in W.V.O. Quine and J.S. Ullian, *The Web of Belief* (New York: Random House, 1970).

experiences since they do have direct access to their experiences. This would require language about objects getting translated into language about experiences. The sentence, "there is a book in front of me" might actually mean, "I am having an appeared-to-bookly experience." There is a lurking problem however with phenomenalism. According to Quine, it relegated ordinary language into merely illusory status. When I utter the sentence: "There is a book in front of me" I do not normally mean to be saying something about my experience of the book, but rather about the object in front of me. On a phenomalist account, this is an illusion of language. This struck Quine as entirely odd and unwarranted.

The alternative account, physicalism claimed that language referred to physical objects and not merely to an experience of them. This seemed to solve the illusion problem, but another issue reared its ugly head. If I am referring to an object in front of me when I utter the words: "There is a ball in front of me," I must also have in mind a particular time, a particular place, a particular way of pointing, a particular way to use definite pronouns, a particular understanding of balls, and so on. I must have an entire conceptual scheme to make sense of the simple sentence. So the sentence is true not simply in virtue of a round object in front of me, but also because my words are placed within a whole language system. This signaled to Quine that knowledge was underdetermined by experience alone.[50] Truth claims were relative to a conceptual scheme which itself was relative in time with respect to a society's language and perspectives. Our best beliefs are still posits according to Quine representing simply our best effort to say what the world is like. In a revealing quotation Quine admits:

> For my part I do, qua lay physicist, believe in physical objects and not in Homer's gods; and I consider it a scientific error to believe otherwise. But in point of epistemological footing the physical objects and the gods differ only in degree and not in kind. Both sorts of entities enter our conception only as cultural posits. The myth of physical objects is epistemologically superior to most in that it has proved more efficacious than other myths as a device for working a manageable structure into the flux of experience.[51]

The physical objects (and the scientific theories which contained them) were a myth precisely because one could never get one's epistemological hands on the objects themselves with any certainty. Quine argued that there was no privileged access to objects in the world. There was no access independent of a perspective.

The consequences for foundationalism were clear. Without privileged access to the world, the "foundations" of knowledge were no longer firm and solid. The atomic particles or building blocks of knowledge were as dependent upon a whole

---

50 Hume seems to have recognized this problem clear enough but strangely retreated back into a phenomenalist account of knowledge. See especially A. Flew, *Hume's Philosophy of Belief* (London: Routledge and Kegan Paul, 1973).

51 "Two Dogmas of Empiricism:" 44.

conceptual system as any other kind of belief. The foundation could not support the weight which modern philosophers had placed upon them. No belief could stand on its own. Every belief was dependent upon the whole web of beliefs and language.

The positivists had believed that a firm commitment to the notion of empirical foundations was sufficient to eradicate all talk of religion and ethics from the philosophical dictionary. The positivists supposed that philosophers simply needed to clearly distinguish statements of science and statements of religion. The statements of science were built upon unshakeable (allegedly) foundations of pure observation of things in the world. Quine's work effectively demolished this key distinction arguing that statements of science and statements of religion were not different in kind, but only degree. Without such a sharp distinction, there was no way to distinguish a (solid) foundation of empirical beliefs from the (less solid) superstructure of derived religious beliefs.

Wilfred Sellar's work took Quine's criticism one step further. His work received less fanfare than Quine's (or Kuhn's) but in hindsight, Sellar's criticism was the crushing blow to the whole metaphor of human knowledge as being built upon scientific foundations. His work was also prepared the way linking the demise of foundationalism to the end of objectivity as a prime virtue of science.

Wilfred Sellars and the Myth of the Given

Wilfred Sellars was a significant voice in the philosophical discussion about the nature of science in the 1950s. This meant that Sellars was an influential participant in the controversies of the English speaking guild dominated by the positivist conceptions of science and philosophy. And indeed Sellars' point of departure in his philosophical work was the classical project of the logical empiricists.

As the son of an eminent philosopher, Sellars was well suited to his philosophical calling.[52] He was a Rhodes scholar at Oxford, and professor of philosophy at Minnesota and Yale before assuming the chair in philosophy at the University of Pittsburgh in 1963. Almost single-handedly he established the university's remarkable reputation in the philosophical guild. He started the first philosophical journal, *Philosophical Studies*, devoted exclusively to the analytic philosophical tradition. His work was devoted to the newly developing discipline of philosophy of science. Sellars' saw himself as crafting a "synoptic vision" which brought together the ordinary (or "manifest') image of the physical world and the technical (or "scientific") image of particle physics and quantum mechanics.[53] Sellars'

[52] Wilfred Sellars' father was the Critical Realist philosopher, Roy Wood Sellars, long time professor of philosophy at the University of Michigan.

[53] This "synoptic vision" is the subject of the interpretive essays on Sellars' work, *The Synoptic Vision: Essays on the Philosophy of Wilfrid Sellars*, Cornelius Delaney, Michael Loux, Gary Gutting, and W. David Solomon (Notre Dame: University of Notre Dame Press, 1977).

intentions were to make philosophical sense of the rise of theoretical physics in a culture still dominated by talk of ordinary objects. How could one reconcile an "observational language" with the technical discourse of physics and quantum mechanics? How could one speak of sub-atomic particles while ordinary people got along quite well without ever having seen or touched such particles? Was an object such as a desk a collection of randomly moving quantum particles, or was it really just a couple of pieces of wood glued together with a large flat surface?

Lurking not far below the surface of this growing controversy was the older positivist conception of science which privileged physical object claims. Sellars called this act of privileging the "myth of the given." Sellars realized that the positivists' love of science was noble in its own right but failed to capture the way in which science was constantly changing and adapting. In the hands of the positivists, modern science with its inviolable laws and infallible self-evident claims, resembled the old religions. The positivists had made claims about a "scientific conception of the world" which looked curiously like the discredited "religious conception of the world" for which the positivists had such great disdain. The foundation-like nature of the new science and the old religion were somehow so strong that they could not be rationally challenged. The empirical claims of science, in the hands of the positivists appeared to have a new kind of privileged access to reality in a remarkably analogous way to the privileged claims of revelation in the older Judaeo-Christian religious order.

Sellars argued that there were no foundational "givens" in science (or religion). There were no beliefs which could not at some future point be revised. All beliefs were mutable. But the basic spirit behind the idea of a "given" in positivist theories was that of providing an immutable foundation for scientific knowledge by exhibiting a set of statements describing the world that are inviolable. These infallible decrees would have been asserted by any adequate scientific account, or so thought the positivists. Sellars smelled something fishy. Religion had been displaced because it failed to distinguish between myth and reality. In a most ironic manner, the positivists had also failed to distinguish adequately between myth and reality. They had embraced what Sellars called the "myth of the given" all the while supposing they were protecting the natural order from supernatural intrusions. Sellars argued that the essential myth of the "myth of the given" was that science was built from a set of true statements that were themselves directly descriptive of the world but were nonetheless *not* testable by the techniques of science.[54] Scientific laws were indeed testable and could in fact change. They were more nearly hypotheses rather than laws. They were hypotheses dependent upon "unobservable" realities, such as the space-time continuum of Einstein's relativity theory.

All beliefs, according to Sellars, gained their meaning and justification by their connection to the system of which they were a part. There were no "givens" independent of the system or framework of other beliefs. There were no beliefs

---

[54] On this point see Gary Gutting, "Sellars' Philosophy of Science" in *The Synoptic Vision*, pp. 73–87.

which had epistemic authority independent of other beliefs. There was no final guarantee that any touchstone of experience was ultimately true because everything was tied to a conceptual scheme, which could someday be revised. As Sellars put it, "science is rational not because it has a foundation but because it is a self-correcting enterprise which can put any claim in jeopardy, though not all at once."[55]

Someday the language of everyday ordinary discourse might be replaced by the language of molecules and electrons. It seemed possible but unlikely in the 1950s. If the change were ever in fact to take place, It would not be because suddenly ordinary people could put their hands on protons, or could see electrons with their ordinary glasses. Rather it would be that the "word pictures" of quantum physics made sense of people's experience. As the language of a flat earth has given way to talk of a globe, it was not because most people do not still experience a mostly flat world. Rather the word picture of the world as a large ball has taken collective hold on people's imaginations. They use the language of the world as a globe despite their ordinary observations, not because of them. The change occurred not because science rested on the bedrock of ordinary observational language and experience. This is what the positivists had mistakenly believed. Scientific knowledge was embedded in an ongoing temporal process of inquiry.[56] Science had never needed a privileged notion of a "given" to sustain itself Sellars claimed, to "reject the myth of the given ... is to commit oneself to the idea that even if [science] does have a rock bottom level, it is *still* in principle replaceable by another conceptual framework in which these predicates [of ordinary observation language] do not, *strictly speaking* occur."[57]

While Sellars was obviously attempting to portray science more accurately, he also undermined the mythology of linear progress attached to science by the positivists and by most modern intellectual traditions. Science did not discover the "givens" through observation and experiment, and then simply build upon them greater and greater scientific theories. If there were no "givens," then science could not be built in ever increasing breadth from the sure and certain foundations. If there were no foundations, science must look differently than the positivists had supposed.

As we have chronicled, the positivist movement was defeated largely from within its own ranks. Both Quine and Sellars were Anglo-American philosophers deeply committed to the project of natural science. Both were wary of fuzzy metaphysics. And both were adamant about the advantages of an increasing influence of secularism in the academy. However, discarding the analytic/synthetic distinction and exposing the myth of the given were important chapters in the

---

55 "Empiricism and the Philosophy of Mind" in *Science Perception and Reality* (London: Routledge and Kegan Paul, 1963, originally published 1956), p. 170.

56 In many ways this was analogous to the arguments of earlier historical critics in their rejection of the allegedly "privileged" claims of religion.

57 "Scientific Realism or Irenic Instrumentalism: A Critique of Nagel and Feyerabend on Theoretical Explanation." reprinted in *Philosophical Perspectives* (Springfield, IL: Charles Thomas, Publishers, 1967, originally published 1965), p. 187. Italics are Sellars'.

demise of the modern intellectual project which they had inherited. They may not have recognized the full consequences of their work, but there is little doubt their works were nails in the coffin of the Enlightenment inspired vision of the positivists. Their work opened the door to sweeping new work re-visioning the large scale project of science altogether. The work of Thomas Kuhn heralded a new theory about theories through which the project of science would be viewed. Part of the impact of Kuhn's research in the history of science was the establishment of the non-neutrality or theory-ladeness of science. Science never could (and never did) operate from a theory-free, objective standpoint. Evidence was evidence only from within a given set of historically conditioned parameters.

Thomas Kuhn and the Paradigms of Science

When Kuhn first published his influential work, *The Structure of Scientific Revolutions* in 1962, there seemed little precedent for its radical argument.[58] It was Kuhn's exposure to a science course for non-scientists while a doctoral student in theoretical physics, that led him to several case studies in the history of science. Kuhn was later to write of those case studies, "To my complete surprise, that exposure to out-of-date scientific theory and practice radically undermined some of my basic conceptions about the nature of science and the reasons for its special success."[59]

Kuhn had received his doctorate in theoretical physics from Harvard in 1949 where he also taught before joining the faculty at University of California at Berkeley. After publishing his early work on the Copernican revolution and his groundbreaking *Structure of Scientific Revolutions*, he moved to Princeton to teach the philosophy and history of science.[60] He taught briefly at MIT and passed away in 1996.

It was a fundamental assumption of the positivists that came under the particular scrutiny of Kuhn, the objectivity of the scientific project in contrast to other theoretical endeavors. Kuhn wrote of the "mythic" character of science, whether it was the hard sciences or the social sciences:

> If these out-of-date beliefs (e.g. Aristotelian dynamics, phlogistic chemistry) are to be called myths, then myths can be produced by the same sorts of methods and held for the same sorts of reasons that now lead to scientific knowledge. If on the other hand they are to be called science, then science has included bodies of belief quite incompatible with the ones we hold today.[61]

---

[58] (Chicago: University of Chicago Press, 1962).

[59] Ibid., second edition 1970, preface, p. v.

[60] His first published work was entitled, *The Copernican Revolution: Planetary Astronomy in the Development of Western Thought* (Cambridge, MA: Harvard University Press, 1957). It foreshadowed many of the controversial claims of *Structures*.

[61] *Structures of Scientific Revolutions*, 2.

What had led Kuhn to these startling conclusions? Having been trained with a positivist bent it was Kuhn's working assumption that science was by definition an accumulation of unchanging knowledge.[62] Once science embraced a particular true theory about empirical data, this theory could not at some later point become false if the data remained the same. Believing in a fixed body of knowledge of science seemed the only reasonable alternative to skepticism. Without an unchanging core, science would be as transitory as birds that fly south in the winter. Had not the history of science proven the stability of the scientific core and wasn't that indeed the "hope" of the modern scientific outlook.

Kuhn argued that the history of science did not in fact bear any of this out. He considered episodes in the history of physics where there were radical changes of a unique variety. Contemporary theories of relativity had replaced older theories of mechanics. The new theories gained traction not by adding new knowledge to an already existing stable core. Rather the new theories replaced the old theories with entirely new ones. A fundamental change in the basic conceptualization of physics had been required.

For Kuhn this realization posed a dilemma. Either one had to admit the radical nature of scientific revolutions and thereby admit that science could essentially change or one had to affirm that Newton and other predecessors were not doing real science in the first place. The latter alternative seemed especially unpalatable to Kuhn and he thereby set out to provide some working constructs to understand the nature of scientific change.

Central to Kuhn's alternative description of science was the much heralded notion of a "paradigm."[63] It was this notion that played a central role in undermining the confidence in the objectivity of science in the old positivist theory. Leaving aside the trenchant criticism which Kuhn's notion itself withstood, it is right to suggest, as Kuhn argued, that all of science took place within theoretic commitments which themselves were not simply objective. There were a set of problems and acceptable solutions with which every scientific paradigm worked. Those sets of problems and solutions did not remain constant across paradigms. They were chosen for many different reasons, the least of which were often non-scientific in the older

---

62 It is significant that *Structures of Scientific Revolutions* was published in the series, *The International Encyclopedia of Unified Science* with positivists luminaries, Otto Neurath and Rudolph Carnap as editors.

63 See Margaret Masterman, "The Nature of a Paradigm," in *Criticism and the Growth of Knowledge*, eds, Imre Lakatos and Alan Musgrave (London: Cambridge University Press, 1970) for a wonderful descriptive treatment of the myriad of ways in which "paradigm" was used in the philosophy of science literature in these early years, and even the widely divergent ways Kuhn put the term to use. Gary Gutting, ed., *Paradigms and Revolutions: Applications and Appraisals of Thomas Kuhn's Philosophy of Science* (Notre Dame: University of Notre Dame Press, 1980) is a helpful collection of essays on the application of Kuhn's construct of "paradigms" across a wide cross section of academic discourse.

sense of that word. Even politics and religion ought to be included in the rationale for shifts in scientific paradigms.

The shifts (or revolutions) among scientific theories were not predictable in any straightforward sense. There was no algorithm which a philosopher of science could construct to explain the choice of a new paradigm in science. The choice of a new paradigm occurred when older paradigms broke down plain and simple. There was no guarantee that the new paradigms would last long either. The reason was that each [scientific revolution] produced a consequent shift in the problems available for scientific scrutiny and in the standards by which the profession determined what should count as an admissible problem or as a legitimate problem solution. And each transformed the scientific imagination in ways that we shall ultimately need to describe as a transformation of the world within which scientific work was done.[64]

Science had not simply discovered biological evolution but was itself a clear example of it. Conflict was the central motivating force in science. There was no external goal towards which the system was headed inextricably, other than survival. No ideal truth served as a magnet drawing science ever closer towards it. Progress in science was random and defined by little more than the community's sense of distance from earlier theories.

All of this seemed to entail that the hard sciences and the theories that the positivists had attached to them, were as "biased" as any of the social sciences or (worse yet) even the previously discredited disciplines of religion, art, literature and ethics. The solid ground under girding physics and astronomy and biology seemed little more than sinking sand now, or so it dawned on many intellectuals in the light of Kuhn's work. Enlightenment hope had turned into suspicion. If all theories could and did change, which theory could one ultimately trust? Maybe none.

Ludwig Wittgenstein and the Final Disenchantment with Positivism

The final nail in the coffin of Enlightenment hope may well have been the later work of Ludwig Wittgenstein. It was Wittgenstein who had attracted such attention near the birth of the positivist movement and in whose genius lay the pristine foundational formula of the positivist picture of truth and knowledge. One of the towering figures of twentieth-century philosophy, Wittgenstein was born in Vienna in 1889, educated at Cambridge under Russell, taught for a time at Cambridge and died in Cambridge in 1951.[65] By most accounts, however, Wittgenstein was ill-suited for life as an academic. He was a meandering soul who felt restless wherever he was and misunderstood by most. He was a genius of the first rank and yet one whose work seemed continually misinterpreted. It is with some irony

64 *Structures of Scientific Revolutions*, 6.

65 Norman Malcolm's biography remains the most compelling and personal picture of Wittgenstein. See his *Ludwig Wittgenstein: A Memoir.*

that Wittgenstein himself seemed to repudiate his earlier writings during the later period of his life.

The early Wittgenstein was often viewed by the logical positivists as the intellectual genius of their movement.[66] He was never actually physically present at any of the meetings of the Vienna circle but his shadow loomed large over the group.[67] It was therefore a very significant surprise that Wittgenstein's later work all but repudiated the earlier vision of epistemology which he had sketched out in the *Tractatus*.[68] It was his later work, *Philosophical Investigations*, in particular which subverted much of the central principles of his earlier "picturing" view of language and meaning.[69] Wittgenstein wrote in the preface to the later work, "For since beginning to occupy myself with philosophy again, sixteen years ago, I have been forced to recognize grave mistakes in what I wrote in that first book."[70] And so it was that the later work sought to correct many of the fundamental assumptions of the earlier work.[71]

Wittgenstein had always been fascinated with language but earlier on he had assumed it had a mathematical quality to it, or at least it could be shown to have a mathematical precision if philosophers would only be careful to say what they intended to say. Later on Wittgenstein recast his whole understanding of language and came to believe that language was a living, unsystematic and polymorphous array of human conventions for a large and not classifiable range of human purposes. This pointed at the bareness of his earlier theory of language. Instead Wittgenstein suggested the meaning of a word derived from its use in a wide variety of human acts of communication. There might be some words which do gather their meaning from their use in "picturing" objects in the real world, but this was a small part of the overall use of language. Words were used to give

---

66 Thomas Eubel notes that during the academic years, 1924–26, under Schlick's leadership the weekly seminars of the Circle was spent reading Wittgenstein's *Tractatus* line by line. See Uebel, "Otto Neurath, the Vienna Circle and the Austrian Tradition," in *German Philosophy Since Kant*, edited by Anthony O'Hear (Cambridge: Cambridge University Press, 1999), p. 251.

67 On the influence of Wittgenstein upon the Vienna Circle see the introduction by Gordon Baker to *The Voices of Wittgenstein, The Vienna Circle and Friedrich Waismann*, transcribed, edited and trans. by Gordon Baker (New York: Routledge, 2003).

68 There are complicated issues in assessing the relationship of the early Wittgenstein to the later Wittgenstein. Some interpreters, such as P.M.S. Hacker argue for a sharp repudiation of the early Wittgenstein by the later. Others such as D.F. Pears argue for a continuity within the greater discontinuity of the two periods in Wittgenstein. See Hacker, *Insight and Illusion* (Oxford: Oxford University Press, 1986) and Pears, *The False Prison: A Study of the Development of Wittgenstein's Philosophy* (Oxford: Clarendon Press, 1987).

69 *Philosophical Investigations*, eds G.E.M. Anscombe and R. Rhees, trans. G.E.M. Anscombe (Oxford: Blackwell Publishers, 1953).

70 Ibid., p. vi.

71 A helpful overview of Wittgenstein's entire philosophical work is Anthony Kenny, *Ludwig Wittgenstein* (Oxford: Blackwell Publishers, 2006, original 1973).

directions, to share emotions, to promise, to play a game and almost an infinite number of other uses.

It was the systematic attempt to tie words down to a small set of uses that inevitably led positivists and many other modern intellectuals to misconstrue the genuine character and diversity of human language. It was the natural and social context of human speech which needed to be understood if actual words themselves were to be useful. Wittgenstein referred to this wider context as a "language game," meaning by it nothing more than the set of rules, intentions and circumstances that give shape to the particular ways in which people communicate.[72] A teacher might raise their voice to get the attention of students. In order for the words to accomplish their intended purpose, the students had to understand the rules which led the teacher to raise the tone of their voice. Words were part of a "game," and could only be understood if the other rules of communication employed were also understood. Miscommunication occurred when speaker and listener were not playing by the same rules. The listener may have "read between the lines" of the speaker's words assuming that they had in mind an earlier event, while the speaker had no such event in mind. The two were not playing by the same rules. Baseball players and cricket players may understand much of what the others are speaking about without however understanding all (or even most) of the conversation. The rules of the game are similar enough to allow for communication but different enough to create misunderstandings. So it is with language in general.

Wittgenstein came to believe philosophers had no special or private access to the real meaning of words. Those who thought carefully might reveal some latent rules or patterns in language but they could not thereby serve as arbiters as to how language was and was not allowed to be used. Philosophers should not think of themselves as linguistic policemen. Rather philosophers like other serious minded folk, ought to think of themselves as no more than thoughtful conversationalists. Conversationalists had no unique authority when it came to language. The philosopher ought not suppose they can reform language or rid it of all religious or ethical or aesthetic terms. It was the business of the human community as a whole to decide what language it wanted to use. At best philosophers might describe the rules by which ordinary language operates in a particular culture at a particular time.

Philosophy might better be described as a kind of therapy. Its intentions were not to solve the perennial and perplexing problems of philosophy but rather to discover the ways in which ordinary language may lead to philosophical confusion. The two sentences: "you have a sore throat" and "you have a nice thought" may appear to have the same "grammar." One may mistakenly conclude on that basis that throats are like thoughts and the description of them ought to occur in philosophically similar ways. But thoughts are not after all like throats. The deception of the history of philosophy has been to treat thoughts as though

[72] There are undoubtedly family resemblances between Wittgenstein's notion of a "language game" and Kuhn's notion of a "paradigm." Nonetheless it is important to see the similarities as a strategy against the positivist notion of language as atomistic.

they were empirical entities just like throats. But if thoughts are not like throats what are they like? Wittgenstein suggested ordinary language will normally reveal how the language of "thoughts" should be used. That is the best we should expect according to Wittgenstein.

Gone were the illusions of the positivists that there were some clear and distinct criteria to distinguish good language (the language of science) from bad language (the language of religion). Gone also was the simple relationship of language to the world which supposed that the foundations of knowledge were those and only those statements which hooked up directly with simple empirical objects in the world. Language was much messier than this. The later Wittgenstein's embrace of this messiness spelled doom to the classic formulations of foundationalism. It also cleared the space to think in post-positivists ways.

Conclusion

In the nineteenth century the notion of philosophy as a foundational discipline was consolidated in the writings of the neo-Kantians. Philosophy had become a substitute for religion for many intellectuals of this period. In the twentieth century the logical positivists had been concerned to keep philosophy rigorous, scientific and clear of any religious commitments. The note of desperation in their voices seemed ironic for the triumph of the secular over the claims of religion had seemed almost complete in the early twentieth century. Religion was still very much alive, and though it may have been privately important it was increasingly publicly irrelevant. At mid-century philosophers were no longer viewed as the intellectual avant-garde, protecting civilization against the forces of superstition. That position had largely been taken over by novelists, poets and increasingly by the singer/musicians of the 1950s and 1960s.[73] Enlightenment intellectuals may have dreamed of a secular culture in centuries previous. Intellectuals in the 1960s saw it become a reality, only to realize they were not much needed any longer in the revolution.

Philosophers had become as remote from mainstream culture as had theologians. The poets of folk music had taken the place of both preachers and philosophers as the (a)moral guides of the youth. One of the important consequences of these social realities was that the more scientific and rigorous philosophy became, the less it had to do with the rest of culture and the more absurd its traditional pretensions

---

[73] Ironically Wittgenstein lamented the loss of the poetic voice in the 1930s and the rise to prominence of the scientific and philosophical voice. Monk cites him as saying:

> "I was walking about in Cambridge and passed a bookshop, and in the window were portraits of Russell, Freud and Einstein. A little further on, in a music shop, I saw portraits of Beethoven, Schubert and Chopin. Comparing these portraits I felt intensely the terrible degeneration that had come over the human spirit in the course of only a hundred years" *Wittgenstein*, p. 299.

seemed. The attempts by philosophers in the positivist tradition to: "ground" this, "analyze" that and "criticize" the other, were shrugged off by those whose activities were purportedly being grounded, analyzed and criticized.[74] Philosophy was just plain too confident of its role to be regarded any longer as relevant.

With the critique of Quine, Sellars, Kuhn and Wittgenstein, there was every good reason to suppose that philosophy might happily give up these pretensions. It was not a foundational discipline for there were no longer foundations upon which to rest human knowledge. Philosophy was just another way to carry on a conversation about what culture thought was important to it at any given time. Nothing more. The 1960s would tell us much about what our culture thought was important but not because it had been told so by professional philosophers. If anything it became apparent that philosophers were following trends, not setting them anymore. The demise of foundationalism was a striking testimony to that end.

---

[74] To this effect Rorty wrote:

> To assert the possibility of a post-Kantian culture, on which there is no all-encompassing discipline which legitimizes or grounds the others, is not necessarily to argue against any particular Kantian doctrine, any more than to glimpse the possibility of a culture in which religion either did not exist, or had no connection with science or politics, was necessarily to argue against Aquinas' claims that God's existence can be proved by natural reason. *Philosophy and the Mirror of Nature*, p. 6.

Chapter 7
The Death Beyond the Death of God: Radical Theology in the 1960s

> I am denying that religion is necessary. Really to travel along this road means that we trust the world, not God, to be our need fulfiller and problem solver, and God, if he is to be for us at all, must come in some other role.
>
> William Hamilton (1965)[1]

In 1966, if the above had been said by a member of the New Left or even Timothy Leary, the American public would have barely noticed. That it was written by a Christian theologian seemed downright puzzling, if also somewhat amusing. It was also becoming relatively familiar to a nation whose collective consciousness included the memory of *Time* magazine's cover from April of that year. In large red letters across the front were written the words: "IS GOD DEAD?" The starkness of the black background against which the red letters appeared came to symbolize the national reaction to the new theological fad. Incredulity marked the mood of official church reactions to the movement. In retrospect, though one might have had suspicions to the contrary, the theological academy with few exceptions looked askance at this burgeoning new movement as well.[2]

The players in this radical movement were few and on the face of it, academically insignificant in the world of professional theology. William Hamilton taught at Colgate-Rochester Divinity School, Thomas J.J. Altizer was an associate professor at Emory University, Paul Van Buren was in the religion department at Temple

---

1 Hamilton, William, "The Death of God Theology," *The Christian Scholar* (Spring 1965) reprinted in *Radical Theology and the Death of God*, Thomas J.J. Altizer and William Hamilton (Indianapolis IN: Bobbs Merrill, 1966), p. 39.

2 Though many theologians commented superficially on the movement, Langdon Gilkey appears to be the lone significant voice calling for serious critical interaction with the writings of the main figures of the movement. See his *Naming the Whirlwind: The Renewal of God-Language* (Indianapolis, IN: Bobbs Merrill, 1969) which is centrally a book length treatment of the Death of God theologies. Another more recent essay, "Thomas J.J. Altizer and the Death of God," Bruce Ritchie and Terrence Tilley, *Postmodern Theologies: The Challenge of Diversity*, ed. Terrence Tilley (Maryknoll: Orbis Press, 1995) places Altizer's work in particular against the construct of postmodernism. Ritchie and Tilley's essay is the work of theological historians attempting to draw a descriptive picture of Altizer in the context of other theologies connected to the postmodern turn.

University and Gabriel Vahanian was a sociologist of religion at Syracuse.[3] None of them were established senior scholars residing in the very elite universities of America. Hamilton and Altizer collaborated on a collection of essays rather late in the life of the movement but the four central individuals were otherwise isolated from each other and from the dominant (and domineering) institutional centers of theological orthodoxy of the early 1960s—New Haven, Chicago, New York and Cambridge, Massachusetts.[4]

Neoorthodoxy was the regnant theological tradition at mid-century and its central voices had an uneasy relationship to the Death of God Movement. To his own personal chagrin, Paul Tillich was viewed as the elder statesmen of the Death of God Movement.[5] Each of the radical theologians in their own way had also been deeply influenced by Barth in their training and early religious commitments. Some commentators noticed a distinct Bultmanian influence in the necrotheologians' treatment of the Bible as well. However, one could barely discern significant theological continuity with the earlier tradition even in the nature of the questions being asked let alone in the answers given. It would not be unfair to say that the Death of God theologians did not view themselves so much as an extension of nor a reaction against neo-orthodoxy as those attempting to rethink and revision the very nature of the theological project itself. The disestablishment of neo-orthodoxy

---

[3] Vahanian, with some justification, refused to think of himself as part of the Death of God Movement. He argued against the idolatry of the modern church with the intention that a more adequate (and accurate) picture of God would be restored to the churches. He is the first of the group to use the phrase "the Death of God" but for Vahanian it remains largely a negative epitaph upon the church in the post-War period. As a result we will abstain from including Vahanian in the Death of God Movement. Harvey Cox also came to be associated with the movement in the minds of some. Cox repeatedly rejected the phrase "the Death of God" and though he was much concerned with the secularization process, his thought moved in fundamentally different directions that Hamilton, Altizer and Van Buren. See Cox, *The Secular City: Secularization and Urbanization in Theological Perspective* (New York: Macmillan, 1965).

[4] Both Altizer and Hamilton protested that there was even such a thing as a "movement." Such little collaboration would seem to justify their assertion. In what follows I will attempt to be sensitive to this reality and to the conflicting one that most people (theologians and otherwise) spoke and thought of these thinkers as constituting a movement if not by their collaborative work, at least by their shared sympathies.

[5] Altizer wrote:

> It was while reading Tillich as an undergraduate that I was led to an acceptance of the Christian faith, and I have found that throughout my teaching and study it was Tillich who exercised the greatest theological influence upon my work. Among twentieth-century theologians, it was Tillich alone who made possible a way to a truly contemporary theology. While I have been forced to resist and oppose Tillich's theological conclusions, I do so with the conviction that they are no yet radical enough, and with the memory of Tillich's words to me, that the real Tillich is the radical Tillich. Certainly, Tillich is the modern father of radical theology. *The Gospel of Christian Atheism* (Philadelphia: Westminster Press, 1966), p. 10.

happened as a by-product of the shifting character of the concerns raised by these radical theologians.[6] For all practical purposes a bewildered public awoke one morning and confronted the reality that theologians (at least four of them) were no longer interested in God nor in his Word. Times were changing![7]

Prophetic Protest (or Not)

The prophetic element so important to the 1960s was in all respects a protest against the status quo. The necrotheologians were undoubtedly protesting the status quo. They viewed themselves as radicals clearly outside the mainstream, making radical claims in radical ways, at least by traditional religious standards. They identified with radical elements within American culture and crafted their rhetoric to challenge deeply held beliefs. But whose status quo were they protesting and were they unwittingly a part of a larger status quo?

The theologians of the Movement saw themselves as protesting the conservative religious sub-culture of America. That sub-culture too often spoke as if evolution were an unproven hypothesis and relativity theory was a piece of science fiction. Many Churches still believed the Bible more trustworthy than science, accepting the centuries old picture of the warfare between science and religion. On this spectrum the church resolutely sided against science (or so it seemed to the necrothelogians) and the Death of God Movement sided squarely with science.

The "action" in the 1960s was taking place not inside the church but outside of it. The necrotheologians understood this and wanted to capture something of that energy on behalf of the church. And so their protest was largely against the traditional structures of the church and its theology. They wanted to push the church outside itself, recognizing that an ingrown church would eventually wither and fade away.

The Death of God theologians frequently appealed to church-going folk to be involved in civil rights, in urban work, in experimental forms of ministry, and in peace movements. They believed that the only religion that could survive must be a religion that wrestled with urgent concerns of ordinary people in the street. This entailed thinking of religion in secular political and historical terms.[8] In this, their

---

6 On this point see William Hamilton, "The New Optimism: From Prufrock to Ringo," in *Radical Theology and the Death of God*, p. 157.

7 Peter Berger remarked in 1967:

> The spectacle afforded by the movement is strange. Indeed, it has all the characteristics of a man-bites-dog story. The phrase "secular theology" itself strikes with intriguing dissonance, while phrases such as "atheist theology" or "religionless Christianity" seem to come from a script for the theatre of the absurd. "A Sociological View of the Secularization of Theology," *Journal of the Scientific Study of Religion* vol. 6, no. 1 (Spring 1967): 3.

8 On this point see Gilkey, *Naming the Whirlwind*, pp. 24 ff.

theology more nearly became a sub-discipline of political theory or sociology. The ethical direction of the Death of God Movement lay in the transition from the world of the cloister to the world of the city:

> In christology, the [new] theologian is sometimes inclined to suspect that Jesus Christ is best understood as neither the object nor the ground of faith, neither as person, event or community, but simply as a place to be, a standpoint. That place is, of course, alongside the neighbor, being for him.[9]

To be a radical Christian was to be involved in mission and service in the world in a secular way (that is, political, worldly and historical), seeking to transform historical existence rather than merely religiously to react to or reflect upon it. To be a radical Christian was not to be traditionally religious (worshipping, praying evangelizing, amongst others) but rather to love and serve one's neighbor in the world. Radical religious faith had collapsed into love, and the Protestant was no longer defined as the forgiven sinner, the *simul justius et peccator* of Luther, but as the one beside the neighbor, beside the enemy, at the disposal of the person in need. The distinctions between the mission of humankind and the mission of the church ceased to be in this new scheme.

This conviction both under girded and was supported by the growing involvement of the theological community in the Civil Rights Movement. What radically moved the new theologians into a position where similarities to the Social gospel could be noted was the extraordinary impact of the Black Civil Rights Movement on the texture of life in the 1960s. That Movement stands now like a divide between two different forms of life. It decisively altered the forms of American social protest. In the Sixties, the Civil Rights Movement constituted a vanguard, with the new theologians bringing up the rear, just as theories of evolution and socialist activity antedate Rauschenbushch's formulation of the Social Gospel earlier in the century. They accepted, as Hamilton wrote, "the value of the technological revolution, the legitimacy of the hopes and claims of the dispossessed, most of all, the moral centrality of the Negro revolution in America today."[10]

To ignore this revolution was reprehensible to the radical theologians and when God was allied with the conserving social forces, he became morally intolerable:

> A God who "causes" or "allows" the suffering of a single child is morally intolerable. God does not solve the problem of suffering: he only magnifies it. To push off evil on to God simply makes him into a Devil—and in any case

9 Hamilton, "Thursday's Child:" 92.

10 Hamilton, "Death of God Theology," in *The Christian Scholar* (Spring 1965) reprinted in *Radical Theology and the Death of God*, Thomas J.J. Altizer and William Hamilton (Indianapolis IN: Bobbs Merrill, 1966), p. 37.

> represents a cowardly evasion. Men must carry the can and refuse the temptation to dissociation or transference.[11]

Protest was the order of the day, and the Death of God Movement saw itself front and central.

It is remarkable given the radical character of the decade, how quickly the Death of God Movement faded. It had an amazingly short shelf life. The Movement's earliest beginnings date to 1961 with the publication of Vahanian's *The Death of God: The Culture of Our Post-Christian Era* and the little noticed (at the time) book by Hamilton, *The New Essence of Christianity*. It was Van Buren's book *The Secular Meaning of the Gospel*, appearing in 1963, which brought the Movement to national attention.[12] The debates exploded onto the national consciousness in 1964 and 1965 with the appearance of the *Time* cover story along with many small articles by the Movement's participants in widely read religious periodicals. The climax of the Movement was reached in 1966 with the publication of Altizer's, *The Gospel of Christian Atheism* and the collection of essays by Altizer and Hamilton, *Radical Theology and the Death of God* later that same year. Within two years the Movement disintegrated, barely able to have enjoyed its fleeting moment in the limelight. As quickly as it came to national attention, so it faded into the national collective unconsciousness and by 1968 Van Buren wrote, "the hot air has leaked out of the recent 'death of God' balloon, ... as we push the flaccid remains to the back of the drawer reserved for mementos of our more foolish exploits."[13]

Public (and theological) attention turned elsewhere. The assassinations of Bobby Kennedy and Martin Luther King along with the race riots of 1967 and 1968 ironically seemed to bring God back to life.

Fundamental questions remain. Was the Movement itself an artificially created fad—much like the "twist" or "nehru shirts"—or did it express at an ideological level genuine socio-theological realities? Secondly, did the Movement signal a theological revolution giving birth to what we now commonly (and in hopelessly ambiguous ways) call postmodern theology or was it the last gasp of Enlightenment optimism? Was it another in the long line of progressive revolutions against a conservative (neorthodox) majority or was it genuinely the herald of a new (a)theological day?

---

11 Bishop John A.T. Robinson, "Can a Truly Contemporary Person Not be an Atheist?" in *The New Reformation* (Philadelphia: Westminster Press, 1965), p. 113. This essay was first delivered as a lecture at the "Exhibition on Atheism, Eastern and Western" held at University of Frankfurt in November 1964.

12 It must not be forgotten that both Bishop John A.T. Robinson's, *Honest to God* and the German evangelical, Dietrich Bonhoffer's *Letters and Papers from Prison*, were published in America in 1963, lending international credence to the secularization impulse of the Death of God Movement.

13 *Theological Explorations* (New York: Macmillan, 1968), p. 6.

The beginnings of answers to these questions lie in part with the intellectual incongruity of the Movement itself. When professional theologians, paid to think and write about God, instead deny the existence of such a being, it would appear that something had gone awry, amusingly so from the vantage point of the outsider. But here lied a clue to its significance. Most Americans were now theological outsiders, neither understanding (nor caring) what theologians were up to. When the necrotheologians claimed that the very Death of God must be affirmed in order that theology and the church might be renewed for the next generation, it must have appeared as the bizarre manifestation of intellectual derangement and/or an attempt at institutional suicide, save only the fact that most of the next generation had already abandoned belief in God, if not at the conceptual level then surely in a profoundly practical fashion. The sheer strangeness of theologians, entrusted with sacred realities, celebrating the secularization of America understandably caught the attention of "inquiring minds" and of a national media that is constitutionally drawn towards sloganeering, regardless of where it could be found. The premature announcements of God's death were understandably rejected by the religious elites, both in universities and churches who realized quickly enough that their vocations were at stake as well as their pay checks. With such factors in mind it is not hard to defend the claim that the Death of God was a mere passing fancy of a few intellectuals looking for some cheap publicity, as wrong as that claim actually is.

Television had only recently become a national force and it is surely not an exaggeration to say that this small group of intellectuals barely grasped its impact let alone manipulated it for their own use. The radical theologians understood well the ethos of their age, one consumed with the modern desires of the flesh; peace, prosperity and happiness.[14] American culture, like these theologians, had long since cashed in most transcendent concerns for immanent ones. Cosmic events were increasingly being translated into events of personal and therapeutic significance. Work had ceased to be a divine calling and had become conceptualized as a means to a paycheck whose primary benefit was the gaining of social status.

In the writings of the Death of God theologians, transcendental ontology became immanent anthropology and Heilsegeschicte became a kind of personal or social biography. They argued that modernity was the stepchild of biblical faith but like every generation, the child must learn to live out their own life independent of the parents. The concept of providence may have been useful in earlier times

[14] As Berger commented:

> The sometimes awe-inspiring eggheadedness of the theologians vocabulary must not be allowed to obscure the "pop" correlates of the movement. For example, existentialist Angst and alienation are not limited to seminary professors who have read Heidegger. To a remarkable degree, these experiences seem to be shared by suburban housewives. As a result, the translations undertaken by the seminary professors can be popularly applied by ministers with suburban housewives in the clientele. "Sociological View:" 6.

when nature was not so well understood, but in a technologically advanced society, providence sounded too much like the fates of ancient mythology. God's presence was no longer a necessary postulate to fill the scientific gaps. A century earlier, similar themes had been sounded out by a few well-known Protestant liberals. Striking in the 1960s was the resonance of these ideas in the mass public.

Yet the ontological absence of God was not the central driving force in the 1960s. Cultural pressure was increasingly being focused around moral and ethical issues. To a generation discovering the enormous material benefits of technology the morality of an earlier age seemed no longer appropriate. God's death was proclaimed by the radical theologians because God was no longer accessible to the modern subjective self. God's death was actually life affirming because it placed the responsibility squarely on the human community to rectify the wrongs of this world through a provisional ethic:

> The Christian, however, cannot escape the fact that he must make a choice. He must either choose the God who is actually manifest and real in the established form of faith, or he must confess the death of God and give himself to a quest for a whole new form of faith. If he follows the latter course, he will sacrifice an established Christian meaning and morality. ... Certainly he will be forced to renounce every moral imperative with a transcendent ground, and this means that he must forswear the possibility of an absolute moral law, and at best look upon all forms of moral judgment as penultimate ways which must inevitably act as barriers to the full realization of energy and life.[15]

These theologians suggested this provisional ethic be grounded on the model of Jesus as the humiliated, humble and neighborly Lord. As the moral sensibilities of culture changed so would its models of those sensibilities. This ought not worry a contemporary Christian.

Modern individuals, the radical theologians said, no longer pursued a view about ultimate reality, but instead acted provisionally according to their immediate interests and commitments. Most people simply accepted the present cultural conditions and hoped that they could be exploited for humane purposes. In this environment the rules were no longer external and timeless but internal and temporary. Morality, like technology, did not have limits.[16]

---

15 Altizer, *The Gospel of Christian Atheism*, p. 147.

16 Two very significant Supreme Court decisions at the outset of the decade opened the floodgates for a revolution of cultural mores with respect to sexual morality. In 1959 the high court overturned the ban on *Lady Chatterly's Lover* by D.H. Lawrence and in 1961 Grove Press (publisher of *Lady Chatterly's Lover*) also received permission to publish Henry Miller's *Tropic of Cancer*. The revolution is illustrated well by the fact that by the end of the decade the Federal Commission on Obscenity and Pornography recommended wiping out all legal restrictions on the acquisition by adults of hard-core pornography.

The only limits were those of the past and they alone held the potential to stop humankind from reaching its potential.[17] They alone could place restraints on human desires. And it was precisely this intuition that led the necrotheologians to abandon the older theologies. Though noble in their day, the older theologies represented by neo-orthodoxy, simply would not fit the modern world. They placed unnatural constraints on desires and they failed to grasp the hope of the new technologies. In the modern world there had been a fundamental:

> deterioration of the portrait of the God-man relation as found in biblical theology and the neo-orthodox tradition. This theological tradition was able to portray a striking and even heroic faith, a sort of holding on by the fingernails to the cliff of faith, a standing terrified before the enemy-God, present to man as terror or threat, comforting only in that he kept us from the worse terrors of life without him. But ... this whole picture has lost its power to persuade ... in our time.[18]

The strength of the necrotheologians lay in the fact that they were brokers of this brave new world to the academy and to the church on behalf of popular culture. They did not speak for God but on behalf of a new generation. Many in this new generation found it surprising that theologians were speaking on their behalf but as Hamilton wrote:

> The academy and the temple can, for now, no longer be trusted as theological guides. Not only our action but our thought belongs with the world of the city, which in our time means power, culture, art, sex, money, the Jew, the Negro, beauty, ugliness, poverty and indifference.[19]

The prophetic character of neo-orthodoxy was turned on its head so to speak. The world now stood as a prophetic renunciation of the church. It was the church that had to undergo radical change if it was to survive. The church needed to listen to the voices of the modern world, not the prophets of the past. The hope of the radical theologians was that:

> by extending and deepening a heritage from liberal Protestantism, the American theologian is now opening himself to the logician and the philosopher, the psychiatrist and the psychoanalyst, the literary critic and the social scientist.[20]

---

17 Altizer wrote: "once we fully live the death of God, we will be liberated from the temptation to return to an epiphany of deity which is present only in the past." *The Gospel of Christian Atheism*, p. 136.

18 Hamilton, "The Death of God Theology:" 35.

19 Ibid.: 45.

20 Altizer, "America:" 17.

What separated the Death of God theologians from nineteenth-century Protestant liberalism was the commitment on the part of the latter to the history of ideas and the former to the institutions of mass culture. Communication technology had "leveled" ideology in the twentieth century and these theologians realized only too well that those on the bottom of the social ladder were now gaining access to the corridors of cultural power as a result. Television captured the beauty of youth. The numerical explosion of students in American universities after World War II swayed the balance of power on many campuses towards the students and away from faculty. The media coverage of the Civil Rights Movement brought unprecedented attention to a black population whose plight was long excluded from the average American conscience.

This social upheaval followed patterns of democratization in other periods of American history in the face of modernization and industrialization. The populist impulses captured the aspirations of society's outsiders, carried along (and in part created by) a revolution in communications seen most clearly in television and mediated to the youth through a unique and new genre of music, rock and roll. Authority was ascribed to modern balladeers ill-equipped to run for public office or to preach a sermon in church. They underscored the increasingly obvious insight: that virtue resided in ordinary people. Heightened in the revolutionary times of the 1960s was the conviction that ordinary people were ordinarily those on the bottom of the social scale. The older generation may have seemed confused that the weak were confounding the mighty and the last were becoming first but there was no mistaking this trend on the part of the radical theologians. The radical theologians had learned the legacy of "relevance" from liberalism and now stated it in terms that would have made even the most radical of the nineteenth-century Protestant Liberals blush.

If we can truly know that God is dead, and can fully actualize the Death of God in our own experience, then we can be liberated from the threat of condemnation, and freed from every terror of a transcendent beyond. Even though we may be mute and speechless in confronting the terror of our time, we cannot evade its pervasive presence, and to relapse into immobility and silence is to foreclose the possibility of being freed from its life-negating power.[21]

The rising tide of secularization was an accepted fact by most intellectuals in the 60s but it was left to the Death of God thinkers to raise the white flag of surrender on behalf of God, all the while declaring victory for religion. Modern consciousness did not countenance a world without God but modern life was everywhere lived in God's absence. If man had "come of age" then he (in the early 60s this did not include "she") needed an ideological foundation for these social realities, or so the radical theologians thought.

The radical theologies affirmed what was important to modern religious sensibilities in the secular terms that pervaded urban life. The external reality of God was vanishing from that life and it was left to the radical theologians to preserve some religious framework to understand and conceptualize this modern existence.

---

[21] Altizer, *The Gospel of Christian Atheism*, p. 145.

The radical theologians genuinely believed that the secularizing process was inevitable and to a large extent irreversible. What explained their short lived notoriety was the attempt to offer a religious justification of this practicing unbelief of the age given its inescapable and certain future. Though the Death of God literature was, on the whole, directed at a middle brow audience, neither overly technical nor extremely popular, it raised the increasingly pressing (and awkward) question of the age: In an allegedly Christian culture, what kind of belief in God can be maintained in the face of the rising tide of practicing unbelief? These theologians were more than willing to assert the post-Christian (and post-theistic) character of America, a conviction that struck at the heart of the generation gap then emerging in the early 1960s. The mind of the older generation was still burning with the memory of the World Wars fought for God and country. That the covenant between God and country could be broken seemed ludicrous to them. To the nascent baby boomers, such covenant arrangements did not mean much, having experienced a land flowing with milk and honey, largely because Dad worked in the booming car or insurance or steel industry and Mom had also found a part time job to keep the future bright for the children. God's providence had been replaced by job security at GM or US Steel or Sun Oil. The new generation sensed a divine call but now it came from the protest of Bob Dylan and Joan Baez, focused largely against the dichotomy in their parents lives between religious beliefs (God, country and church) and their lives (money, money, money). John Lennon of the Beatles captured the sentiments of the nascent youth culture:

> Christianity will go. It will vanish and shrink. I needn't argue with that; I'm right and I will be proved right. We're more popular than Jesus now; I don't know which will go first—rock and roll or Christianity.[22]

That radical theologians joined in the protest (against God and church) seemed ludicrous to the older generation but somewhat amusing to the youth.

The radical theologians sought common cause with the student radicals, with the civil rights protesters and with the emerging Feminist Movement, all of whom conceptualized their task as the disestablishment of the status quo in some deep and profound sense. Though the necrotheologians may have been formally in dialogue with Tillich, Bultmann and Wittgenstein, it was the revolutionary social movements on American soil that provided the necessary fertilizer for the Death of God Movement to grow and flourish. The events and moral issues of Mississippi and Vietnam were very real to the person in the street. The traditional religious affirmations about God, world, and human nature may have seemed true enough though not of much importance. The radical theologians (with support from an English bishop and a martyred German pastor) recognized this and sought to give cognitive as well as practical priority to the reality presuppositions of the younger generation over those of the older and religious generation.

---

[22] As quoted in an interview by Maureen Cleve, *Evening Standard* (4 March 1966).

Part of the problem the radical theologians faced was translation. The radical elements of culture did not speak the language of Tillich nor of Wittgenstein any more than did the emerging youth culture. With rare exceptions, the academy looked down its very long intellectual nose at the pop icons of the day, Jimmy Dean, Marilyn Monroe and Marlon Brando. The ideological conversations of the intellectual elite mirrored in important ways the secularizing trends of popular culture but there was little actual contact between them, until of course the boomers went to college in unprecedented numbers in the 1960s. Here the worlds of pop culture and academic culture intersected as never before, in some measure because of the sheer volume of students and thereby new young faculty requisite to teach all the newly needed classes. Echoes of protest reverberated throughout the universities of America. College campuses served as the breeding ground and the justification of the new theologies.

The radical theologians sensed clearly enough that they were no longer at home in the church. They inhabited the world of the academy where the church was distant and where professional concerns dominated. Hamilton asked the poignant question:

> Does the theologian go to church? The answer is no. He may, in the past have concealed this "no" from himself by escaping into church work, speaking to church groups, preaching at church or college, slaking his thirst for worship and word in more protected communities. But now he is facing up to this banal answer to the banal question, and he will say "no" openly.[23]

The "alienated theologian" was concerned (and in part commissioned) with the articulation of the confession of the Christian community but who was himself as much a doubter as a believer.[24] He now accepted the premises of unbelief of his academic colleagues in other departments and saw those colleagues as the ones to whom it was necessary to justify his own calling. Some of these theologians tried straightforwardly to pour the new atheistic wine into the old Christian wineskins. Others did it in subversive but often hidden ways. What was common to them was the acceptance of the naturalistic temper of their disciplinary home, the modern university, and with it the realization that their ecclesiastical home was no longer inhabitable.[25]

---

[23] "Thursday's Child," *Theology Today*, January 1964. Reprinted in *Radical Theology and the Death of God*, Thomas J.J. Altizer and William Hamilton (Indianapolis IN: Bobbs Merrill, 1966), p. 88.

[24] This is from the title of Van Harvey's influential essay "The Alienated Theologian," in *The Future of Philosophical Theology*, ed. Robert A. Evans (Philadelphia: Westminster Press, 1970), pp. 113–43.

[25] "The new theologian is confessing that the Word has ceased to be truly or decisively present in the established and traditional forms of faith." Altizer, *Christian Atheism*, p. 16.

At Home with Modern Science

Entering the second half of the twentieth century God was intellectually superfluous to many of the academic elite in the West and the radical theologies accepted this naturalistic viewpoint characteristic of the post-War academy and the corresponding morality of knowledge that undergirded it.[26] This part of the "tradition" of the academy embodied such virtues as skepticism against unfounded assertions, including (and maybe especially including) the dictates of traditional metaphysics, the suspicion bordering on cynicism of institutionally sanctioned forms of authority, the valuing of logical clarity, the appeal to evidence and experiences of certain varieties and the non-certainty of all claims to final truth.[27] Hamilton stated this as almost a matter of fact:

> But it is, I think we should agree, a mark of education and good sense to refrain from dogmatic statements which necessarily deny all merit to all other positions and points of view. One can hold serious commitments without universalizing them and without insisting that all who disagree are either knaves or fools. If relativism has an unpleasant sound, then let us call it tolerance. By whatever name, it is an important feature of the (secular) spirit of our age; and when we run into its denial, as in McCarthyism or Goldwaterism, most of us are at least uncomfortable.[28]

Herein lay the legacy inherited from the Enlightenment that was part of the normal working fabric of the alienated theologian's environment. It was part of their professional "duty" to be estranged from the ethics of traditional Christianity which conceived of credulity and belief based upon ancient texts as virtues and skepticism as sinful.

The radical theologians tried to state these sets of epistemic duties in theological prose though cognizant that their intended audience no longer sat in pews but behind desks in their classrooms. To them the unreality of God formed a fundamental postulate and thus all language about this Being ought to be thought of as meaningless and in some sense irrelevant. This claim had been made rather starkly by many prominent philosophers of the early twentieth century on the grounds that modern science no longer needed such a Being. One finds many of the same ideological justifications of this unbelief in the Death of God theologians. Looming on the horizon of the 1960s, absent in the philosophers however, was the increasingly apparent connection between institutional religion and evil. Philosophers in the empiricist tradition had sought to protect science from the

---

[26] See George Marsden, *The Soul of the American University* (New York: Oxford University Press, 1994).

[27] Gilkey referred to these epistemic duties collectively as "the principle of personal intellectual honesty." *Naming the Whirlwind*, p. 114.

[28] Hamilton, *Theological Explorations*, p. 41.

unwanted invasion of the transcendent. The Death of God theologians sought to protect the modern world from the religious justification of bigotry and violence. It was impossible for them to understand the experience of evil if belief in God is blind and thereby serves an axe to grind one's prejudices. If humankind was to be responsible, they must be free and if they were free they could serve no masters, especially not a distant transcendent one.

Analogous to the philosophical guild's embrace of modern science, so the radical theologians affirmed the modern "world" in all of its secularity. This world became the sole relevant environment in which necrotheologians lived and thought, establishing the norms for adequate inquiry and the criteria for acceptable living. Having come of age in the twentieth century, humankind was no longer *homo religius* but *homo seculare*. God was no longer the glue that held human existence together. He was but a peripheral part of reality consigned to play the role of an odd character in an ancient storybook. Humankind had shown themselves eminently capable of getting along in the world without God.

Common cause with an important philosophical school of the 1930s and 1940s, logical positivism, was the tendency of the necrotheologians to dispense with all metaphysical, suprahistorical, divine or otherwise invisible entities or categories. Attention had to be focused and confined to this world, to what is directly visible, experienceable and verifiable. On this rendering, language about "God" should be translated into terms more readily accessible for modern secular people.

The meaning of the word "God," even its reference to the "transcendent," can be developed and understood entirely in terms of this-worldly (therefore "secular") experiences and conceptions—that is, in terms fully comprehensible and significant to the most "modern" of men.[29]

Van Buren, more than the other figures in the Death of God Movement was cognizant of logical positivism though even he seemed unaware in the early 1960s of the important internal criticisms of the Movement which had arisen within positivist circles in the 1950s. He thought the Anglo-American school of philosophy could provide tools of immense benefit to modern theology. As many of the positivists had urged in the 1920s, so Van Buren argued in the 1960s that post-Kantian idealism which had furnished the modern German theological house, was now hopelessly out of date.[30] Conversant with the influential "University

---

[29] Gordon Kaufman, "On the Meaning of 'God;' Transcendence without Mythology," *Harvard Theological Review*, vol. 59, no. 2 (April 1966): 106. Kaufman had been one of Van Buren's professors at Harvard and was viewed by Van Buren at least, as a soulmate to the Death of God Movement. See the final chapter of *Theological Explorations* for this connection.

[30] As logical positivism dismissed British Idealism for making nonsensical metaphysical claims, so the necrotheologians dismissed traditional religion for making nonsensical metaphysical claims. Van Buren wrote:

> This way of doing philosophy [i.e. linguistic analysis] challenges the Christian to think clearly, speak simply, and say what he means without using words in

Discussion" in the mid-50s, Van Buren cited Anthony Flew's parable of the gardener from that discussion as substantiating the claim that the problem with traditional Christian theism was a language problem.[31] Christian theism used terms that were meaningless if understood in their modern secular senses. Like the explorer in Flew's parable who continued to defend his belief in the invisible, intangible and insensible-to-electric shocks gardener (God), so the church at its peril continued to defend belief in a God who existed in some timeless, non-spatial, transcendent realm. In an earlier mythological age, these beliefs may have seemed reasonable, but the "modern" person could no longer countenance them as meaningful in light of their experience. Science and technology had brought the modern world into existence and as gaps in scientific knowledge narrowed, God lost his place in the world. The older religious language just did not make sense any more.

The positivists had started out with similar aims. They had sought to come to grips with the tremendous impact that empirical science had had upon the modern world. Most of them were trained in one or another of the sciences and only later in life turned to the classic problems which philosophy had sought to address.[32] Their movement was straightforwardly anti-metaphysical and they very clearly believed that the only important philosophical questions left were questions about the meaning of language. Philosophy could be useful only as a handmaiden to science, clarifying the language of science. "Philosophy should be defined as the 'pursuit of meaning' and science as the 'pursuit of truth.'"[33]

The similarities between the Positivist Movement and the Death of God Movement are striking. The logical positivists defended an older Enlightenment understanding of science as objective and neutral. The radical theologians were less interested in science, *per se*, but rather in the consequent worldview, which the modern world had inherited from it. For both Movements there was no useful distinction any longer available between a theological starting point relevant for the Church and one relevant for the world. Belief and unbelief must now operate

---

unusual ways, unless he makes it quite clear what he is doing. A sentence from [Schubert] Ogden's book illustrates the appropriateness of this challenge; "When we say, then, that the integral significance of the event of Jesus is to re-present as a possibility demanding decision the final truth about man's existence *coram deo*, we are actually saying the reality this truth seeks to express is literally present 'in, with, and under' that same event." ... One wonders what Ogden is "actually saying." The purpose of linguistic analysis is to rid us of such cases of language cramps, when we cannot say just what we mean and do not seem to mean just what we say. *The Secular Meaning of the Gospel* (New York: The Macmillan Co., 1963), p. 18.

31 Van Buren, *The Secular Meaning of the Gospel*, pp. 1–20.

32 This is especially so with the members of the Vienna Circle. See Chapter 6 of the present work for a fuller treatment of the Vienna Circle.

33 Moritz Schlick, "The Future of Philosophy," in his *Philosophical Papers*, vol. 2, edited by Henk L. Mulder and Barbara F.B. van de Velde-Schlick; translated by Peter Heath (Dordrecht: D. Reidel, 1979), p. 48.

off the same premises.[34] They also both lived in ontological deserts whose only apparent vegetation consisted in the finite realities science could describe and ordinary experiences of secular people. They found meaningless or irrelevant any category of the transcendent or the sacred. They were consistently naturalistic in character, rejecting any peculiarly religious means of knowing reality be it called revelation or religious experience.

Both Movements were committed to the death of metaphysics in the traditional sense and to an optimistic understanding of the benefits of secularism. Logical positivism deeply believed in an optimistic appraisal of the powers of science and the necrotheologians in an optimistic appraisal of the powers of the new secular society.

There is also a remarkable similarity between logical positivism and radical theology in terms of their quick rise to prominence and equally quick demise. The intellectual tenure for both Movements was amazingly short. The Death of God movement died, as it were, from benign neglect. No one picked up their mantle. But it was the death of optimism, which is finally the explanation for the demise of both of the Movements. In respect of the logical positivists, this was most clearly in the work of Thomas Kuhn. It was he who raised the most disturbing questions about the historical character of science and of its claim to provide unbiased access to the real world. After Kuhn, it became harder and harder for philosophers to view science as the fundamental source of human progress.[35] It was as tangled in the mire of personal politics as was any form of intellectual inquiry.

The Death of Optimism and the Death of God

Key to the death of the Death of God Movement was the death of American liberalism in its optimistic phase. The death of both began around 1965 and culminated by 1968. The Death of God theologians believed they were riding the wave of optimism as the tumultuous decade began. Representatively, Hamilton went so far as to suggest that neo-orthodoxy died after the War because the pessimistic spirit of America had died.[36] The necrotheologian sounded radical but they were in part echoing themes similar to Kennedy and Johnson. Change would come if enough

---

34 This is what Anthony Flew refers to as the "presumption of atheism." See his *The Presumption of Atheism and Other Philosophical Essays on God, Freedom and Immortality* (New York: Barnes and Noble, 1976).

35 Distinctive theologies arising from a particular paradigm experience of the world emerged in the 1970s and 1980s. They were not directly related to the shift of Kuhn, Quine, and Sellars amongst others. However these theologies gained a legitimating force (plausibility structure) with the work of these philosophers in epistemology and the philosophy of science. I know of no work that has made this connection explicit though it is surely worth exploring further.

36 "The New Optimism:" 157–9.

moral courage could be mustered and if people simply believed it could happen. Kennedy banked on this in his inaugural address and Johnson used it effectively to push landmark legislation on civil rights and poverty through Congress early in his presidency. The necrotheologians had spoken of this hope in theological garb and added a radical twist. In retrospect the latter was very dependent upon the former. Hamilton believed his was an age of "resolute confidence and optimism that even the really intractable problems that have marked our civilized period can be overcome, problems as apparently irreducible as war and mental illness."[37]

Hamilton thought this optimism began to peak in 1965 concurrent with the passage of Johnson's major Civil Rights legislation. However, the Civil Rights Movement's lurch towards violence shortly thereafter, the riots of the urban landscape and the intensifying protest against Vietnam progressively destroyed this fundamental trust in modern secularism. With it were dashed the prospects of finding a prophetic hope within the confines of contemporary secular society. If God had died and American culture was left with nothing but this world, by 1968 it appeared this was worse than if God had somehow managed to survive.

The Death of God Movement lasted such a short time because it allowed for such a narrow range of meaning to human existence and experience, failing to account for radical flaws within the human constitution and the need for meaning beyond a secular existence. However, the genius of the Movement lay precisely in its weakness. The modern world of experience had been "flattened" ontologically, but when it was flattened the religious questions came much closer to the surface and it was imperative to come to grips with that reality. The Death of God Movement finally signaled something genuinely true about modernity, that it was deeply alienating and despairing.

The legacy of the Death of God Movement is still to be sorted out, but it seems in hindsight that the Enlightenment-inspired optimism in secularity ended when the Death of God Movement vanished. With the rise of liberation theologies on the left and the post-liberal theologies on the right in the last decades of the twentieth century, the theological answer to the radical sixties is less than settled. Theology inevitably lives now on the other side of the crash of optimism in modern secular culture.

Liberation theologies were rooted in the experience of oppression within that culture whereas post-liberal theology raised anew the neo-orthodox insistence upon the prophetic distance between the gospel and the world. Both were/are very wary of "modern man" though that wariness leads in two different directions. The seriousness of the concern to wrestle with the alienating character of modern secularity continues, and in part continues because the Death of God theologians were so bold as to bring it center stage. Theologies after the Death of God cannot help but wrestle with that "problem of modernity." They can also not help but reckon with the loss of optimism so characteristic of the period after the 1960s. Science itself is no less pervasive but its secular moorings are viewed with

[37] Ibid.: 160.

deeper suspicion after the 1960s. It is a suspicion profoundly characteristic of the postmodern age.

The Death of God theologians had argued that the status quo must be protested on largely secular grounds. But the embrace of secularity left little room to protest the deformations of that secular arena. There was too little "bite" in their protest without some transcendent vantage point. But it was that transcendent vantage point which the Death of God theologians explicitly repudiated. Neither did their criticism of the church have much "bite" to it either, for the church's identity lay precisely in its distance from the secular arena. The church that looked too much like the world would have nothing prophetic to say to it. This was Martin Luther King's central claim, that a voice from outside the system was needed for meaningful change to take place. None of the necrotheologians anticipated the rise of black or feminist theologies nor were they conscious of how Martin Luther King's prophetic voice assumed an active and living God.[38] Many church folk, black and white, dismissed the Death of God Movement as lacking an authentic prophetic voice.

The desire to be prophetic lingered on beyond the 1960s and remained a part of the postmodern mood. More nearly it was the power of the establishment which explained the desire to protest, rather than fundamentally new intuitions about the secular life. Partisan protest continued because the establishment remained so entrenched by virtue of the power of its tools and its organizations. The Death of God theologians prophetically realized that religion must be prophetic if it was to survive but little realized that it was the "secular life" which cried out for change. The death of the Death of God Movement signaled a new anxiety about secularity and a surprising revival of robust religious faith at the end of the 1960s. This is seen nowhere more clearly than in the work of the young Alisdair MacIntyre to which we turn in the next chapter.

---

[38] On this point see the interesting and mostly sympathetic article on the Death of God Movement shortly after its death by John Rathbun, "God is Dead: Avant-garde Theology for the Sixties," *The Canadian Review of American Studies*, vol. 5, no. 2 (Fall 1974): 166–80.

PART IV
Hesitant Radicals

Chapter 8
A Secular Voice Against Secularity

> In our ordinary secular vocabulary we have no language to express common needs, hopes and fears that go beyond the immediacies of technique and social structure. ... We should therefore expect to find continual attempts to use religious language to mask an atheistic vacuum.
>
> Alasdair MacIntyre (1963)[1]

It was not an uncommon prophecy through the first half of the twentieth century that religious belief of any substance would soon go the way of the horse-drawn buggy and the oil-burning lantern. This was not simply a statement of intellectual confidence by atheists but more often grounded in the obvious sociological realities that religious conviction was slowly eroding under the forces of secularization.[2] The confidence in the impending demise of theism was different than the conviction of David Hume in the eighteenth century that belief in God was no longer tenable in light of the pervasive presence of evil or Ludwig Feuerbach's insistence that belief in God could be better explained as a projection of human ideals. It was different because many in the twentieth century believed that the social structures of modernity would soon make Christianity obsolete, forever abandoned to the dustbin of an earlier primitive time. There would be no grand intellectual battle. Christian faith would die not because of its intellectual inferiority (though it was) nor because of its immoral consequences (though it had many) but rather because of its irrelevance to modern life.

The fear of irrelevance lay in part behind the long tradition of remaking theism after the image of modernity. Toning down the miraculous and construing Jesus as a social prophet were strategies along the way to achieve the accommodation of Christianity to its cultural context. By the middle of the twentieth century the practical irrelevance of religious belief to many in the English-speaking world appeared to threaten even these watered-down versions of Christianity. There remained a slight few, who, though they had abandoned Christian trappings openly, still seemed to have an uneasy conscience about the impact of secularization upon the religious vigor of the English-speaking world, and prime among them was

---

1 "God and the Theologians," *Encounter* (September 1963) reprinted in *Against the Self Images of the Age* (Notre Dame: University of Notre Dame Press, 1971), p. 23.

2 Secularization is "simply the transition from beliefs and activities and institutions presupposing beliefs of a traditional Christian kind to beliefs and activities and institutions of an atheistic kind." Alasdair MacIntyre, *Secularization and Moral Change* (New York: Oxford University Press, 1967), p. 7.

the young Alasdair MacIntyre.[3] He was born and raised in Scotland, educated in London, and taught at prestigious universities on both sides of the Atlantic during a long teaching career. MacIntyre's early work had been inspired by Marxist critiques of religion in the U.K. but he seemed increasingly suspicious of Marxism as the decade of the 1960s wore on, in large measure because he came to abandon its vision of a secular utopia free from the shackles of religious belief. He espoused a confidence in modern science, but he nonetheless seemed uncomfortable with the moral declension brought on by the structures of modernity. He could not envision any other viable alternative outside of a secular future, but neither was he content with that possibility. With hindsight MacIntyre's uneasy conscience expressed in his early work was one of the signs of the complicated role religious belief played in the 1960s and as a prelude to MacIntyre's later work on religion and moral traditions.[4] The moral incongruities of modern life to MacIntyre were too great to be ignored, even if he was not yet ready to retrieve the moral traditions of Christianity. In light of these misgivings about modern secularity, his religious conversion in the early 1980s in retrospect ought not be as surprising as it might have been when it first happened.[5] MacIntyre has remained a committed member of the Roman Catholic Church since his conversion.[6]

---

[3] His early works include: "Visions" in Anthony Flew and Alasdair MacIntyre, eds, *New Essays in Philosophical Theology* (New York: MacMillan Co., 1955); *Difficulties in Christian Belief* (London: SCM Press, 1959), *The Religious Significance of Atheism* (New York: Columbia University Press, 1969), "God and the Theologians," *Encounter* (September 1963), *Secularization and Moral Change* (London: Oxford University Press, 1967) and "The End of Ideology and the End of the End of Ideology," in *Against the Images of the Age* (London: Gerald Duckworth and Co. Limited, 1971).

[4] MacIntyre is a figure of interest in charting the beginnings of postmodernity in the Anglo-American world because of his complicated and complicating response to the intellectual turmoil of the 1960s. In his major triology of works: *After Virtue* (1981); *Whose Justice, Which Rationality* (1988), and *Three Rival Versions of Moral Enquiry* (1990), MacIntyre criticized the whole Enlightenment project as providing a neutered and neutral rationality. In this sense he is a window that allows us to see the intellectual revolt against modernity in their early and formative stages.

[5] John Horton and Susan Mendes, remark, "*After Virtue*, which was published in 1981, surprised the philosophical world by the depth of its disillusion with modern morality in general and what MacIntyre called 'the Enlightenment project' in particular." See Horton and Mendes, "Alasdair MacIntyre: After Virtue and After" in John Horton and Susan Mendes, *After MacIntyre: Critical Perspectives on the Work of Alasdair MacIntyre* (Notre Dame: University of Notre Dame Press, 1994), p. 1. "With the benefit of hindsight" Horton and Mendes go on to write: "the seeds of the still more radical critique of modernity can be found [much earlier]."

[6] A brief biography of MacIntyre can be found in Mark C. Murphy, "Introduction" in Mark C. Murphy, ed., *Alasdair MacIntyre* (Cambridge: Cambridge University Press, 2003), pp. 1–9.

In his 1966 Bampton lectures, MacIntyre argued that the difference between theists and atheists had a radical new look in the twentieth century as opposed to the nineteenth century. Until midway through the nineteenth century the differences between theism and atheism were conceived largely in metaphysical terms and the debate wrestled with the requisite evidence for the best explanation of the competing metaphysical claims. On this score David Hume's arguments against theism looked similar to the arguments batted back and forth by sophisticated skeptics in the third and fourth centuries. In the latter half of the nineteenth century, there developed an uncomfortable doubt about the intellectual viability of religious belief among several significant English thinkers. It was uncomfortable precisely because of the social implications of religious doubt. Standing against the tide of religious conviction in England seemed somewhat risky in the nineteenth century. By the beginning decades of the twentieth century opposition to religious belief had become something of a fait accompli. In MacIntyre's mind this was unique and without historical precedent. MacIntyre illustrated the point by referencing two well known religious skeptics, Henry Sidgwick (1838–1900) and John Maynard Keynes (1883–1946). MacIntyre wrote:

> Sidgwick agonized over whether he could continue conscientiously to hold his Cambridge fellowship given his religious doubts, whereas Keynes an intellectual generation later could put aside any social worries about unbelief. Keynes was certain as to the falsity of Christianity and this replaced doubt. For Sidgwick there was an agonizing doubt as a way of life in which the connection between the Christian religion and the actual choices that men have to make in their moral and social lives had become remote.[7]

MacIntyre supposed that Darwinian biology, Marxist economics and Freudian psychology had gained such currency in the academy through the first half of the twentieth century as to grant religious unbelief a certain smug overconfidence. The alleged "war between science and religion" may have given the appearance of putting theists on the defensive at the end of the nineteenth century, but the battle seemed entirely over by mid-century to British intellectuals. Religion was the clear loser.[8] The new techniques of historical criticism and its consequent ideology became so ensconced in the intellectual guild by the middle of the twentieth century, that there was no longer much credence given to a notion of a transcendent reality.

---

[7] *Secularization and Moral Change*, p. 37.

[8] Two works of the late nineteenth century illustrate the cultural tension in the emerging conflicts between religious belief and scientific commitments. The theologically liberal, but tempered, work of Frederick Temple, *The Relations between Religion and Science* (London, 1884) and the more radical work by Andrew D. White, *A History of the Warfare of Science and Theology in Christendom* (1896).

These changes in the mood of religious unbelief were unusual not because of any newly available evidence which had undermined religious belief but rather because most people were embedded in a set of cultural processes where technology and affluence increasingly displaced religious conviction as the practical motivation of their actions. Religion no longer occupied the central space in the public domains of people's lives. Under the conditions of modernity religion had been relegated to the private functions of an individual's conscience. Religious behavior persisted but in greatly truncated forms. Less than 10 per cent of the British population attended services in a church on a weekly basis at mid-century, but nearly 70 per cent of them were still baptizing their children in a local Church of England parish. The majority of marriages and funerals were still performed by the clergy though one respected survey of religious conviction in the 1950s argued that a sizeable portion of the "English population held a view of the universe which can most properly be designated as magical."[9] This all assumed an essentially secular framework and yet it was shrouded in a vestigial religiosity with no signs of abating. These were puzzling realities to MacIntyre.

For a host of complicated reasons the intellectual gulf between traditional theism and the ethos of contemporary culture grew ever wider and wider as the twentieth century wore on. Theism was no longer an enemy, it appeared as simply irrelevant. But as irrelevant as it seemed to many social philosophers, religious behaviors persisted and showed no signs of being fully extinguished. The prophesies by Marx and Engles that total secularization was inevitable were proving woefully untrue according to MacIntyre. Secular thinkers seemed overly confident regarding the eventual demise of religion, but the sociological realities suggested to MacIntyre that total secularization itself was the one with a dubious future. Why were many religious sensibilities still present? Why was the easy confidence in unbelief misplaced? The answer to those questions animated much of MacIntyre's work in the 1960s and thus serve as a window on this revolutionary decade.

Rationality and the Religious Dilemma

With a characteristic Enlightenment-inspired hope in human reason, MacIntyre supposed that the fundamental change in the terms of the science-religion debate lay in the realization that science progressed on its own merits independent of the cultural forms in which it took place. By contrast religious belief was embedded in a peculiarly primitive social context and could not intellectually survive outside of that context.[10] Although both science and religion carried on their activities in socially sanctioned institutions, science (or so thought MacIntyre at the time) alone had the capacity to transform and replace earlier (outmoded) theories. This

[9] Thomas Harrison, *Britain Revisited* (London: V. Gollancz, 1961) as cited in MacIntyre, *Secularization and Moral Change*, p. 17.

[10] This is the heart of the argument in *The Religious Significance of Atheism*.

was part of the very character of empirical research upon which modern science had been built. On the other hand, religion was characteristically reluctant to tolerate whatever was anomalous or exceptional to its own established constructs. It presupposed one way of looking at the world that would not and could not change. The Church's commitment to certain historical events prohibited it from countenancing any set of phenomena of such a kind that their occurrence would show that God did not exist or that God lacked the attributes traditionally ascribed to him.[11] While not therefore strictly unfalsifiable in a positivist sense, theism had always been conceived as irrefutable by Christians.[12] The resurrection of Jesus was a foundational Christian belief but in so far as it was a historical event, was it open to be proven false or not? Christianity could not countenance the possibility that there was no such resurrection, but what if present day evidence suggested otherwise. What would Christians do? The most likely option would be to make the resurrection immune from the evidence, and thus to make it immune from scientific scrutiny. But in the age of science this seemed entirely implausible. In this light the rise of modern science and its commitment to be led wherever the evidence mandated, could not but create a crisis for religion, MacIntyre believed. If traditional theism were to be subjected to the critical standards of modern science it would not long survive, or so it appeared.

MacIntyre supposed that in a culture where refutability was embraced as a criteria of rationality, two alternatives for religious belief would be to reformulate itself as deism or to refuse to acquiesce to rational standards. Whenever it refused to acquiesce, religion did so by segregating itself from the secular intellectual disciplines. This was the option of religious fundamentalists. On the other hand reformulation was the strategy employed by theological liberals such as Paul Tillich and Bishop John Robinson. Fundamentalism and Liberalism both attempted to create theistic enclaves protected by two very different sorts of strategies. Liberalism supposed that modern secular culture was a given and that Christian faith would have to remove the "offensive" elements from its own repertoire to retain a place at the table. Notions of judgment and hell would have to be jettisoned, especially as applicable to adherents of other world religions. The miracles recorded in the Bible would also have to be reinterpreted. Broadly speaking, liberal religion engaged in a process of distinguishing worthy beliefs from unworthy ones according to a vague notion of scientific respectability. This strategy was instantiated in the ecumenical movements associated with theological liberalism during the opening decades of the twentieth century. In contrasting fashion fundamentalists attempted to retain Christian orthodoxy by

---

[11] In the 1960s all discussion relative to God still occurred using the male pronouns.

[12] Refutability is merely the claim that reasonable beliefs are those beliefs about which there are possible ways to refute them. A true belief is reasonable, not because it has been refuted, but because it is refutable, if there were possible evidences to the contrary.

denouncing contemporary secular culture and its criteria of scientific rationality.[13] They supposed there were irreducibly religious elements in reality that could not be explained away by science. However, the depth of secular culture showed no signs of vanishing in the face of the fundamentalist challenge.

The common outcome of both strategies was the irrelevance of substantive religious belief, or so it seemed to MacIntyre and many other secular intellectuals in the 1960s. Liberal religion watered down theism to virtual irrelevance, and fundamentalist made themselves irrelevant by their parochial views of modern culture. MacIntyre saw no point in making much of denying the existence of God because he saw little point in affirming God. As a result, the death of theism remained a matter of historical curiosity but little more than that to him. Christianity seemed incompatible with the technical industrial society of the twentieth century, but why did certain religious practices persist nonetheless. At some point MacIntyre grew uneasy about the too-glib dismissal of theism but groped for reasons to explain his own uneasiness.[14] He denied that Christianity could retain any of its traditional viability, but he also sensed that secular society could not develop a common morality that would be sustainable. He wrote: "On secular terms, there is no moral scheme available with a clear view of good and evil."[15] Without such a scheme, there was no notion of a common good to which secular communities could strive and be sustained in their efforts.

Superstitious Secularism

The secular spirit was far from clearly victorious in MacIntyre's England of the 1960s, though clearly neither was the traditional religion of Christianity. Most people stood somewhere in the superstitious middle, using the church when convenient but giving little heed to religion when it was inconvenient. A very small percentage of the British population regularly attended church (less than 10 per cent) but a much larger percentage of the population used the church during the great events of the life cycle; birth, marriage, and death—as if these required a religious context even though the population on other accounts did not really

---

13 The self-styled evangelical prophet, Francis Schaeffer seemed a particularly clear proponent of this strategy, though MacIntyre and other mainstream intellectuals never gave any evidence of having read Schaeffer or any other fundamentalists/evangelicals of the period. See Francis Schaeffer, *The God Who is There* (InterVarsity Press, 1968).

14 In the mid-1950s MacIntyre still supposed that theism could survive the challenge of evidence. By the late 1950s and throughout the 1960s his convictions underwent a significant change. He abandoned the project he had begun with Anthony Flew of assessing theism/atheism relative to the evidence. See *Difficulties in Christian Belief* for the clearest statement of this earlier strategy.

15 *Secularization and Moral Change*, p. 69.

believe one existed. Over half of all English citizens were still married in the church and even more were buried there.

A sizable percentage of regular church attenders did not believe in life after death while nearly 20 per cent of avowed atheists said they prayed and believed that Jesus was more than a man. Behind this seemed a belief that Christianity was false and a wish that it were not, which at other levels appeared as a kind of half-belief. As MacIntyre remarked, "The creed of the English is that there is no God and that it is wise to pray to him from time to time."[16]

MacIntrye cited the ironic case of the Marxist inspired Labor Churches of the early twentieth century as prime evidence that the English wanted religion without being religious.[17] The Labor Churches were made up exclusively of working class union members. In these churches, the name of Jesus was often accompanied by loud cheers as if Jesus were a real working-class hero. There were hot disputes in the Labor Churches as to whether prayers were permitted or not. Some argued against praying because such practices committed the church to a belief in God, a belief that they thought unduly connected to the dogma of the ruling class. Others argued that prayer often appeared to do good for those who prayed, and thus the church ought to pray whether there is a God or not. The odd marriage of Marxism and Christianity did not last long, though the attempt was itself instructive.

The secular party line supposed this was but a remnant of nostalgia for earlier times, a remnant that would soon diminish and fade away altogether. MacIntyre was not so convinced though he was not particularly religious himself in any identifiable sense. The survival of religious habits and modes of feeling and questioning at widely different levels in the culture pointed to something that the prophets of God's death (Marx, Engels and Nietzsche in the last century and Altizer and Hamilton in the 1960s) missed. But what was it?

The religion of English society prior to the Industrial Revolution provided a framework within which eternal and transcendent questions could be asked and answered, even if there were slightly different and sometimes even rival answers given. What does it mean to be human? From whence did we come? What happens at death? Is there a meaning to life other than the meaning we choose to give it? Is there a moral governor outside our own private interests? The old religious order at least asked these questions even if its answers no longer seemed reasonable. The dissolution of the old religious order seemed to presage a declension of the moral order in such a fashion that these questions were no longer asked in the public square. This inevitably led to a set of vestigial religious practices that tried to hold onto the questions without supposing that they could be meaningfully answered.

---

16 "God and the Theologians:" 27.

17 Ibid.: 26–7.

Atheism and Moral Change

MacIntyre supposed that public morality was so integrally tied to Christian theism that the loss of the latter presaged the loss of the former. This seemed the only ground for retaining some remnant of religious belief. However, MacIntyre in this period captured the spirit of the times in arguing not only that morality can thrive without religious belief but that in separating it from religious belief it would more nearly acclimate to the demands of modernity. In agrarian contexts the stability of the family unit may have been important but in industrialized contexts marital fidelity was no longer necessary, morally or economically.[18] To a generation discovering the enormous material benefits of technology the public morality of an earlier age seemed no longer appropriate. As the moral sensibilities of culture changed so would its models of those sensibilities. At times MacIntrye seemed unfazed by this, but other times he seemed to mourn the loss of the old moral order. The belief in a sovereign and transcendent God no longer could serve as a standard of morality. The old picture of God just did not fit the times. But the new morality seemed especially vacuous to MacIntrye. The new replacement virtues of cooperativeness, fair-play, tolerance and compromise were secondary types of virtues, parasitic upon the notion of another set of virtues which were directly related to the goals which humans pursued as ends of their life. Virtue itself depended upon ultimate ends. Without primary virtues, the secondary virtues seemed pointless. In the new morality, there were acceptable means, but no ends. This may have provided a spirit of tolerance for other moralities, but it also emptied the meaning of right and wrong in any strong sense:

> The secondary virtues of Britain rule out any kind of metaphysical exclusivism. They are virtues which express an attitude to the world in which the making of cosmic and universal claims for one's own group as against other groups, is no longer possible.[19]

But if there were no cosmic and universal claims against other groups, there were also none in favor of any group. There were no longer grounds for distinguishing right from wrong other than expediency. Lost were the virtues which sustained a moral identity and by which moral norms could protest radical evils such as injustice and oppression. This cost seemed to MacIntyre quite high.

The abundant prosperity of the 1950s, deeply appreciated by the generation which had lived through the Great Depression in the 1930s, was increasingly viewed by the new generation in the 1960s as a source of moral emptiness. The uneven distribution of the new affluence was especially repugnant to those inspired by the older Marxist notions of economic justice such as MacIntyre. One of the radical theologians wrote:

---

18 See Ch. 2 of *The Religious Significance of Atheism* entitled "Atheism and Morals."

19 *Secularization and Moral Change*, p. 24.

> One might imagine that existence in a vacuous society (like technological and urban America) effects a liberation from the past, a liberation that is potentially demonic to be sure, but a liberation that likewise provides the occasion for the deepest kind of creativity.[20]

It was this creativity which was the promise of the era, and also its danger. The British Prime Minister, Harold MacMillan delivered his famous "Winds of Change" speech in 1960 in Cape Town, South Africa. In that speech, MacMillan announced the impending freedom from Colonial rule of the British colonies of Africa. The right of self rule of black Africans by black Africans must be respected. The independence movements spawned by the speech changed the political equation throughout much of Africa in the decades ahead, often in violent revolts against oppressive regimes. The result was also a changing of the moral equation upon which the British Empire had relied. Traditional British culture was no longer viewed as the civilizing force, but the oppressing tryant as the 1960s wore on.

On the other side of the Atlantic, John Kennedy had sounded the motif of change as well in his inaugural address in 1961. The youngest president in American history proclaimed the torch was being passed onto a new generation. He promised major new legislative efforts aimed at ending the troubles of American society - the responsibility for which lay squarely on the shoulders of the young, for good and for ill as the decade was to manifest ever too clearly.

Part of the decade's hopes lay also with the burgeoning new world of technology whose creative energies would finally be harnessed for the betterment of humanity. Technology appeared to under gird the freedom for individuals from the drudgery of the past. Individuals now possessed a power over their destinies because of the power of their tools. These creative energies would also have a profound moral impact. The tools themselves allowed for the possibility of reshaping the norms governing the human community in accord with the deepest longings and desires of the modern world. Poverty could be eliminated. Hunger and starvation would likewise be vanished. New moral norms would govern the relations between the haves and the have-nots in society. Morality would mirror technology in its inevitable march towards progress as the second half of the twentieth century unfolded. This is why it seemed so precarious to some to hold onto outdated and outmoded moral frameworks. Morality ought to be unhinged from traditional religious conviction and attach itself rather to the changing ethos of a technocratic culture.[21] Peace and prosperity were just around the corner if the moral norms

---

20 Thomas Altizer, "America and the Future of Theology," *Antaios*, September 1963, reprinted in *Radical Theology and the Death of God*, Thomas J.J. Altizer and William Hamilton (Indianapolis IN: Bobbs Merrill, 1966), p. 9.

21 I do not want to suggest that this general cultural picture of the malleability of morality coincides with MacIntyre's views. The picture is rather representative of the views of the popular culture which dovetail the philosophical justification of the independence of morality that MacIntyre championed at the time.

would acclimate themselves to the emerging new technologies. Together they held the hope of the new generation.

It was this utopian-inspired hope which appeared to presage the end of substantive religious belief at the mid-point of the twentieth century. It is reasonable to suppose that the harbinger of this was the secular protest movements of the early 1960s. They supposed that secularity could be celebrated religiously. The end of religion was cause for religious celebration. Sociologists of religion supposed that the secularizing process was inevitable and to a large extent irreversible. It was strange that bishops in the Church of England actually embraced this prophesy as well. In the mid-1960s it seemed that Britain had lost its religious convictions, but strangely held onto its religious habits. The prophets of secularity held out the hope that the demise of religion presaged the end of those religious practices as well. The end of religion would signal the end of bigotry, hypocrisy and inequity. These attitudes associated with religious belief would soon be eradicated and would give way to new cultural attitudes of tolerance, freedom and openness. The window of optimism did not last long in the 1960s.

Often unseen at the time, morality was also being reshaped by the immediate interests and desires of a younger generation. These in turn were framed by the common world of experience with its vast complex of business, technology, power, money, sex, culture, race, and poverty. Most people accepted the modern world in all its gaudy plasticity and dreadful humors with the ironic hope that it would lead to a better life. In youth culture, the holy trinity of drugs, sex and rock-and-roll, grew out of the utopian aspirations of the era. In this era the rules were no longer external and timeless but ever more nearly attached to technological progress. Morality, like technology, ought to look to the present rather than the past. This was the spirit of the times in which MacIntyre's uneasy conscience played itself out. Progress was a primary value in modernity, but MacIntyre often noticed moral decline as much as moral progress in the post-Industrial Revolution era. Technological morality could as easily reflect itself in a pragmatic selfishness as in a pragmatic altruism. Selfishness was as old as humankind, but the post-Industrial world had simply baptized it for economic reasons rather than treat as the pariah of traditional religious sanctions. This worried MacIntyre.

The Theological Climate of the 1960s

Many religious figures, unlike MacIntyre, seemed to be at peace with the terms of modernity. According to Bishop John Robinson the future survival of the church lay in its ability to adapt to the realities of modern secular, industrial, urban, and mass culture, rather than to speak prophetically against the ills of modernity. Even such a significant religious figure as Robinson in the Church of England had unflinchingly accepted the terms of modernity. He argued that modernity was a natural evolution of biblical faith. Religious people of earlier times had confessed the regularity of nature was rooted in the regularity of God's providence over nature.

In a technologically advanced society, providence sounded too much like the fates of ancient mythology. Nature still had laws, but these were not divinely imposed, but rather naturally evolving. Nature's laws could be explained without reference to God. The ontological foundations had changed. Nature had become foundational and super-nature was but an unnecessary parasite on it. Nature displaced God as an explanatory framework. The categories of the transcendent, the sacred and the holy were conceptually empty if they also retained some importance for religious persons. Robinson hoped that religious beliefs could be translated in non-religious terms. God ought to be seen in friendlier terms and divine morality must be more sympathetic with the changing political and social mores of the modern period. Robinson supposed Christian ethics could be effectively reinterpreted if it was reduced to an ethic of love, plain and simple. MacIntyre was not so persuaded. Love must be given some content in the actual behaviors of people, he argued. There must be actions which are in fact loving, while other behaviors, regardless of intentions are not loving. This supposed "love" could not be the sole guiding force of ethics. There had to be a greater and more concrete ethical framework. MacIntyre was not sure from whence that ethical framework would emerge, but he doubted whether it could emerge simply from secular modernity. Once actual concrete behaviors are prescribed, there must be a return to a moral scheme with a clear view of good and evil. A secular technocratic culture did not appear to have the resources for such a scheme. Surely, a secular ethic of love fails miserably at this precise point, thought MacIntyre.

Some supposed that God would be less offensive if God were thought as identical with an inner state of feeling. Rather than supposing God is "out there," the sentiment was to put God "in here" freed from the critical scrutiny of empirical observations. This appeared to salvage religion by retreating into an ontological ambiguity, and avoiding the age old dilemma of how the infinite and the finite could relate. In MacIntyre's words:

> Behind these difficulties [with religious language] which arise from the claim that the divine is revealed in a certain inner *Bewusstseinslage* lies one of the simplest and crudest difficulties of orthodox theism. If God is infinite, how can he be manifest in any particular finite object or experience? The definition of God as infinite is intended precisely to distinguish between God and everything finite, but to take the divine out of the finite is to remove it from the entire world of human experience. The inexorable demands of religiously adequate language seem to make experience of God a notion that is a contradiction in terms.[22]

The dilemma was partially addressed with the claim that theological statements were finally statements about what ultimately concerned human beings, not about some independently existing and transcendent being called "God." Since there

---

22 "Visions:" 256.

was no ontological overlap between an infinite God and a finite human, religious "God-talk" must in fact only be about ultimate concerns.

MacIntyre reasoned however, if the object of theological discourse is our own ultimate concern, what of God? Had "ultimate concern" in fact transformed God into little more than a "nobodaddy?"[23] Was this just "merely a familiar form of atheism with a new name?"[24] If it turned out that religious belief just was the name for that concern and no more, what were the grounds for supposing those ultimate concerns actually ever got addressed? Who was to be entrusted with delivering any of the ultimate goods which might satisfy those ultimate concerns? In the 1960s many who occupied the pews still confessed a belief in those ultimate goods even if they did not live as if they mattered much. MacIntrye was perplexed by this scandal of religious belief encased in a non-religious world view, but could not settle for a straightforward modern solution; to suppose that secularism had enough conceptual resources to eradicate the concern for ultimate goods. MacIntyre was troubled by an accommodated religious belief and by an unremitting belief in secularity. However, MacIntrye could see no other alternative in the 1960s.

Liberal theology through the first half of the twentieth century sought to assimilate Christianity to modernity to such an extent that it ceased to be an external adversary of modernity and became instead an embodiment of the forms and values of modern culture and society. Here was the dilemma facing theologians in the aftermath of the crisis of belief, supposed MacIntyre. Any presentation of theism able to secure a hearing from a secular audience, would have to undergo a transformation that had evacuated it entirely of its theistic content. Conversely any presentation which retained such theistic content would be unable to secure a place in contemporary culture which those theologians desired for it.[25] Religion without theism was simply another name for atheism. Religion with theism was too offensive to be relevant. Atheism in a technocratic world was perilously close to being a simple sanction of the moral declension everywhere present in the technocratic world. MacIntyre strongly suspected this because atheism did not have the moral resources sufficient to protest the inequities of the technocratic world.

The Nobodaddy of Secularism

As the decade wore on it became painfully clear that no non-religious utopia would be produced. MacIntyre understood the celebration of secularity was premature. The hope that a secular tradition could provide the culturally stable

---

23 MacIntyre borrowed this term from H.A. Williams, "Psychological Objections to Christianity," in *Objections to Christian Belief, Four Lectures by D.M.MacKinnon, H.A. Williams, A.R. Vidler and J.S. Bezzant* (London: Constable Press, 1964).

24 MacIntyre, *Secularization and Moral Change*, p. 68.

25 This is the summary of the argument found in his *The Religious Significance of Atheism*.

conditions under which deep conflicts would dissolve could not be realized. Having survived the devastation and tragedies of World War II, Britain opened up its immigration policies and in the 1960s quickly ceased to be a monocultural society. Immigrants were welcomed and then resented for having torn apart the unified fabric of English society. The conflicts simmered below the surface for a time, but everywhere the tension seemed manifest. The uneasy truce in Northern Ireland through the 1960s also begged for an enduring answer to British cultural conflict. The Londonderry riots of 1968 and the Belfast riots of 1969 removed any optimism about an easily attainable peace between Protestants and Catholics. The protests against the American war in Vietnam spilled over onto British soil and anti-American sentiment arose with disturbing speed.[26]

Without a common religious framework, how would these cultural conflicts be resolved? Did the new secularism hold any promise for dealing with these apparently intractable conflicts? Increasingly hope seemed to dissipate from the secular balloon even if there were no other ideological framework to replace it. In the middle of the 1960s, MacIntyre saw something important in religious discourse but did not yet grasp its enduring significance in the diagnoses of the secular dream. He thought there was a danger that atheism was being treated as if it too was the private creed of yet another minority religious group offering a means to locate meaning and purpose. He knew better. He knew that atheism was nothing more than the expression of a social fabric without meaning and purpose. He warned that secularists should "wince who have turned conscientious atheism into a substitute Nobodaddy of our own."[27] Secularism had not set British society free from the fragileness of human life. It had simply masked that fragileness by celebrating the freedom which modern life had allegedly brought. This freedom itself was mostly an illusion for the vast majority of people in technologically advanced cultures.

> [The secular theologian] holds onto a heroic Promethian secularity where secular man has come of age at last, and is now able to control his own destiny. This is just not true. Certainly industrial growth and technological change can now be

---

26 The protest of Vietnam was voiced through a vocal minority on both sides of the Atlantic. In any nuanced treatment of the theological implications of Vietnam, it ought to be clear that the conflict was also about informational authority (or secrecy) with which the war was waged. The loudest protest came from the media and the student left who were fundamentally protesting the right to know. The protest then may be understood both as a conflict about the morality of war as such and the morality of knowledge and information. These larger questions are endemic throughout the shift from modernity to postmodernity. See, for example, Bruce Pollock, *When the Music Mattered: Rock in the 1960's* (New York: Holt Rinehart and Winston, 1983) who argues that rock music was able to bypass the normal channels of institutional information control and thereby create a mass following connected with moral causes such as Vietnam.

27 "God and the Theologians:" 25.

> predicted in new ways, but the proportion of human beings who are in a position to participate in this kind of prediction and the consequent decision-making is very small. It is not clear that those who do participate feel themselves able to affect more than a very small area of their lives.[28]

This was MacIntyre's uneasy conscience at work. The discrediting of theism left a religious vacuum but secularism had no resources to fill it. MacIntyre was increasingly wary of secularists who attempted to sneak in a vocabulary of meaning and hope. He knew industrial society had never been able to accommodate a religious interpretation of its own activities.[29] In modern industrial contexts, the substance of religious belief was no longer available, but the replacement secular vocabulary had no language to express common needs, hopes and fears that went beyond the immediacies of technique and social structure. MacIntyre thought it was not unexpected to find persistent attempts to use religious language to mask an atheistic vacuum. He realized the only cure for this vacuum in a secular framework lied in the transformation of modern social structures but the vocabulary of the secular culture had no means to express the underlying vacuum. Therefore it had no resources to criticize the peculiar oppressions of secularity nor the means to encourage significant social change.[30]

Religion now inevitably lives on the other side of the crash of optimism in modern secular culture which MacIntyre foresaw. The birth of the "paradigm theologies" (that is theological visions arising from particular paradigm experiences in the world—feminist, African-American, Latin American, Charismatic, even postliberalism to some extent) at the end of the 1960s grew out of the demise of modern optimism and in part contributed to its death.[31] Those theologies rooted in the experience of oppression within secular culture came to express a prophetic critique of the empty consumerist impulses of secularity. Other theologies raised anew the older insistence upon the prophetic distance between the gospel and the world. Both sorts of theological strategies were/are very wary of "modern man" though that wariness led in different directions It seems clear enough that no single interpretation has proved dominant yet and may never within the confines of the

---

[28] *Secularization and Moral Change*, p. 70.

[29] "God and the Theologians:" 22.

[30] It is not surprising then the MacIntyre is one of the early secular critics of the Marxist social project.

[31] Little seen at the time were the legitimating shifts taking place in the other arenas of the intellectual community. Other episodes highlighted in previous chapters include the demise of foundationalism, the rise of feminism and the dissent over mass culture. Not insignificant are MacIntyre's own sympathies about the end of the end of ideology. Though not stated at the time in the language now familiar, it was MacIntyre's contention then that all rationality is rooted in a tradition; the end of ideology is still ideological. See his "The End of Ideology and the End of the End of Ideology," in MacIntyre, *Against the Self Images of the Age: Essays on Ideology and Philosophy* (London: Gerald Duckworth and Co., 1971).

postmodern paradigm. The seriousness of the concern to wrestle with modern secularity continues, and in part continues because a non-religious interpretation of that secularity is not adequate to the human realities of late modernity. MacIntyre's portrayal of the "nobodaddy" of modern secularity was a pungent signal of that. He reminded us that we cannot help but wrestle with the "problem of modernity." In his early period, MacIntyre may not have predicted such a rapid loss of optimism in the prophets of secularity, but his uneasy conscience all but assured that the loss of optimism would come. That uneasy conscience manifested a suspicion prophetically related to the tumultuous decade of the 1960s.

Chapter 9

Radical Retrieval: Evangelicals and the Story of the 1960s

> I had no time for the church matrix. The churches weren't going to accept me looking like a street person with long hair and faded jeans. They did not like the music I was recording. And I had no desire to preach the gospel to the converted. I wanted to be out on the sidewalk preaching to the runaways and the druggies and the prostitutes.
>
> Larry Norman[1]

Introduction

Curiously the story of religion in the 1960s, with few exceptions, has been told in such a way as to suggest that evangelicalism was but a peripheral part of the decade. If given a role at all, evangelicalism was assigned the function of providing a safe-haven against the inroads of secularism and religious liberalism.[2] Evangelicals were culturally significant in large measure because they provided a link to safer, more secure days in the American past.[3] If God was dead, at least his memory was kept alive in evangelical circles, or so the consensus historiography suggests of this period.[4]

---

1 Interview with Larry Norman, http://www.larrynorman.com/press/1.html, Norman was the most prominent of the evangelical counter-cultural musicians of the 1960s. His influence led to the creation of the contemporary Christian music movement.

2 I should mention my indebtedness to Christopher Lasch, *The True and Only Heaven* (New York: Norton, 1991) and Nathan Hatch, *The Democratization of American Christianity* (New Haven: Yale University Press, 1989) for some of the underlying framework which follows. Neither applies their insights directly to the 1960s though the analogies with their respective concerns are not difficult to make, as the following will make clear.

3 The evangelical Peter Marshall's best selling text of American history is self-conscious attempt at persuading his readers that the best traditions of the American past were evangelical in origin. See *The Light and The Glory: Did God Have a Plan for America?* (New York: Fleming Revell Publishing Co., 1978). A fellow evangelical, Tim LaHaye, wrote the following recommendation on the dust jacket for Marshall's book, "The Light and the Glory reveals our true national heritage and inspires us to stay on God's course as a nation."

4 As early as (and as late as) 1978, the dean of American church historians, Sydney Ahlstrom, wrote, "Evangelical growth in this period can be explained essentially by the role

The underlying assumption of this historiography has been the powerful paradigm of the "culture wars" which supposed that American culture was divided along religious/political/social lines in roughly symmetrical ways.[5] On one side of the culture war lay those who believed in the progressive notions of equality and liberty at the cost of moral ambiguity and social splintering. On the other side of the culture war were conservatives who believed in cultural hierarchies and moral authority, at the expense of individual freedoms and wide civil tolerance. On this rendering, the fault lines within American religious life no longer occurred across denominational lines, but rather across the culture war boundaries.[6]

Without undermining the usefulness of this framework, I want to suggest that it does not adequately account for the resurgence of evangelicalism at the very nadir of the radical 60s. In particular the culture war typology underemphasizes the radical and progressive character of evangelicalism which permitted it to thrive in an age of individual freedoms. The "culture war" paradigm strongly emphasized the traditionalist and conserving side of evangelicalism—a "safe haven" from progressive agendas, but failed to take seriously the adaptive abilities of much of the evangelical world.[7] On the culture war rendering, the 1960s was a time of horror for evangelicals who thankfully woke the faithful up and launched America into a search for and a potential recovery of significant aspects of its Judeo-Christian heritage.[8] This supposed that evangelicalism was fundamentally a conserving force in American culture, analogous with religious and social conservatives in earlier periods of American history. It also supposed that evangelicalism was not significantly different from religious fundamentalism. Evangelicals, as a subset of

it played in countering secularization." "National Trauma and Changing religious values," *Daedalus* (1978): 22.

5 James Hunter offers the clearest and the most nuanced map to chart the culture wars of the last half of the twentieth century. See his *Culture Wars* (New York: Basic Books, 1992).

6 Borrowing a metaphor from Peter Berger wherein he speaks of the 60s as a psychological earthquake. "A Call for Christian Authority in the Christian Community," *Christian Century* 98 (27 October 1981).

7 It may be no accident that the traditional interpretation of the culture wars is given most definitive expression during the Bicentennial of America. It was that context which occasioned reflection upon the character of America's soul and thus the "revolutionary" character of the 60s was framed early on along these progressivist/traditionalist lines. Most interpretations of the 60s written in the 1970s were of this type. Representative of this view were Sydney Ahlstrom, "National Trauma" and William G. McCloughlin, *Reform, Revival and Awakenings* (Chicago: University of Chicago Press, 1978). Later studies which appeared to operate with a more nuance polarization thesis in view were Robert Wuthnow, *The Struggle for America's Soul: Evangelicals, Liberals and Secularism* (Grand Rapids: Eerdmans, 1989) and Langdon Gilkey, *Society and the Sacred* (New York: Crossroad, 1981).

8 It is now almost historical orthodoxy to consider the succeeding two decades (the 1970s and 1980s) as repudiations of the ideals of the 60s. This is to claim that there was a fundamental disjunction between the earlier and later periods. Without debunking that orthodoxy entirely, I will suggest that it represents a partial reading of the events at best.

fundamentalism were Biblical/traditional in their outlook and under the pressure of radicalizing events of the 1960s, they offered the large silent majority of Americans an alternative world view that harkened back to safer and more secure days. On this interpretation, evangelicals were centrally arrayed against the godless forces of secularism and communism.[9] Or to use the paradigms present elsewhere in this volume, evangelicals were centrally premodern in their world view and in many respects, thoroughly anti-modern in their distaste of contemporary culture. The religious underpinnings of the evangelical worldview could not tolerate the moral chaos that the institutions of democracy had foisted upon the modern world, nor could they tolerate the spiritual anarchy that seemed to be popping up all across the nation. And though evangelicals could not see the cultural revolutions coming, they would have been aghast at the prospects of the impending religious pluralism of the post 1960s era. Or so the story goes.

At the beginning of the 1960s the mainline churches provided the vital center of American religious life.[10] The period of the 1950s marked the greatest period of numerical growth for establishment churches in American history. But at the very point of their nadir, they suddenly underwent a reversal in membership size of cataclysmic proportions, which continues to this day. Church membership as a percentage of the total population peaked in the late 1950s and for the first time in more than a century, declined significantly throughout the 1960s.[11] Most striking was the decline in membership of the Protestant Establishment Churches associated with the National Council of Churches (NCC).[12] From 1960 to 1980, these churches combined lost nearly 15 per cent of total membership—over

---

[9] Daniel Bell foreshadowed this argument in the early 1960s in his work, Daniel Bell, ed., *The Radical Right* (New York: Doubleday, 1963) in which he connected political and religious conservatives. He (and his collaborators) argued that ideological forces arrayed against communism in the 1950s were motivated in part by an enduring religious conservativism that had the ironic force of political tyranny upon the American democracy.

[10] The language of the "center" is used cautiously here, especially against the backdrop of the right and left "extremes" of the culture war paradigm. The terminology supposes that the "middle" is an appropriate balance between two other positions and therefore ought to be favored. However, this can mask a hidden assumption that to be between two extremes is somehow rationally superior, simply in virtue of being in the middle. But why should one suppose there is a "geography of rationality or morality?" On this point see Michael Horton, "Who's Got the Center?" in *Books and Culture*, vol. 7, no. 2 (March/April 2001). It was this assumption that was so radically challenged in the 1960s and which led to another in the long line of disestablishment episodes in American history. The "center" was displaced in virtue of more persuasive arguments represented elsewhere on the religious and political spectrum.

[11] Figures taken from Robert Wuthnow, *The Restructuring of American Religion* (Princeton: Princeton University Press, 1988), p. 159.

[12] The list of these churches includes the American Baptist Church, the Christian Church, The Lutheran Church in America, The Protestant Episcopal Church, the United Church of Christ, the United Methodist Church and the United Presbyterian Church.

four million members.[13] The loss was even greater in the urban centers of the 1960s. Urban Protestant Establishment Churches lost nearly 50 per cent of their membership during the decade. Much of that population left for the suburbs but it ought to be remembered that it was not replaced by immigrants from abroad or those who left the rural South and moved into the cities in that decade. It was a slide entirely unexpected and unexplainable at the time. The mainline churches and the NCC had been far more supportive of the policies and politics of the establishment than churches associated with the National Association of Evangelicals (NAE). The mainline churches appeared to be in lock step with larger cultural trends and thus seemed assured of their place of increasing prominence and prestige. But as the 1960s wore on, the mainline churches were pulled at from too many directions and the religious center eventually frayed. The center attempted to be all things culturally, politically and religiously and ended up being vacuous to many. The way in which the old line churches came to terms with the cultural upheaval and the consequent crisis of authority of the 1960s led to a profound loss of Protestant identity and consequent evacuation of meaning, confusion of purpose, and frustration of mission in much of American religious life.[14]

Religious realignment did take place and undoubtedly occurred in polarizing fashion.[15] However, the character of the realignment suggests that it was not entirely driven by nor originated in two different religious ways of looking at the world. Evangelicals were far friendlier to the modern world than most historians recognized at the time, and which much of American populace seemed blissfully unaware. It is not a stretch to argue that evangelicals were as strongly a protest movement as any of the other radical movements of the decade. In what follows I will not argue that evangelicals provided a strong ideological protest to the establishment. But they did importantly serve to legitimate the protest against the establishment by bringing a radical democratization of piety and by religiously affirming the tools and economies of technology. Allied with these were the deep suspicions most evangelicals felt towards establishment liberalism of the 1950s, primarily the liberalism ensconced in the major theological schools of the period and in the major political institutions of the time.

One of the great ironies of the 1960s lay in the "radical" character of the conservative religious movements of the decade. Since 1972 and the publication of Dean Kelley's work, *Why Conservative Churches Are Growing*,[16] we have been

---

13 The total loss figure comes from Grant Wacker, "Searching for Norman Rockwell: Popular Evangelicalism in Contemporary America," in Leonard Sweet, ed., *The Evangelical Tradition in America* (Macon, GA: Mercer University Press, 1984).

14 On this point see, Leonard Sweet, "The 1960s: The Crises of Liberal Christianity and the Public Emergence of Evangelicalism," in George Marsden, ed., *Evangelicalism and Modern America* (Grand Rapids: Eerdmans, 1984), pp. 29–45.

15 On the realignment of religious conservatives and religious liberals see the masterful study by Robert Wuthnow, *The Restructuring of American Religion*.

16 (New York: Harper and Row, 1972).

aware of this unexpected conservative resurgence in a secular age though less clear as to the reasons for it. Kelley had supposed that conservative churches were growing precisely because they were an alternative to the confusion in the secular culture and its profound instability. People retreated into these isolated pockets as a measure of self-defense against an overly aggressive secularism. The Pentecostal and charismatic branches of evangelicalism were viewed as especially clear illustrations of the conservative thrust to seek a haven from the storm of modern (secular) consciousness.[17] Undoubtedly there is an element of truth in this, but not as the central explanation of the resurgence. The paradigm of polarization rather legitimated a wider sense of cultural unease felt across the religious spectrum at the end of the 1960s, though it submerged elements of the interpretive grid that might have more fully explained the unease.

In its earliest phase, the evangelical movement garnered strength in unexpected places—most notably among youth. And so to the question, "why did conservative churches grow in this period?" It is important to remember that the central growth of the conservative churches in this period was among the youth. It was growth along baby boomer lines. It was the baby boomers who were notoriously dissatisfied over the material blessings bestowed upon the nation as a result of the economic boom of the late 1940s and throughout the 1950s while being embedded themselves in that affluence. The music of the new generation became increasingly defined by a sense of protest and rebellion, both among the hippies as well as the Jesus people.[18] The music may well have ended up being captured by the very economic forces against which it was arrayed in the first place, but in the beginning of the decade, the music quite clearly was intended to separate the boomers from their parents. In this it is important to remember that the new Jesus music of the era sought to wage a protest against the religious status quo, mostly in terms of the concern to be radical followers of Jesus in a culture of material abundance.[19] This was not a conserving force in American culture, but rather a voice of radical protest.

Historical Prelude

The history of the evangelical movement finds its origins in the post-War period of the late 1940s and early 1950s. The reemergence of a public evangelicalism in this period caught many observers by surprise. It was not uncommon to have assumed that the defeat of fundamentalism in the modernist/fundamentalist wars

---

17 So Alhstrom argues in "National Trauma and Changing Religious Values."

18 On the notion of music as protest, see Bruce Pollock, *When the Music Mattered: Rock in the 1960's* (New York: Holt Rinhart and Winston, 1983).

19 This is especially true in the music of the most notable originator of Jesus rock, Larry Norman. For a brief historical account of Jesus rock and its commercial step-child, Contemporary Christian Music (CCM), see Paul Baker, *Contemporary Christian Music* (Westchester: Crossway Books, 1985).

of the 1920s would have meant the virtual end of the movement as a cohesive force in American public life.[20] Conservative religionists were considered cultural outsiders without access to the main organs of mass communication throughout the 1930s and 1940s.[21] But the cultural defeat in the 1920s in fact actually reenergized fundamentalism even as it split into two main factions somewhere during the period from 1930–50. There were those who saw separation (theologically and culturally) as the only viable strategy. This group more nearly kept the name of fundamentalism.[22] Marsden refers to the fundamentalists of this era as those who were "militantly anti-modernist evangelical Protestants."[23] There were others who insisted on engaging the culture in a more direct fashion and came to be referred as neo-evangelicals. The lines drawn were not largely theological lines but tactical lines. The fundamentalist/evangelical movement separated over how the encroaching secularity of modernity was to be most effectively challenged.

Typical of this divided strategy were two educational institutions representative of neo-evangelical integrationist and fundamentalist separationist strategies. In the late 1940s, Fuller Theological Seminary was founded under the leadership of Wilbur Smith and Carl Henry, leading intellectuals of a conservative religious

---

[20] George Marsden, *Fundamentalism and American Culture: The Shaping of Twentieth Century Evangelicalism, 1870–1925* (New York: Oxford University Press, 1980) remains the best treatment of fundamentalism/evangelicalism prior to its cultural defeat in the 1920s.

[21] Laurence Moore, *Selling God* (Oxford, 1994) tells the story of the virtual monopoly which liberal churches held over the public airwaves until the mid-1960s. The popularity of the evangelical televangelists of the 1970s (James Bakker, Jimmy Swaggert, Jerry Falwell, amongst others) was in fact so striking precisely because evangelicals were previously given such little airtime previously. The FCC essentially had handed the license to all religious broadcasting to the NCC in the 1950s so as virtually to exclude evangelical and fundamentalist voices from the airwaves.

[22] The origins of the fundamentalist movement lie in the revivalism of the nineteenth century, the millenarian movements of the end of the nineteenth century, and the holiness movements associated with the Keswick conferences also at the end of the nineteenth century. Ernest Sandeen, *The Roots of Fundamentalism: British and American Millenarianism 1800–1930* (Chicago: University of Chicago Press, 1970) is the standard treatment of the rise of fundamentalism. Joel Carpenter's study, *Revive Us Again: The Reawakening of American Fundamentalism* (Oxford: Oxford University Press, 1997) is the best historiographic study of fundamentalism through the twentieth century.

[23] "Fundamentalism" in Eerdmans' *Handbook of Christianity in American*, eds, George Marsden, Mark Noll, Nathan Hatch, David Wells, John Woodbridge (Grand Rapids, MI; Eerdmans, 1983) p. 384. Likewise Bruce Lawrence, *Defenders of God: The Fundamentalist Revolt Against the Modern Age* (San Francisco: Harper and Row, 1989) defines fundamentalism as "the affirmation of religious authority as holistic and absolute, admitting of neither criticism nor reduction; it is expressed through the collective demand that specific creedal and ethical dictates derived from scripture be publicly recognized and legally enforced."

bent.[24] Smith had long taught at Moody Bible Institute in Chicago, one of the bastions of the early fundamentalist and dispensationalist movement. Henry was a young theologian and journalist, who would later become a significant public voice of evangelicalism through his editorship of the monthly journal, *Christianity Today*. Smith and Henry put together a distinguished evangelical faculty with the express intention of creating an evangelical alternative to the mainline university divinity schools, and Princeton Seminary in particular. In contrast to an earlier attempt at replacing Princeton's theological voice which led to the birth of Westminster Theological Seminary, Fuller was non-denominational and not distinctively Presbyterian nor reformed in theological orientation. The vestiges of Old Princeton remained at Fuller largely through its vision to engage the liberal scholarship of the day in a responsible and thoroughly evangelical fashion.[25]

On the other side of the divide, the fundamentalist Bob Jones University resolutely set itself against engagement of secular scholarship. Started in 1927 shortly after the Scopes Trial, the university was founded by the well known evangelist, Bob Jones Sr. with the express intention of rescuing young people from the godless modernism of the era.[26] The university was born out of a specific kind of religious ideology that was anti-modern, which was nonetheless friendly to the tools of modernity. It rejected the philosophical rationalism and individualism that accompanied modernity and sought to remain separate institutionally from all those who had compromised with the values of modernism. Ironically, it also sought to take full advantage of certain technological advances that characterized the modern age and developed a full print and telecast industry of its own. It was the leader in establishing a conservative home-school movement that sought to replace public education with direct parental education. In all of this Bob Jones was remarkably successful while being remarkably separate from the rest of religious world.

The separatist strategy of fundamentalism survived in isolated pockets (by necessity and in principle) but gradually it became clear in the post-War period that the strategy of neo-Evangelicalism would become the dominant strand within conservative Protestant circles. And by the late 1960s and early 1970s it became evident that neo-Evangelicalism would also more centrally set the social and political agenda for the conservative Protestant movement as a whole, though notable

---

[24] George Marsden's fine work *Reforming Fundamentalism: Fuller Seminary and the New Evangelicalism* (Grand Rapids: Eerdmans, 1987) charts the early history of the institution specifically against the backdrop of the evangelicalism/fundamentalism typology.

[25] "Old Princeton" refers to that group of theologians associated with Princeton Seminary in the nineteenth century committed to an intellectual exposition and defense of conservative Presbyterianism, men like Charles Hodge, B.B. Warfield and A.A. Hodge. With respect to the chronology of this study, Old Princeton refers to Princeton Theological Seminary prior to its liberalizing phase of the first half of the twentieth century.

[26] A very fine recent treatment of the Scopes Trial and its enduring implications is Edward Larson, *Summer for the Gods: The Scopes Trial and America's Continuing Debate Over Science and Religion* (Cambridge, MA: Harvard University Press, 1997).

fundamentalist preachers would retain a public following of immense proportions and would remain enemy number one for the liberal religious establishment.[27]

In the eyes of both fundamentalists and evangelicals, modernism posed grave threats to religious belief and practice. They dealt with that threat in different ways and in sharp contrast to theological liberals, Protestant conservatives were entirely opposed to changing the confessional structures of historic Christendom to meet the mandates of modernism. Liberals adapted to modernity by a passive ecumenicity, treating the increasing cultural pluralism with kid gloves. They gave up all claims to the uniqueness of the Christian message and of any distinctive Biblical kerygma. They thereby hoped that all the diverse cultural forces might live together peacefully. This contrasted sharply with the impatient stance of evangelicals and the downright intolerant stance of fundamentalism. For them, Christianity made exclusive truth claims, which increasingly became the centerpiece of their message. What was not so readily recognized was the influence of modernity upon this strategy. Intolerant on one level, evangelicals were highly tolerant of modernity on another level.

The paradigmatic intransigence to the secularizing impulse of modernism expressed itself most clearly in the debates about morality: abortion, gender roles, sexual orientation, divorce, and so on. This public face of resistance gave sharpest focus to the nascent culture wars of the 1960s and 1970s.[28] Below the culture war radar however, was the enormous amount of accommodation taking place within the evangelical movement as the very means of rapprochement with the wider secular culture. Modernism may have been the ideological enemy but modernity construed as a set of social structures proved to be quite a friend for conservative Protestantism of many stripes. Evidence of this was translation of the specifically religious dimension of evangelicalism into rigorously standardized prescriptions (when previously these had been taken to be plain and self-evident). James Hunter referred to this as the growth of a "spiritual positivism."[29] The proliferation of "how-to" manuals and the "four easy steps to salvation" were signs of this accommodation to the technological rationality of the age. Recent commentators

---

[27] Jerry Falwell's rapprochement with mainstream evangelicals in his book, *The Fundamentalist Phenomena: The Resurgence of Conservative Christianity* (Garden City, NJ: Doubleday Press, 1981) was a strong indication of the cultural strength of the neo-Evangelical movement in comparison to the fundamentalist movement.

[28] Cf. James Hunter, *Culture Wars*. Michael Horton, *Beyond the Culture Wars* (Chicago: Moody Press, 1994) manifests the evangelical frustration with the culture war paradigm as the best explanation of religious disagreement in the decades after the 1960s.

[29] He goes on to note, "Likewise the reduction of the gospel to its distilled essence and the methodization of the conversion process make widespread distribution of the gospel possible, while maintaining a cognitive uniformity in substantive quality of the message and an experiential uniformity in functional quality of the process." James D. Hunter, *American Evangelicalism: Conservative Religion and the Quandary of Modernity* (New Brunswick: Rutgers University Press, 1983), pp. 83–4.

have argued that the innovative use of market techniques for evangelism was uniquely characteristic of the accommodating temper of evangelicalism.[30]

The defense of orthodox dogma separated from theological tradition and attached itself to an anti-modern stance appearing in the most modern of styles. The urge to resist all things modern and secular was realized by acquiescing at key points with the technological and consumerist impulses of that very secularized modernity. In the modern free market, truth does not always win out. The best set of packaged goods normally does. And ironically, it was the evangelicals' enigmatic mass marketing of exclusive truth which helped to make evangelicals as successful as they were.

Truth became allied with success as a criteria of the presence of the Holy Spirit. God could be found where there was truth (primarily in the Bible) and where evangelistic efforts were successful.[31] Increasingly, these two criteria moved further apart. The Bible appeared to remain the touchstone in matters of doctrine, but in matters of practice the presence of the Spirit was intuited, not correlated with the framework of the Scriptures. Evangelism oriented itself towards the production of results, and the biblical record became of secondary importance.[32] Many evangelicals during the first half of the twentieth century had hoped and worked for a restoration of religion to purer ways.[33] What was unforeseen was the implicit capitulation to many of the characteristically modern ways, against which evangelicals had reacted so strongly. The climactic beginning to this compromise manifested itself most clearly in the 1960s. Three particular themes appear in that decade which underscore the ironic relationship between the emergence of conservative religion as a part of a radical decade: the pervasive embrace of liberty, the democratizing of God's presence and the marriage of technology and piety. The strange result was the disestablishment of liberalism—the goal for which fundamentalism had yearned, but which when it occurred, was nothing like expected.

---

30 Representatively see David F. Wells, *No Place for Truth: Whatever Happened to Evangelical Theology* (Grand Rapids: Eerdmans, 1993), Os Guinness, *Dining with the Devil: The Megachurch Movement Flirts with Modernity* (Grand Rapids, Mich.: Baker Book House, 1993) and Mark Noll, *The Scandal of the Evangelical Mind* (Grand Rapids: Eerdmans, 1994).

31 An extended argument to this effect can be found in Richard Lints, *The Fabric of Theology* (Grand Rapids: Eerdmans, 1993).

32 This is helpfully pointed out in an unpublished essay by a former colleague of mine, T. David Gordon, "Old and New School Christianity."

33 Joel Carpenter shows that "restorationism" was not the sole and most likely not the dominant motive in the evangelical coalition at the turn of the century. See his "Contending for the Faith Once Delivered: Primitivist Impulses in American Fundamentalism" in Richard T. Hughes, ed. *The American Quest for the Primitive Church* (Urbana: University of Illinois Press, 1988), pp. 99–119. That being the case, it is still undeniable that many evangelicals were motivated, at least in part, by a concern to return to the purer, simpler ways of the past.

From Fate to Freedom

The divergent political/religious glosses of the 1960s were overlaid upon a complex foundation, which mitigated against appearances being identical with reality. Evangelicals carried their own radical subplots throughout much of the decade, which helped explain their resurgence during the radical 1960s.[34] The cultural revolutions of the sixties neither created a religious tension nor were centrally about the conflicting religious visions of America. Rather the decade of the sixties partially radicalized the religious polarities of the past two centuries while also submerging these polarities in strange and unexpected ways. The left hand side of the spiritual revolution pinned its hopes on human potential by way of participatory democracy while the right hand side committed itself to human potential by way of religious individualism. Both saw human freedom at the heart of the crisis and thereby were centrally concerned whether individuals were free to pursue ends they deemed important.[35]

Why did the language of "freedom" serve as the new found rhetorical paradigm, at this particular time, in a country that had recently fought world wars in defense of freedom? Why did rebellion in the name of "freedom" take root at this particular time? The answer is complicated and one ought not overlook patterns of these cultural protests in earlier episodes of American history.[36] Undoubtedly the answer lies in part with the power of the new found tools of technology that emerged

---

[34] Steven Tipton's significant work, *Getting Saved From the Sixties* (Berkeley: University of California Press, 1981) actually argued for a complex religious synthesis between the left and the right at the end of the decade. This is a controversial conjecture and it must be nuanced in important ways. So for example, Langdon Gilkey notices this synthesis as a distant possibility but believes the polarization thesis still adequately explains religious realities. See his *Society and the Sacred.* Even Harvey Cox supposes that evangelicalism cannot be understood as a simple retreat from the progressivist vision and revolution of the 60s though he still does suppose there are in reality two fundamental ways to respond to the death of neo-orthodoxy; either in a conservative/evangelical or a progressive/liberationist fashion. See his, *Religion in the Secular City: Towards a Postmodern Theology* (New York: Simon and Schuster, 1984).

[35] The conservative Roman Catholic, E. Michael Jones has long queried the relationship between liberty and license, arguing in effect that the former cannot be embraced without the embrace of the latter, precisely what conservative Protestant movements fear the most and to which they are most susceptible. See especially his *Degenerate Moderns* (San Francisco: Ignatius Press, 1993). Without the same theological axes to grind, David Wells argues much the same point relative the worldliness of contemporary evangelicalism in its embrace of the self-movement. See Wells, *Losing our Virtue: Why the Church Must Recover its Moral Vision* (Grand Rapids: Eerdmans, 1998).

[36] Nathan Hatch's masterful work, *The Democratization of American Christianity* (New Haven: Yale University Press, 1989) argued that this pattern of religious protest on American soil has been present at least since the time of the American Revolution.

in the post-War period.[37] Eisenhower's commitment to build a national highway system in the 1950s created a deeply felt consciousness of mobility and freedom. The medical advances, paradigmatically found in the arena of sexual reproductive technologies, created freedoms of sexual relations which had not been known previously. The vast new wealth created in the post-War boom, brought new possibilities for suddenly affluent teenagers of which their parents were hardly aware. The newly affluent suburbs of American cities brought both new found senses of security and a new found sense of sterility. For better and for worse, the cultivation of affluent privacy impacted the spirituality of suburban Christianity. And maybe most importantly in hindsight, the virtual explosion of television on the American scene during the 1950s brought an entirely new mindset of mass culture and thereby mass protest. It proved too good to be true, in an ironic way. Teenagers vicariously experienced a reality on television too good to be true, and yearned for a utopia of their own. Theirs was a utopia of peace and love and purpose. The tools of technology were powerless to craft such a utopia and to newly converted evangelical teenagers, it was the secular world of materialism and the liberal power establishment which seemed the greatest of all modern idols.

The cry for freedom could be heard everywhere.[38] Evangelicals participated in the radical rhetoric of freedom in the decade of the 1960s. The new evangelical hymnody celebrated a radical Jesus. Evangelical youth rallies manifested all the characteristic signs of radical protest against an entrenched status quo. Following Jesus was attractive in large measure because it was deemed radically different by evangelical youth.

The clearest expression of the evangelical protest for freedom lay in its recovery of its own revivalist heritage within a modern mass culture context. The language of evangelicalism in the late 1950s and throughout the 1960s was of "deciding for Jesus." This was not fundamentally new in evangelicalism, but the context of the social protests for freedom, placed the evangelistic question in different perspective. The mass rallies of Billy Graham throughout the 1950s and the 1960s served as a conduit through which a whole generation of evangelicals was raised to think about Christianity. In the hands of the Jesus people, this freedom to choose Jesus replaced the freedom to do your own thing. "Choosing Jesus" was most definitely a form of cultural protest.

---

[37] The same question emerged with the American Revolution of the 1770s as well. Why did the protest in favor of freedom take place at that time in that place? There were a confluence of factors which (oversimplifying) included; newly emerging capitalist markets, a bureaucratic nation state, the pluralistic metropolis from which the Americans had come in Europe, and the ideologies of the Renaissance and the Reformation in the relatively recent past. See Hatch, *Democratization of American Christianity*.

[38] The movement from fate to choice was not a minor subplot of the era, but a dominating strand of human experience during this decade. See Peter Berger, *The Heretical Imperative* (New York: Anchor Books, 1979).

If the rhetoric of freedom was a form of social protest, it also permitted the self movement to flourish throughout the 1960s in radical ways among evangelicals. At mid-century, the self under the pressures of consumerism had become a bundle of desires and needs gratified primarily in the free expression of the will. Self-determination became an end in its own right. In evangelical garb this manifested itself most clearly in the repudiation of traditional structures of the church: its hymnody, its liturgical prayers and its ordained hierarchy. Freedom was well suited to a religion that had historically been suspect about history and the shackles of tradition that history brought. In all of this the emphasis upon freedom within evangelical circles was not a move to a safe haven of the past, but rather an intentional departure from the status quo.

God's Presence Democratized

In the 1960s theologies and theologians no longer led culture but had become the spokespersons of wider cultural trends. The explosion of popular culture thoroughly invaded religious culture by mid-century. The leading religious spokesmen in mass culture were entertaining television personalities like Norman Vincent Peale and Bishop Fulton Sheen. Laurence Moore remarks of the religious renaissance of the 1950s:

> For many Americans the spiritual help available in churches or in movie houses or on television or in a best-selling book or at a businessmen's prayer breakfast tended to become equivalent. From one perspective (i.e. the establishment) it was becoming hard to view religion as something distinct from popular culture.[39]

The "cultural elites" who occupied chairs in the religion departments of major universities no longer exerted the pervasive influence of an earlier generation. Instead the shapers of culture (and importantly the religious elements of culture) were those able to rally large segments of the populace to an awareness of their own rights.[40] It was the fundamental challenge to the perceived oppression of the status quo which helped explain the resurgence of groups as diverse as students, women, people of color, religious dissidents, evangelicals and charismatics. All of them were outsiders to the corridors of power as the 1960s dawned. As Gerard Howard aptly remarks:

---

[39] *Selling God*, p. 241.

[40] I want to be careful not to claim that this phenomena has no historical precedent in North America. It surely does and therefore the claim here is that the cycle of populist religious leadership was likely repeating itself in the 1960s as it had in earlier periods of America's religious history.

> All of a sudden it was the lower orders who were creating the new styles and setting the fashion, society and art worlds on their heads—a new democracy of culture. The distinctions between high and low culture, the *haute monde* and the *hoi polloi*, became impossibly blurred.[41]

As was the case in the Second Great Awakening, the cultural outsiders in the 1960s took center stage, in part, because of the success of their democratic impulses in the face of institutionalization.[42] Near the heart of the evangelical and charismatic responses in the 1960s was a resolute unwillingness to cognitively negotiate the transcendence of God. On this score they appeared at odds with other radical movements of the decade. But in common with the other movements of protest, evangelicalism and the charismatic movement were deeply anti-institutional in character and driven by a concern to contextualize the gospel in light of the contemporary situation. In all the revolutionary movements of the 1960s, both evangelical and progressive, God was not known in the atemporal, timeless fashion of neo-orthodoxy, nor in the creeds and confessions of historic Protestantism, nor in the decrees of the Roman Catholic magisterium. Rather God was known at the center of an individual's unique and unrepeatable experience. God was found not "out there" but "in here." In the devotional piety of the newly resurgent evangelicals, this was very much true.[43] The rallying cry of evangelical crusades was a "personal relationship with Jesus." It was true of the charismatic movement as they interpreted their own religious experience as a map for larger religious directions.

In different ways both the Jesus movement and later the charismatic movements were variants of that subjectivist search for meaning and significance.[44] Both movements were profoundly consumed with "religious feelings" and exhibited a strong desire to romp spiritually through new fields of consciousness and new dimensions of experience. From one vantage point conservatives were answering

---

[41] *The Sixties* (New York: Washington Square Press, 1982), p. 15.

[42] Though Nathan Hatch, *The Democratization of American Christianity*, does not draw the parallel directly between the Second and Fourth Great Awakening, his framework for understanding the Second Great Awakening seems well suited for the Fourth Great Awakening as well. William G. McLoughlin, *Revivals, Awakenings and Reform*, does draw the explicit parallel between the second Great Awakening and the 1960s on the democratizing impulse—but does not pay any attention to evangelicals in the 1960s.

[43] See David Wells, *God in the Wasteland* (Grand Rapids: Eerdmans, 1994) for an astute treatment of the cognitive bargaining inherent in evangelicalism's alliance with modernity, especially as it relates to their understanding of the transcendence of God.

[44] It would be unfair to suppose that the Jesus movement was stereotypical of the evangelical movement. Even in their heyday, the Jesus movement was but a fringe movement within the larger umbrella of evangelicalism. However, it is not unfair to say that the Jesus movement presaged many trends that would become central with the baby boomer spirituality of evangelicalism in the 1970s.

the question: Why should I become/stay a Christian? By offering inducements that were experiential and pragmatic. In this regard the movements appealed to the aesthetic of the experience.[45]

To borrow Steven Tipton's term, evangelicalism evidenced being an "alternative religion" in the 1960s. It neither repeated the traditions from which it arose nor completely abandoned them. By that tenuous compromise it negotiated its separation from the mainstream religious culture. The traditions were reinterpreted to allow adherents to make sense of their lives in the America of the 1960s and granted them an answer as to why they were cultural outsiders. Though God's presence and existence may have been questionable in the academy of this period, it was the radical democratization of God's presence which captivated the vision of evangelicalism during this period and which promised solace in the midst of cultural alienation. God's presence was manifest most clearly in the very fabric of personal experience—in particular the experience of those who stood outside the corridors of cultural power, and this very much included evangelicals during this period. The democratization of God's presence was neither voted upon nor legislated, though the evangelical music of the era amply recorded it. Neither the academy nor the mainline churches were genuine alternatives for the counterculture in the 1960s. The funeral procession gathering in culture was not for God. In the oft repeated phrase of Robert Fitch, "the real candidate for interment was a lesser chap by the name of Liberal Protestantism."[46] The religious mainstream of Liberal Protestantism had held onto a God who was too far away, and who seemed too remote from daily life. The genius of the evangelical and charismatic revivals of this period lay in their ability to grant immediate access to the corridors of power, not simply the corridors of temporal political power, but the power of God, bypassing the cultural powers in the process.

The evangelical and charismatic movements were alternatives to the status quo. In reality the battle over the death of God was not a cognitive battle but a battle about institutional authority and on this reading evangelicalism was as firmly countercultural as were the liberation movements related to race, gender and ethnicity of the period. The theology of Barth and Niebuhr in the 1950s emphasized the depravity, corruption and imperfection intrinsic to human nature,

---

45 Leonard Sweet writes"

> Expressions of the self as a new source of authority could be seen in the simpering self-exhibition of Christian authors and celebrities, the various movements for "self-help," "self-discovery," "self-realization," the "show and tell" style of evangelism, and the "Let it all hang out" countercultural styles where people were encouraged to "do your own thing." People began to journey with anyone who promised them either some new insight about the self or some escape from the burden of building a self, and Americans pursued a variety of religious options from A(rica) to Z(en). "The 1960s: The Crises of Liberal Christianity and the Public Emergence of Evangelicalism:" 38.

46 Robert E. Fitch, "The Protestant Sickness," *Religion in Life* 35 (Autumn 1966): 503.

which became manifest in the will to power and the place of pride in human actions. Allied with this was a fear of politics and mass action and emphasis on law and social restraint as a means of holding down the fanaticism latent in political passions. Astonishingly these concerns and cautions vanished in the religious revivals of the 1960s. New optimism about human nature and human powers appeared. What emerged was a theology that was far more optimistic about human nature and yet driven by a deep sense of the corruption of American culture. This was as true of the Jesus people as it was of black theologians.[47]

There were deep flaws manifesting themselves in the American experiment, at least to those who had not been the full recipients of the benefits of economic and corresponding political expansion in the post-War period. The reach of the federal government increased rapidly in the post-War economic boom, and many conservative churchmen were suspicious of the increasing powers of Washington. It was evangelicals who captured the religious momentum in the 1950s by wholly bypassing the traditional corridors of power, taking the message directly to the people. It was not uncommon that these attempts were treated with some disdain by the powers that be. Reinhold Niebuhr was deeply critical of Billy Graham and the simple minded optimism of his religious crusades. Graham may have been less a problem in Niebuhr's eyes than Norman Vincent Peale and his "gospel of success," but Niebuhr was wary of any attempt to hitch the gospel to popular and populist culture, bypassing the critical faculties of the university and the other organs of intellectual reflection.[48] The horrors of World War II and the sober realities of the Cold War chastened many intellectuals, but they failed to realize the enormous explosion and power of popular culture that the post-War era brought. It

---

[47] Writing at the end of the decade, Peter Berger commented:

> the celebration of secularity that came to the fore in the theology of more recent years, of which John Robinson's *Honest to God* and Harvey Cox's *The Secular City* were popular high points, naturally turned to more cheerful anthropological perspectives. The moral mood came closer to an endorsement of "enjoy enjoy!" than to the earlier recommendations to be as anxious as possible. The social world was once more seen as an arena of purposeful action for human betterment rather than as a quagmire of futilities. *A Rumor of Angels: Modern Society and the Rediscovery of the Supernatural* (New York: Doubleday, 1970), p. 64.

[48] It would be unfair to paint the entirety of evangelicalism as being opposed to scholarly reflection. Carl Henry's call to repudiate the divorce the head and the heart in matters pertaining to religious faith in his *The Uneasy Conscience of Modern Fundamentalism* (Grand Rapids, MI: Eerdmans 1947) typified a small but significant voice within evangelical circles that urged a greater engagement with scholarship. One of the earliest respectable treatments of the counterculture of the 1960s was actually by a professing evangelical scholar, Os Guinness, *The Dust of Death* (Downers Grove, IL: InterVarsity, 1971). This presaged the so-called renaissance of evangelical scholarship that would emerge in the 1980s and the 1990s in the fields of history, philosophy and sociology. On this renaissance see George Marsden, *The Outrageous Idea of Christian Scholarship* (New York: Oxford University Press, 1999), Chapter 6.

was left to evangelicals like Billy Graham and Charles Fuller to capture orthodox religious believers in the maelstrom of religious revivals, as a means of protest against the Pharisee like quality of American elite religious culture. This theme had worked well in earlier periods of American history for evangelicals and it worked surprisingly well as the decade of the 1960s began.[49]

Televangelism and The Information Revolution

It was a much lamented fact among conservative Christians at mid-century that American universities had become bastions of secularism and religious liberalism. With few exceptions, they believed the academy had become a foe of Christian belief. As a result, serious theological reflection, at least of the sort practiced in the academy, became distasteful to many evangelicals for it represented an unhealthy imbibing of the style and agenda of the academy. The strategy of evangelicals was to bypass the university and take the battle directly to the people.[50] Billy Graham's voice in this was key. In the 1950s Graham came to represent the hopes of evangelicals in the key task of evangelizing American culture.[51] Graham had many rivals among the traveling evangelists, but his real peers were media figures who did not fit easily into traditional categories of itinerant evangelist or media star. The sheer size of Graham's audience also dwarfed earlier revivalists. He reached millions of people weekly through a 900 station radio network along with several yearly special national television broadcasts. Graham's *Decision* magazine had a circulation of over four million and a syndicated column appeared in more

---

[49] Hofstater, Richard, *Anti-Intellectualism in American Life* (New York: Alfred Knopf, 1962) was the most significant warning by the elite culture of the invading hordes of evangelicals as the decade began. He effectively argued that evangelical religion required an anti-intellectual stance throughout its history on American soil. His claims did not take seriously the long tradition of conservative religious scholarship of either the eighteenth or the nineteenth century, but it did capture popular sentiment among intellectuals in the 1960s that fundamentalism and its related cousin, evangelicalism, were founded on a blind faith that did not take seriously critical questions of modern scholarship. Thirty years later, Mark Noll, *The Scandal of the Evangelical Mind*, makes essentially the same argument about the populist evangelical sub-culture of the twentieth century, but with the important caveat that evangelical faith, in principle, ought to honor the life of the mind.

[50] During the last twenty five years of the nineteenth century, a corresponding strategy of evangelicals was to create institutions of higher learning of their own. Though giving the appearance of being committed to honest intellectual inquiry, it only further removed the movement from sensitive public debate on the issues. What occurred was the retreat of the movement into safe bastions of orthodoxy and the result was a relatively sterile and repetitious presentation of orthodox theology.

[51] John Pollock, *To All The Nations: The Billy Graham Story* (San Francisco: Harper & Row, 1985) and William Martin, *A Prophet with Honor: The Billy Graham Story* (New York: W. Morrow, 1991) remain the best sympathetic biographies of Graham.

than 200 newspapers.[52] Graham's message was in many ways resonant of earlier evangelical revivalists. But none of the earlier revivalists of the twentieth century had crafted such a prominent public persona as Graham, owing to his masterful use of modern media.[53] As in earlier periods, so now the revivalist required adaptation to new media in the form of easily remembered slogans and well packaged presentations of the gospel.[54] There was serious work being done by evangelical scholars in this period but the hopes of the movement were not attached to the conservative scholarship of the period. Rather it was the mass religious culture, which captivated the newly emerging evangelical movement.

Television was the prime organ for the distribution of knowledge in the new mass culture. Television shouted forth in fragmented ways, the pictures which educated an entire generation of evangelicals. While it motivated them to be more involved with the world, it also created a high degree of worldliness in them. By the early 1960s television had been successfully adapted for evangelistic use and the period witnessed phenomenal growth in televangelism, remarkably analogous in form to the mass protests of the left, if markedly different in content.

The emerging evangelical movement was not particularly involved in the social protests against the war nor particularly happy with Kennedy or Nixon. Most sat on the sidelines (embarrassingly) during the civil rights conflict. The radical character of evangelicalism was expressed vicariously by contrast to these direct action movements. By personally responding to evangelistic appeals evangelicals saw themselves rebelling against the secular as well as the religious establishment.

When intellectual battles were engaged by evangelicals, it was ordinarily accomplished by establishing new institutions of theological education—evangelical seminaries sprouted up during this period in increasing numbers. The three seminaries most often associated with the neo-evangelical movement all

---

52 These figures come from in Eerdmans' *Handbook of Christianity in American*, eds, George Marsden, Mark Noll, Nathan Hatch, David Wells, John Woodbridge (Grand Rapids, MI: Eerdmans, 1983), p. 436.

53 The exception here may well be George Whitefield, the prominent itinerant evangelist of the First Great Awakening (1740–45). Whitefield preached in open fields outside of church sanctuaries and spoke in rough populist vernacular. He was also a person known well by many of the prominent founding fathers of the American republic. On this point, see the compelling biography by Arnold Dallimore, *George Whitefield* (Westchester, IL.: Crossway Publishers, 1980). On Whitefield as the prototypical American revivalist see the fine work by Harry Stout, *George Whitefield: The Divine Dramatist* (Grand Rapids: Eerdmans, 1990).

54 *The Fundamentals: A Testimony to Truth* (Chicago, 1910–1915) was an earlier illustration of this. These were originally published in 12 volumes. These volumes were not widely used in the academy though they were widely distributed among the fundamentalist constituency. They were significant in setting the symbolic boundaries of the fundamentalist movement and manifest an early skill of the use of mass communication and mass marketing to bypass the corridors of authority of the cultural elites.

sprang up near mid-century. Fuller Theological Seminary was founded in 1947. Trinity Evangelical Divinity School was founded in 1963 and Gordon-Conwell Theological Seminary was established in 1968.[55]

The energy of the movement lay outside of the academy. The leadership of the movement lay with those skilled in mass evangelism, either directly as in the crusades of Graham, or on radio and television. There were a variety of attempts to keep the evangelical message off the airwaves most notably in the alliance between the Federal Communications Council (FCC) and the National Council of Churches (NCC) which lasted until overturned by federal regulation in 1960. The earlier arrangements had mandated that the national television networks give away their public-service airtime to religious broadcasters approved by the NCC.[56] As a result of being officially excluded from the national airwaves, evangelicals learned the lesson well of "buying" airtime and freeing themselves from the shackles of federal regulations. They also understood well what would sell on television and went about producing it in great quantity. The first national religious television hit was Charles E. Fuller's *The Old Fashioned Revival Hour* in the late 1930s. It was produced for NBC, the last of the national networks to be founded. It was also the network which did not form an alliance with the NCC until the 1940s. Evangelicals learned to deal with many of the independent local television stations in scooping up airtime when it could not otherwise be sold to national sponsors. The first explicit religious television network was founded by the evangelical, Pat Robertson in 1960.[57]

Most of their prominence on national television (until their fall from grace in the televangelists scandals of the late 1980s[58]) came by producing successful religious shows as adaptations of evangelical worship services. It was not unusual to add several entertaining segments such as interviews with famous people or an elaborate musical production. They realized that if religion could be clearly communicated and entertaining at the same time, people would invariably respond.

The normal evangelistic television service would begin with several songs pitched at the right emotional level to create a solemn but expectant atmosphere. The music made people feel comfortable and the heart vulnerable. From the 1960s onward, the music tended toward "praise music" which echoed the genre of music

---

55 Gordon-Conwell came into existence with the merger of Gordon Divinity School in Wenham, MA and Conwell School of Theology in Philadelphia. Gordon was under the influence of Harold John Ockenga, long time pastor of Park St. Church in Boston and founding President of Fuller Theological Seminary in California while Conwell (formerly the Temple University School of Religion) was under the influence of Billy Graham.

56 For a helpful recounting of this alliance as well as a summary of the intersection of television and religion, see Moore, *Selling God*.

57 It was called at the time, Christian Broadcast Network, CBN.

58 The best sympathetic treatment of this episode can be found in David Harrell, *Pat Robertson: A Personal, Religious and Political Portrait* (San Francisco: Harper and Row, 1987).

available (with different lyrics) from mainstream popular sources. Very personal and individual prayers came next. Prayers were never offered in the third person for this was too abstract for simple lay folk in the television audience. The climax of the service was the preaching of an evangelistic sermon built around several key stories or illustrations and demanding some immediate response on the part of the audience. The effectiveness of the sermon was judged by the number of people who sent in money or how many listeners tuned in each week.[59] There was rarely emphasis on the Lord's Supper or on corporate prayers. The television preacher was a story-teller who directed the service at each individual and not at the gathered community (even if there was one in the television studio). God's people become spectators, whose "faithfulness" could be measured by their viewing habits or their monetary gifts to the shows.[60]

Almost every revivalist of this period, and Graham preeminent among them, argued that theirs was the simple message of the Bible. In this, the authoritative caste of the revivalist project hearkened back to a day when authorities were respected. From this angle the message often appeared on the "conservative" side of the religious spectrum. But the use of the Bible on television or in the crusades was centrally an organ to simplify a complicated modern life, to give purpose beyond the material well being of an affluent culture, or to protest the cultural powers in the ordinary language of the listener.

Evangelicals also were well ahead of the cultural curve on religious publishing. They had fought battles over the reliability of the Bible back in the fundamentalist/modernist wars of the 1920s and saw themselves as protecting the integrity of the original message of the Bible, albeit one now translated into innumerable evangelical translations. What seemed so surprising about the abundance of new evangelical translations, was the earlier insistence that the sacredness of the Scriptures mandated no external messages be superimposed upon the Scriptures. Higher critical scholarship of the early twentieth century had sorted through which passages were reliable in the Bible and their translations followed suit. This seemed anathema to many evangelicals. As one historian wryly notes:

---

59 The parallels with frontier revivalism of the 1820s and 1830s are striking, the central difference being that the medium has changed the nature of the response. Typically the audience of televangelism was asked to "call in" or to "send money" rather than to "step forward and come to the anxious bench." Oral Roberts, the Pentecostal televangelist, actually created "blessing pacts" by which if a member of his television audience mailed him a hundred dollars, he would promise to refund if they did not within the year receive the gift back from an unexpected source.

60 See *The Electronic Golden Calf: Images, Religion, and the Making of Meaning*, Gregor T. (Cambridge, Mass.: Cowley Publications, 1990) and especially Quentin J. Schultze, *Televangelism and American Culture: The Business of Popular Religion* (Grand Rapids, MI.: Baker Book House, 1991).

> After virulently criticizing liberals over the years for their bible translations, especially the RSV, evangelicals did an about-face in the late 1960s and became very busy turning out biblical paraphrases and amplified versions, each one a rewriting of Scripture (the one basis on which evangelicals had stood up to modernity) in the writers' own image.[61]

At stake implicitly was the control of knowledge in the age of the information revolution. The newly ubiquitous presence of the media assured that the sense of cultural crisis would be larger than life, that "crisis" itself would become a defining aspect of 1960s existence.[62] It carried over into the "battle for the Bible" fought now by evangelicals through the translating of the Bible as they saw fit. A strange irony indeed.

Legacy—Dislodging the Powers that Be

The revolutionary character of rebellion was as much a part of the fabric of the so-called conservative wing in the 1960s as it was of the progressive wing. Evangelicals emerged as culturally significant in part because they tapped into the "radical" rhetoric of the era. Part of the self-consciousness of the expanding evangelical constituency was the conviction that their faith was every bit as "radical" as anything the death of God theologians were championing. Oddly enough, to establishment liberalism, the hippies and the Jesus People looked strangely alike in their revolutionary animus. The radical character of the movement was manifest in the new Jesus music, the parachurch thrust of the movement, the emergence of the "miraculous" in daily religious life and the decentering of theological commitments from the identity of the movement.[63] All of these were reactions against tradition and against the status quo. Evangelicalism was not simply a safe haven from the ever threatening secularization of the larger culture. It was a radical response to the idols of the age.[64]

---

[61] Leonard Sweet, "The 1960s: The Crises of Liberal Christianity and the Public Emergence of Evangelicalism:" 45.

[62] It is not unimportant to know that there were 10,000 TV sets in American households in 1947 and over 40 million ten years later. By 1965, 94 per cent of all American homes had a television. This is reported in William L. O'Neill *Coming Apart: An Informal History of America in the 1960's* (Chicago: Quandrangle Books, 1971) and William E. Leuchtenburg, *A Troubled Feast: American Society Since 1945* (Boston: Little Brown and Co., 1973).

[63] I have traced this in my book, *The Fabric of Theology* (Eerdmans, 1993), Chs 1–3. David F. Wells has provided an analysis of the decentering of theology within the evangelical community in his work, *No Place For Truth* (Eerdmans, 1993).

[64] Some representative evangelical titles in the period bear this out: *Go!: Revolutionary New Testament Christianity*, Charles W. Kingsley and George Delamarter. (Zondervan, 1965), *A Revolutionary Gospel*, Vernon C. Grounds (Conservative Baptist Press, 1969),

The counterculture had both a left and right wing to it and both clearly saw the enemy not in ideological terms but in cultural and often religious terms. The conservative wing of the counterculture was as deeply populist, as profoundly committed to participatory democracy and as extreme in its commitment to diversity as SDS or SNCC or any other of the organs of the New Left. Both shared an antipathy to big business, government by the elite, and the Protestant Establishment. Both spoke through the modern medium of rock music and both thought of themselves as a distinct "generation."

To the counterculture on the left and the right felt it felt like post-War America was no longer home. Traditional American ways neither communicated security nor significance to a generation born in the aftermath of World War II. The Vietnam vet returned home only to find he was little appreciated for his heroism. The yippies, the hippies, the Jesus people, and the Black Muslims all felt like strangers in a strange land. The common thread in all of these narratives was a sense of cosmic alienation from their America, that land which had by virtue of its existence granted purpose to its citizens.[65] The place seemed now a foreign and even evil land to these outcasts. The wrinkle in the story was that these foreigners were waging a war as if this land was rightfully their home.

Evangelicalism grew because it effectively captured the radical impulses of the day as a mechanism of revolt against the religious establishment and a recovery of their spiritual home.[66] In their hands, religion was a radicalizing force, preparing for a revolutionary era when a democratized religious spirituality would surprisingly come front and central on the national consciousness.

Christ the Controversialist, John Stott, ed. (InterVarsity Press, 1970), William Cannon, *The Jesus Revolution*: A *New Inspiration for Evangelicals* (Nashville: Broadman Press 1971), *Jesus the Revolutionary*, H. S. Vigeveno (Regal Books, 1966), *The Christian Revolutionary*, Dale W. Brown (Grand Rapids: Eerdmans, 1971), *The Revolutionary Masses & Christ's Will*, Donald McGavran (William Carey Library, 1969).

65 I have borrowed the term "cosmic alienation" from William Becker but put it to slightly different use. See his, "The 1960s and Today's Vision of America," *The Christian Century*, 29 May 1985.

66 One further though ironic confirmation of this disestablishment dynamic at work was lay in the experience of many Roman Catholic children in this period. They rejoiced and quickly adapted to the demise of the Latin mass and the emergence of the folk mass. Enthusiasm also accompanied the permission to eat meat on Fridays. At the outset of the decade, these children experienced life in America as outsiders. By the end of the decade, they had found a new home—by way of a new president, new music, and a new openness to things American.

PART V
Conclusion

Chapter 10

The Migration of Conviction: From Protest to Retrieval and Back Again

> With the intellectual idealism of folk music attached to the nature and abandon of rock 'n' roll, there was nothing a generation burned by Kennedy's assassination couldn't envision. Even without him we would save the world, unite the races. ... White kids would play the blues. Black kids would play quarterback.
>
> Bruce Pollock[1]

The cultural and conceptual upheavals of the 1960s were undoubtedly forms of protest against a perception about the "way things are." Dissent against the status quo was lodged from many diverse angles and extended into domains previously considered untouchable. Above all the 1960s held out hope that life could change and structural problems could be solved. Hope seemed limitless though it appeared dangerous as well. Standing against the powers that be is rarely comfortable. However dissent was a thoroughly traditional activity rooted and grounded in American ideology. This was the irony to the diverse movements of the 1960s.

In retrospect the protests may seem to have been too simple at times because it betrays the fact that realities are never finally simple. Quite simply, the decade was quite complex. Americans tended to believe the future was bright and the possibilities for change real. In the decades since, we have lived through the consequences of believing in those possibilities for change. Ours may be an age that feels uneasy about the future, but it knows that things are not the way they used to be. Times have changed.

The 1960s contained the watershed events that marked the passing of an era. The 1960s also provided conceptual signals of the changes that were coming. Those conceptual signals, often overlooked, have served as the primary lens through which the decade has been viewed in the preceding chapters. The conceptual signals were interwoven with concrete historical episodes and movements whose significance were bound up with the signals themselves. The story of the 1960s manifested a fusion of belief and behavior, of the ideological and the social, of the public and the personal, in such a fashion that an explosion was bound to occur. In the aftermath of that explosion it is important to wrestle with its character and its causes.

---

1 *When the Music Mattered: Rock in the 1960's* (New York: Holt Rinehart and Winston, 1983), p. 18.

The democratizing forces unleashed in the first half of the twentieth century finally wrecked conceptual havoc in the decade of the 1960s. Nowhere is this more clearly seen than in the revolutions of race and gender. African-Americans and women had been culturally excluded from the blessings of the American dream even if they had also played significant roles in the defense of that dream in the World Wars. The irony was not lost on the Civil Rights Movement nor on the early feminists. In retrospect, the contours of those protests may seem clear even if the legacy of feminism is more deeply fractured than that of the Civil Rights Movement. Neither Movement accepted the social identities of the status quo. It was left to feminism to provide conceptual arguments that deconstructed stereotyped social identities (of gender). Social identity was not fixed and permanent and the early feminists clearly believed social identity could not be easily equated with physiological realities. The radical calls for greater democratization which both Movements trumpeted may seem now almost inevitable outgrowths of social conditions at mid-century. The conceptual framework in which that democratization would be extended was anything but inevitable at mid-century.

One of the significant ironies of the decade was the radical rhetoric of evangelicals against the establishment in the 1960s. Far too frequently, religious belief has been viewed as a conserving social force and the mythology of secular progress so widely heralded in the 1960s appeared to exclude conservative religious movements from revolutionary roles. Here was the catch. Evangelicals felt excluded at mid-century and saw the liberalizing trends within the church and the secularizing trends in the culture, as providing impetus for the radical religious revolution. Evangelicals grew significantly in the 1960s because they effectively captured the radical impulses of the day as the means to revolt against the liberal religious establishment. In their hands, religion was a radicalizing force, preparing for a spiritually democratized age. Religion would not be controlled by the liberal elites. The status quo of a comfortable civil religion would be replaced by religious movements focused on decentralized authority. Ironically the radical rhetoric of evangelicals was accompanied by the retrieving of lost traditions, especially those traditions supposing that a religious elite was always to be distrusted. Whether the elite were "liberal" or "conservative" made little difference to the dynamic of disestablishment. What mattered was that those in control were seen as inevitably corrupting the "true essence" of religion by virtue of their control.

The culture of consumption so widely felt in the 1950s radically imploded in the decade that followed. The economic boom of the post-War period held out the promise that poverty would be defeated soon. It became apparent that those most left behind in the economic boom, African-Americans, were deeply suspicious of such national prosperity. The American dream proved to be a nightmare for many embedded in the social systems of inequalities. Wealth may have been more widely distributed but there still remained large pockets of Americans who remained well below the poverty line. The problem was not a more efficient economy, but a different social fabric in which the economy played a much smaller role. Racial justice was not simply one subset of the system of economic justice but had different criteria in view, more deeply ethical and religious. In America, race proved to be a far more powerful social glue than class. Not incidentally the Civil Rights Movement possessed a radical religious ethic not satisfied with an American dream which excluded African-Americans.

The end of ideology debates illuminated a central conundrum of the 1960s. If the culture of consumption was a leveling force on entrenched cultural conflicts, why were there so many eruptions in the culture in the decade? Did not the end of ideology promise a mass culture in which conformity rather than conflict would be dominant? The prophets of the New Left understood better than most that the end of ideology theorists were themselves deeply embedded in an ideology. It was an ideology that came to be identified as the status quo. This permitted it to be attacked from the left as well as the right. There was no neutral vantage point from which social conflicts could be resolved. There was no middle objective perspective which representatively embraced all other perspectives. All participants in the narratives of a culture were ideologically invested. Theory is always value laden, even that theory which supposed that there was to be an end to theory.

God's death was proclaimed on the front cover of national magazines in the 1960s only for many to be surprised that God made a remarkable comeback a few years later. The irrelevance of God to a materially saturated and affluent culture made much sense to the prophets of secularity in the decade. Most Americans still believed in God, but few lived as if that belief made any difference. The secularization thesis in its many varieties early in the 1960s simply recognized this incontrovertible truth. America may have thought itself a Christian nation, but it behaved as if the Christian faith mattered little. The necrotheologians were merely trying to proclaim as true what seemed obvious to so many. God was no longer needed. The radical response to this came strangely enough not from the Death of God theologians, but the long haired bell-bottom-wearing Jesus people.

However irreligious America may have seemed in its economic and social behaviors, it remained a deeply spiritual nation. It needed conceptual resources outside of the secular status quo not only to maintain human dignity, but also to protest the abuses of the very secular mode of life in which it was embedded. The early MacIntyre was a powerful reminder of this. Without a sense of the sacred, there were no moral restraints on a secular state. Without God, there was the ever present danger of emerging dictators. God, in the 1960s may have little resembled the God of the seventeenth-century American Puritans but MacIntyre seemed to understand the danger when secularity itself posed as the new sacred being. Religious authority was increasingly diffused into many diverse individuals who claimed a religious voice outside the controls of the establishment. The necrotheologians may have correctly supposed that the God "out there" had little influence in the lives of Americans. However, they were wrong to suppose that the God "in here" was not a potent social force with which a secular people must reckon.

The world was growing smaller and larger in the 1960s. The end of the colonial empires was still mostly a decade away, but the colonizing impulse had given way to the melting pot mythology at mid-century. Western Europe was quickly losing its cultural hegemony. It was being replaced with a respect for the diversity of cultures and the diversity of perspectives. The story of civilization could no longer be told as belonging monolithically to Europe any longer. The story from those on the margins mattered as much (or more) as those in the corridors of power. The democratizing character of the mass media assured this as did the demise of the older Enlightenment privileging of objective scholarship.

The death of foundationalism represented a much wider demise of socially constructed hierarchies upon which cultural hegemony was based. Knowledge was not built like a pyramid with solid and unalterable foundations. And the arbiters of truth and meaning no longer were the academic policeman of the philosophical guild. The growth of intellectuals as a distinctive class isolated inside the walls of the academy was part of a much more general evolution and devolution in the West. Their distinctive identity was fueled by the decline of the sense of community, the tendency of the mass society to break down into its component parts, each having its own autonomous culture and maintaining only the most tenuous connections with other people in the culture. Intellectuals had formerly represented the class most likely to revolt against the powers that be. By the 1960s they revolted against their own hegemony of ideas. They carved the intellectual space that permitted their own obsolescence. They also crafted a new conceptual project in which the ordinary discourse of culture held greater weight. This permitted those on the margins (blacks, women, students, evangelicals and others) to gain a voice that had hitherto been denied them.

The fragmenting of cultural authorities led to a greater interest in as well as a greater appreciation of diverse cultures. The seeds of globalization in the 1960s were the conceptual interest of people outside of fixed social stereotypes. The malleability of those social identities were beginning to dawn on many, though it did not yet include much interest in those in the two thirds world. Americans were still enamored with Americans, though they began to see (and respect) a greater diversity in their own nation. The demise of a universal perspective allowed them to take other perspectives more seriously, if not more charitably.

In Conclusion: Hope in the Midst of Irony, Irony in the Midst of Hope[2]

The 1960s was neither an unmixed blessing nor an unmitigated disaster. The possibility for substantive and lasting change seemed almost palpable to a generation come of age in the 1960s. The status quo was profoundly shaken and the future seemed both disquieting and important. When the bubble of optimism

[2] I am indebted in loose ways to Nathan Hatch, *The Democratization of American Christianity* (New Haven: Yale University Press, 1989), Nicholas Wolterstorff, "An Engagement with Rorty" *Journal of Religious Ethics* 31/1 (2003): 129–39, and Albert Borgmann, *Crossing the Postmodern Divide* (Chicago: University of Chicago Press, 1992) for the framework of this final section.

burst as the decade came to a close, the status quo was no longer and ambiguity was regnant.

The great ironies of the 1960s lay in their repudiation of long cherished traditions and the recovery in changed form of those very same traditions. The democratic impulses which ignited the protest movements of the period echoed the impulses which had given shape and substance to the American experiment from the beginning. Those very same democratic impulses had also legitimated social structures by which some individual voices were more powerful than others. The free exercise of individuals inevitably resulted in inequities themselves only remedied by a renewed exercise of individual freedoms. The reluctant radicals of our story, Alisdair MacIntyre and evangelicals were pungent and diverse reminders of this.

The mythology of the melting pot in American history both exploded and imploded in the 1960s giving rise to central ambiguities in the decades ahead. Diverse people groups on the margins in American history gained a hearing in the revolutionary decade, but did so in large measure by asserting a distinctive identity that would not be assimilated into the melting pot. The hope of revolution in the 1960s gave way to despair as distinctive social identities refused to participate in the amalgamation process. The Black Power Movement was a natural outgrowth of the Civil Rights Movement, and one which intentionally excluded the affluent and middle-class white students who had risked so much to revolt against the structures of segregation. Second phase feminism fragmented over the very identity of feminism and intuitions about the nature of gender and sexuality. The intention to protest on behalf of women eventually sounded hierarchical by virtue of the claim to speak on behalf of all women.

Old verities gave way to new ambiguities even if the revolutionaries viewed the old certainties as certainly wrong. There was a deep suspicion of tradition, which was itself a deep tradition on American soil. The distrust of authority as the central narrative of the 1960s had also been a central part of the story of America from the beginning. The disestablishment impulse of the 1960s echoed the disestablishment themes of American history. One could be forgiven for supposing that the 1960s was but one more sequel in the story of America.

There is no clearer "metanarrative" to the 1960s than that Americans were nervous about metanarratives. Americans like stories so far as the story is about them and their dissent from the other controlling narratives. The widespread "cultural dissent" of the 1960s was a reflection of this dissenting impulse, but also one that appeared more robust than normal because of its accompanying ideological framework. There was a "story" which warranted American intuitions about the "way life really is" and about "the way life could be." Those "stories" were partly conceptual and partly concrete. This work has tried to tell that story from both vantage points, cognizant that the vantage points were sometimes at odds with each other. Without the conceptual story the dissenting impulses would not have taken collective hold in the wider culture. In that sense the conceptual story provides an intellectual grid map(s) marking out the terrain in which the culture lived out its intuitions.

The great cultural revolution of the 1960s was under girded by an antecedent (and often subsequent) ideological revolution. The two were not related in precise causal fashion. Great ideas sometimes led but often those ideas served as retrospective justifications for the notion of change already well underway in the wider culture. They provided a plausibility to the emergence of trends which otherwise might have been stopped in their tracks.

In the aftermath of the tumultuous decade it may have seemed hard to know how persons who embraced profoundly different comprehensive perspectives on reality, human life, and the good, could nonetheless live together as equals in a just, stable and peaceful society. Some supposed the end of religion was the answer, though that answer was religious in its own peculiar way. Others supposed the end of ideology, though that answer was ideological in its own peculiar way.

The anti-traditional traditionalism of public discourse in America has always been wary of institutionalized religion getting the "final say" on matters. That same suspicion extended to politicians and academics as well. The 1960s manifest the intrinsic wariness of anyone stopping the conversation of our public life together. Deep disagreements always usher in a hope for resolution, but on American soil deep disagreement is a reality with which most are willing to live, even if they disagree about the nature of disagreement.

The legacy of the decade might simply be that anything that human beings care deeply about can be a menace to freedom, including ironically caring deeply about freedom. Genuine dialogue does not demand that the conversation be limited only to foundational beliefs held in common. The public conversation should start wherever it starts. Keeping the conversation going is important. The great risk is to suppose that keeping the conversation going is the final good rather than merely a wise way of thinking about final goods. The tumultuous decade was another reminder of the importance of guaranteeing basic rights and liberties to citizens and resident aliens, and to assure access to the public conversation by all, even when it got quite contentious. This was an important prelude to the story of the fragile times in which we presently reside.

Bibliography

Albert, Judith and Stewart, eds. *The Sixties Papers: Documents of a Rebellious Decade*. New York: Praeger, 1984.

Andrew, John A. *The Other Side of the Sixties: Young Americans for Freedom and the Rise of Conservative Politics*. New Brunswick, NJ: Rutgers University Press, 1997.

Arlen, Michael J. *Living Room War*. New York: Penguin Books, 1982.

Audi, Robert. *Epistemology*. New York: Routledge, 1998.

Ayer, A.J. *Language Truth and Logic*. New York: Oxford University Press, 1936.

———, ed. *The Revolution in Philosophy*. New York: St. Martin's Press 1956.

———, ed. *Logical Positivism*. New York: Free Press, 1959.

Baer, Hans A. and Merrill Singer. *African-American Religion in the Twentieth Century: Varieties of Protest and Accommodation*. Knoxville: University of Tennessee Press, 1992.

Baker, Gordon. *The Voices of Wittgenstein, the Vienna Circle and Friedrich Waismann*, transcribed, edited and trans. by Gordon Baker. New York: Routledge, 2003.

Baker, Jean H. *Sisters: The Lives of America's Suffragists*. New York: Hill and Wang, 2005.

Baldwin, Thomas, ed. *The Cambridge History of Philosophy 1870–1945*. Cambridge: Cambridge University Press, 2003.

Bauman, Zygmunt. *Intimations of Postmodernity*. London: Routledge, 1992.

Beauvoir, Simone de. *The Second Sex*, trans. and ed. H.M. Parshley. New York: Knopf 1952 [orig. 1949].

———. *Memoirs of a Dutiful Daughter*. New York: Harper and Row, 1958.

———. *The Prime of Life*. Cleveland: World Publishing Co., 1962.

———. *Force of Circumstance*. New York: Putnam, 1965.

———. *All Said and Done*. New York: Putnam, 1974.

Bell, Daniel. *The End of Ideology*. Cambridge, MA: Harvard University Press, 1960.

———, ed. *The Radical Right*. New York: Doubleday, 1963 [orig. 1955].

Bellah, Robert, *Habits of the Heart Individualism and Commitment in American Life*. Berkeley CA: University of California Press, 1985.

Benhabib, Seyla. *Situating the Self: Gender, Community and Postmodernism in Contemporary Ethics*. New York: Routledge, 1992.

Benhabib, Seyla and Drucilla Cornell, eds. *Feminism as Critique*. Minneapolis: University of Minnesota Press, 1987.

Berger, Peter L. *A Rumor of Angels: Modern Society and the Rediscovery of the Supernatural*. New York: Doubleday, 1970.

———. *The Heretical Imperative: Contemporary Possibilities of Religious Affirmation*. Garden City, NY: Anchor Press, 1979.

———. *Modernity, Pluralism and the Crisis of Meaning: The Orientation of Modern Man*. Gütersloh: Bertelsmann Foundation Publishers, 1995.

Berger, Peter L. and Peter Luckman. *The Social Construction of Reality*. New York: Anchor Books, 1967.

Berger, Peter L. and Samuel P. Huntington, eds. *Many Globalizations: Cultural Diversity in the Contemporary World*. New York: Oxford University Press, 2002.

Berman, Marshall. *All That is Solid Melts into Air*. New York: Simon and Schuster, 1982.

Bertens, Willem. *The Idea of the Postmodern: A History*. New York: Routledge, 1995.

Bloom, Jack. *Class, Race and the Civil Rights Movement*. Bloomington, IN: Indiana University Press, 1987.

Borgmann, Albert. *Technology and the Character of Contemporary Life: A Philosophical Inquiry*. Chicago, IL: University of Chicago Press, 1984.

———. *Crossing the Postmodern Divide*. Chicago, IL: University of Chicago Press, 1992.

———. *Power Failure: Christianity in the Culture of Technology*. Grand Rapids, MI: Brazos Press, 2003.

Bove, Paul A. ed. *Early Postmodernism: Foundational Essays*. Durham, NC: Duke University Press, 1995.

Branch, Taylor. *Parting the Waters: America in the King Years 1954–1963*. New York: Simon and Schuster, 1988.

———. *Pillar of Fire: America in the King Years 1963–1965*. New York: Simon and Schuster, 1998.

Brown, Norman O. *Life Against Death: The Psychoanalytic Meaning of History*. Middletown, CT: Wesleyan University Press, 1985 [orig. 1959].

Brownmiller, Susan. *In Our Time: Memoir of a Revolution*. New York: Dell, 1999.

Burns, Stewart. *To the Mountaintop: Martin's Luther King Jr.'s Sacred Mission to Save America, 1955–1968*. New York: HarperSanFrancisco, 2004.

Calvert, Greg and Carol Neiman Calvert. *A Disrupted History: The New Left and the New Capitalism*. New York: Random House, 1971.

Cantor, Norman. *Twentieth Century Culture: Modernism to Deconstruction*. New York: Peter Lang, 1988.

Capps, Walter H. *The Unfinished War: Vietnam and the American Conscience*. Boston: Beacon Press, 1982.

Carmichael, Thomas and Alison Lee, eds. *Postmodern Times: A Critical Guide to the Contemporary*. DeKalb, IL: Northern Illinois University Press, 2000.

Carpenter, Joel. *Revive Us Again: The Reawakening of American Fundamentalism*. New York: Oxford 1997.

Carson, Clayborne. *In Struggle: SNCC and the Black Awakening of the 1960s*. Cambridge, MA: Harvard University Press, 1981.

Castro, Ginette. *American Feminism: A Contemporary History.* New York: New York University Press, 1990.

Collier, Peter and David Horowitz. *Destructive Generation: Second Thoughts about the Sixties*. New York: Summit Books, 1989.

Collini, Stefan, ed. *Interpretation and Overinterpretation with Umberto Eco with Richard Rorty, Jonathan Culler, Christine Brooke-Rose.* Cambridge: Cambridge University Press, 1992.

Cone, James. *Black Theology and Black Power.* New York: Seabury Press, 1969.

———. *A Black Theology of Liberation.* Philadelphia, PA: Lippincott, 1970.

Cott, Nancy F., ed. *No Small Courage: A History of Women in the United States*. New York: Oxford University Press, 2000.

Cox, Harvey. *The Secular City: Secularization and Urbanization in Theological Perspective*. New York: Macmillan, 1965.

———. *Religion in the Secular City: Towards a Postmodern Theology*. New York: Simon and Schuster, 1984.

Cross, Gary. *An All Consuming Century: Why Commercialism Won in Modern America*. New York: Columbia University Press, 2002.

Delaney, Cornelius, Michael Loux, Gary Gutting, and W. David Solomon. *The Synoptic Vision: Essays on the Philosophy of Wilfrid Sellars*. Notre Dame, IN: University of Notre Dame Press, 1977.

Douglas, Ann. *The Feminization of American Culture.* New York: Knopf, 1977.

Dubois, Ellen Carol. *Harriot Stanton Blatch and the Winning of Women Suffrage*. New Haven: Yale University Press, 1997.

———. *Feminism and Suffrage: The Emergence of an Independent Women's Movement in America, 1848–1869*. Ithaca: Cornell University Press, 1999.

Dubois, Ellen Carol and Lynn Dumenil. *Through Women's Eyes: An American History with Documents*. Boston, MA: Bedford/St. Martin's, 2005.

Dummett, Michael. *Origins of Analytical Philosophy.* Cambridge, MA: Harvard University Press, 1993.

Dylan, Bob. *Chronicles*. New York: Simon and Schuster, 2004.

Echols, Alice. *Shaky Ground: The 60s and Its Aftershocks.* New York: Columbia University Press, 2002.

Elliot, Michael. *The Day Before Yesterday: Reconsidering America's Past, Rediscovering the Present*. New York: Simon and Schuster, 1996.

Ellul, Jacques. *The Technological Society*, trans. John Wilkinson. New York: Knopf, 1964 [orig. 1954].

———. *On Religion, Technology, and Politics / Conversations with Patrick Troude-Chastenet*, trans. Joan Mendès France. Atlanta, GA: Scholars Press, 1998.

Ellwood, Robert S. *The 60s Spiritual Awakening*. New Brunswick, NJ: Rutgers University Press, 1994.

Eubel, Thomas. "Otto Neurath, the Vienna Circle and the Austrian Tradition," in Anthony O'Hear, ed. *German Philosophy Since Kant*. Cambridge: Cambridge University Press, 1999.

Evans, Mary. "Simone de Beauvoir: Dilemmas of a Feminist Radical," in Dale Spender, ed. *Feminist Theorists: Three Centuries of Key Women Thinkers*. New York: Pantheon Books, 1983.

Evans, Sarah M. *Personal Politics*. New York: Vintage Books, 1980.

———. *Born for Liberty: A History of Women in America*. New York: Free Press 1997.

———. *Journeys That Opened Up the World: Women, Student Christian Movements, and Social Justice, 1955–1975*. Philadelphia, PA: Temple University Press, 2003.

Farber, David. *The Age of Great Dreams: America in the 1960s*. New York: Hill and Wang, 1994.

Featherstone, Mike. *Undoing Culture: Globalization, Postmodernism and Identity*. London: Sage, 1995.

Fjellman, Stephen. *Vinyl Leaves: Walt Disney World and America*. Boulder, CO: Westview Press, 1992.

Flax, Jane. *Thinking Fragments: Psychoanalysis, Feminism and Postmodernism in the Contemporary West*. Berkeley: University of California Press, 1990.

Flew, Anthony. *The Presumption of Atheism and Other Philosophical Essays on God, Freedom and Immortality*. New York: Barnes and Noble, 1976.

Flowers, Ronald B. *Religion in Strange Times: The 1960s and the 1970s*. Macon, GA: Mercer University Press, 1984.

Foucault, Michel. *The Archaeology of Knowledge and the Discourse on Language*, trans. A.M. Sheridan Smith. New York: Pantheon Books, 1972.

———. *The History of Madness*. London: Routledge, 2006 [orig. 1961].

Fox-Genovese, Elizabeth. *Feminism is Not the Story of My Life*. New York: Doubleday, 1996.

Frazier, E. Franklin. *The Negro Church in America*. New York: Schocken Books, 1963.

Freedman, Estelle. *No Turning Back: The History of Feminism and the Future of Women.* New York: Ballantine Books, 2002.

Fricker, Mrianda and Jennifer Hornsby, eds. *The Cambridge Companion to Feminism in Philosophy*. Cambridge: Cambridge University Press, 2000.

Friedan, Betty. *The Feminine Mystique*. New York: Norton, 1963.

Friedman, Michael. *Reconsidering Logical Positivism*. Cambridge: Cambridge University Press, 1999.

Galbraith, John Kenneth. *The Affluent Society*. Boston, MA: Houghton Mifflin, 1958.

Garrow, David. *Bearing the Cross: Martin Luther King, Jr., and the Southern Christian Leadership Conference*. New York: Morrow, 1986.

Gergen, Kenneth J. *The Saturated Self: Dilemmas of Identity in Contemporary Life*. New York: Basic Books, 1990.

Giddens, Anthony. *The Consequences of Modernity*. Stanford, CA: Stanford University Press, 1990.

Gilkey, Langdon. *Naming the Whirlwind: The Renewal of God-Language*. Indianapolis, IN: Bobbs-Merrill, 1969.

———. *Society and the Sacred*. New York: Crossroad, 1981.

Gitlin, Todd. *The Sixties: Year of Hope, Days of Rage*. New York: Bantam, 1987.

Glock, Hans-Johann. "Vorsprung durch Logik: The German Analytic Tradition," in Anthony O'Hear, ed. *German Philosophy Since Kant*. Cambridge: Cambridge University Press, 1999.

Goethals, Gregor T. *The Electronic Golden Calf: Images, Religion, and the Making of Meaning*. Cambridge, MA: Cowley Publications, 1990.

Goodman, Paul. *Growing Up Absurd*. New York: Vintage Books, 1956.

Griffin, David Ray. *God and Religion in a Post-Modern World*. New York: State University of New York Press, 1992.

Gross, Barry R. *Analytic Philosophy: An Historical Introduction*. New York: Pegasus Books, 1970.

Guinness, Os. *The American Hour*. New York: Free Press, 1992.

———. *The Dust of Death: The Sixties Counterculture and How It Changed America*. Chicago, IL: Crossway, 1994.

Gutting, Gary, ed. *Paradigms and Revolutions: Applications and Appraisals of Thomas Kuhn's Philosophy of Science*. Notre Dame, IN: University of Notre Dame Press, 1980.

Hacker, Andrew. *The End of An American Era*. New York: Athenaeum, 1968.

Hacker, P.M.S. *Insight and Illusion*. Oxford: Oxford University Press, 1986.

Hahn, Hann, Rudolph Carnap and Otto Neurath, "The Scientific Conception of the World: The Vienna Circle," trans. Paul Foulkes and Marie Neurath, in Marie Meurath and Robert S. Cohen, eds. *Empiricism and Sociology*. Boston, MA: Reidel, 1973 [orig. 1929].

Hamilton, William. *The Gospel of Christian Atheism*. Philadelphia, PA: Westminster Press, 1966.

———. *Theological Explorations*. New York: Macmillan, 1968.

Hamilton, William and Thomas J.J. Altizer, eds. *Radical Theology and the Death of God*. Indianapolis, IN: Bobbs Merrill, 1966.

Hanfling, Oswald. *Philosophy and Ordinary Language: The Bent and Genius of Our Tongue*. New York: Routledge, 2000.

Harrington, Michael. *Fragments of a Century*. New York: Simon and Schuster, 1973.

Harvey, David. *The Condition of Postmodernity: An Enquiry into the Origins of Cultural Change*. Oxford: Basil Blackwell, 1989.

Harvey, Van. "The Alienated Theologian," in Robert A. Evans, ed. *The Future of Philosophical Theology*. Philadelphia, PA: Westminster Press, 1970.

Hassan, Ihab Habib. *The Postmodern Turn: Essays in Postmodern Theory and Culture*. Columbus: Ohio State University Press, 1987.

Hatch, Nathan. *The Democratization of American Christianity*. New Haven, CT: Yale University Press, 1989.

Helbig, Jorg, Jurgen Heidekin and Anke Ortlepp, eds. *The Sixties Revisited: Culture, Society, Politics*. Heidelberg: Universitatsverlag C. Winter, 2001.

Henry, Carl F.H. *The Uneasy Conscience of Modern Fundamentalism.* Grand Rapids, MI: Eerdmans. 1947.

Hofstater, Richard *Anti-Intellectualism in American Life*. New York: Alfred Knopf, 1962.

Horowitz, Daniel. *Betty Friedan and the Making of the Feminine Mystique: The American Left, the Cold War, and Modern Feminism*. Amherst: University of Massachusetts Press, 1998.

Horton, John and Susan Mendes, eds. *After MacIntyre: Critical Perspectives on the Work of Alasdair MacIntyre.* Notre Dame, IN: University of Notre Dame Press, 1994.

Howard, Gerald, ed. *The Sixties*. New York: Washington Square Press, 1982.

Hunter, James Davison. *American Evangelicalism: Conservative Religion and the Quandary of Modernity*. New Brunswick, NJ: Rutgers University Press, 1983.

———. *Culture Wars: The Struggle to Define America*. New York: Basic Books, 1991.

Huyssen, Andreas. *After the Great Divide: Modernism, Mass Culture and Postmodernism*. Indianapolis: Indiana University Press, 1986.

Hylton, Peter. *Russell, Idealism and the Emergence of Analytic Philosophy*. Oxford: Clarendon Press, 1990.

Isserman, Maurice. *If I Had a Hammer ... The Death of the Old Left and the Birth of the New Left*. New York: Basic Books, 1987.

Isserman, Maurice and Michael Kasin. *America Divided: The Civil War of the 1960s*. New York: Oxford University Press, 2004.

Jameson, Fredrick. *Postmodernism, or The Cultural Logic of Late Capitalism*. Durham, NC: Duke University Press, 1991.

Kaledin, Eugenia. *Mothers and More: American Women in the 1950s*. Boston, MA: Twayne, 1984.

Kenny, Anthony. *Wittgenstein*. Oxford: Blackwell, 2006 [orig. 1973].

Kitcher, Philip. *The Advancement of Science: Science without Legend, Objectivity without Illusions*. New York: Oxford University Press, 1993.

Kuhn, Thomas. *The Copernican Revolution: Planetary Astronomy in the Development of Western Thought.* Cambridge, MA: Harvard University Press, 1957.

Kuklick, Bruce. *A History of Philosophy in America: 1720–2000*. New York: Oxford, 2001.

Lasch, Christopher. *Haven in a Heartless World: The Family Besieged.* New York: Basic Books, 1977.

———. *The True and Only Heaven: Progress and Its Critics*. New York: Norton, 1991.

———. *Women and the Common Life: Love, Marriage and Feminism.* New York: Norton, 1997.

Lawrence, Bruce. *Defenders of God: The Fundamentalist Revolt Against the Modern Age*. San Francisco: Harper and Row, 1989.

Leuchtenburg, William E. *A Troubled Feast: American Society Since 1945*. Boston, MA: Little Brown and Co., 1973.

Levy, Peter. *The Civil Rights Movement*. Westport, CT: Greenwood Press, 1998.

Lewis, Anthony. *Portrait of a Decade: The Second American Revolution*. New York: Random House, 1965.

Lincoln, C. Eric. *The Black Church Since Frazier*. New York: Schocken, 1974.

———. *Black Muslims in America*. Grand Rapids, MI: Eerdmans, 1994 [orig. 1966].

Lincoln, C. Eric and Lawrence H. Mamiya, *The Black Church in the African American Experience*. Durham, NC: Duke University Press, 1990.

Lints, Richard. *The Fabric of Theology*. Grand Rapids, MI: Eerdmans, 1993.

Lipset, Martin. *Political Man: The Social Bases of Politics*. Garden City, NY: Doubleday, 1960.

Litwack, Leon. *Been in the Storm So Long*. New York: Vintage Books, 1980.

Lora, Ronald, ed. *America in the 1960s*. New York: Wiley, 1974.

Lyon, David. *The Steeple's Shadow: On the Myths and Realities of Secularization*. Grand Rapids, MI: Eerdmans, 1987.

———. *Postmodernity*, 2nd edn. Minneapolis: University of Minnesota Press, 1999.

McAdam, Douglas. *Political Process and the Development of Black Insurgency 1930–1970*. Chicago, IL: University of Chicago Press, 1982.

McCloughlin, William. *Revival, Awakenings and Reform*. Chicago, IL: University of Chicago Press, 1978.

MacIntyre, Alisdair. *Difficulties in Christian Belief*. London: SCM Press, 1959.

———. *Secularization and Moral Change*. New York: Oxford University Press, 1967.

———. *The Religious Significance of Atheism*. New York: Columbia University Press, 1969.

———. *Against the Self Images of the Age: Essays on Ideology and Philosophy*. London: Gerald Duckworth and Co., 1971.

———. *After Virtue*. Notre Dame, IN: University of Notre Dame Press, 1981.

———. *Whose Justice? Which Rationality?* Notre Dame, IN: University of Notre Dame Press, 1988.

———. *Three Rival Versions of Moral Enquiry*. Notre Dame: University of Notre Dame Press, 1990.

Malcolm, Norman. *Ludwig Wittgenstein: A Memoir*, 2nd edn. New York: Oxford University Press, 2001.

Malcolm X. *The Autobiography of Malcolm X*. With the assistance of Alex Haley. Intro. by M.S. Handler. Epilogue by Alex Haley. New York: Grove Press 1965.

Marsden, George. *The Soul of the American University*. New York: Oxford University Press, 1994.

Marsden George M. and Bradley J. Longfield, eds. *The Secularization of the Academy*. New York: Oxford University Press, 1992.

Marsh, Charles. *God's Long Summer: Stories of Faith and Civil Rights*. Princeton NJ: Princeton University Press, 1997.

———. "The Civil Rights Movement as Theological Drama – Interpretation and Application," *Modern Theology* 18/2 (April 2002).

Martin, William. *A Prophet with Honor: The Billy Graham Story*. New York: W. Morrow, 1991.

Matthews, Donald. *Honoring the Ancestors: An African Cultural Interpretation of Black Religion and Literature*. New York: Oxford University Press, 1998.

Matusow, Allen J. *The Unraveling of America: A History of Liberalism in the 1960s*. New York: Harper and Row, 1984.

May, Elaine Tyler. "Pushing the limits: 1940–1961," in Nancy F. Cott, ed. *No Small Courage: A History of Women in the United States*. New York: Oxford University Press, 2000.

Meier, August and Elliot Rudwick. *CORE: A Study in the Civil Rights Movement 1942–1968*. New York: Oxford University Press, 1973.

———. *From Plantation to Ghetto*. New York: Hill and Wang, 1976.

Miller, James. *Democracy is in the Streets: From Port Huron to the Siege in Chicago*. New York: Simon and Schuster, 1987.

Mills, C. Wright. *The Power Elite*. New York: Oxford University Press, 2000 [orig. 1956].

Monk, Ray. *Ludwig Wittgenstein: The Duty of Genius*. New York: Penguin Books, 1991.

Morris, Aldon. *The Origins of the Civil Rights Movement: Black Communities Organizing for Change*. New York: The Free Press, 1984.

Murphy, Mark C., ed. *Alasdair MacIntyre*. Cambridge: Cambridge University Press, 2003.

Myrdal, Gunnar. *An American Dilemma: The Negro Problem and Modern Democracy*. New York: Harper and Brothers, 1944.

Nash, Roderick. *The Nervous Generation*. Chicago, IL: Rand McNally, 1970.

Nelsen, Hart, and Anne Nelsen. *The Black Church in the Sixties*. Lexington: University Press of Kentucky, 1975.

Nelsen, Hart, Raytha Yokley and Anne Nelsen, eds. *The Black Church in America*. New York: Basic Books, 1971.

Newman, Fred. *The End of Knowing: and the Rediscovery of Development in the Performance of Conversation*. New York: Routledge, 1997.

Nicholson, Linda, ed. *Feminism/Postmodernism*. New York: Routledge, 1990.

Noll, Mark. *The Scandal of the Evangelical Mind*. Grand Rapids, MI: Eerdmans, 1994.

Nussbaum, Martha. *Sex and Social Justice*. New York: Oxford, 1999.

O'Neill, William L. *Coming Apart: An Informal History of America in the 1960s*. Chicago, IL: Quadrangle Books, 1971.

O'Neill, William. *Feminism in America: A History*, 2nd edn. New Brunswick, NJ: Transaction Books, 1989.

Oppenheimer, Martin. *The Sit-In Movement of 1960*. New York: Carlson Press, 1989.

Parks, Rosa. *Quiet strength: The Faith, The Hope, and The Heart of a Woman Who Changed a Nation. Reflections by Rosa Parks with Gregory J. Reed*. Grand Rapids, MI: Zondervan, 1994.

Patterson, Orlando. *Rituals of Blood: Consequences of Slavery in Two American Centuries*. Washington DC: Civitas/Counterpoint Books, 1998.

Peake, Thomas R. *Keeping the Dream Alive: A History of the Southern Christian Leadership conference from King to the Nineteen-Eighties*. New York: Peter Lang, 1987.

Pears, Angela. *Feminist Christian Encounters: The Methods and Strategies of Feminist Informed Christian Theologies*. London: Ashgate, 2004.

Pears, David F. *The False Prison: A Study of the Development of Wittgenstein's Philosophy*. Oxford: Clarendon Press, 1987.

Pells, Richard. *The Liberal Mind in a Conservative Age: American Intellectuals in the 1940s and 1950s*. New York: Harper and Row, 1985.

Peterson, David J. *Revoking the Moral Order: The Ideology of Positivism and the Vienna Circle*. Lanham, MD: Lexington Books, 1999.

Pichaske, David. *A Generation in Motion: Popular Music and Culture in the Sixties*. New York: Schirmer, 1979.

Piven, Francis and Richard Cloward. *Poor Peoples Movements: Why They Succeed, Why They Fail*. New York: Vintage Books, 1977.

Podhoretz, Norman. *Breaking Ranks: A Political Memoir*. New York: Harper and Row, 1979.

Pollock, Bruce. *When the Music Mattered: Rock in the 1960s*. New York: Holt Rinehart and Winston, 1983.

Pollock, John. *To All The Nations: The Billy Graham Story*. San Francisco: Harper & Row, 1985.

Postman, Neil. *Technopoly*. New York: Knopf, 1992.

Quine, W.V.O. *From a Logical Point of View*. Cambridge, MA: Harvard University Press, 1953.

———. "Autobiography of W.V. Quine," in *The Philosophy of W.V. Quine*, edited by Lew Edwin Hahn and Paul Arthur Schilpp. La Salle, IL: Open Court Press, 1986.

Quine, W.V.O. and J.S. Ullian. *The Web of Belief*. New York: Random House, 1970.

Raboteau, Albert. *Slave Religion*. New York: Oxford University Press, 1978.

———. "The Black Church: Continuity within Change," in David W. Lotz, ed. *Altered Landscapes: Christianity in America, 1935–1985*. Grand Rapids, MI: Eerdmans, 1989.

———. *Fire in My Bones: Reflections on African-American Religious History*. Boston, MA: Beacon Press, 1995.

———. *Canaan Land: A Religious History of African Americans*. New York: Oxford University Press, 2001.

Reiff, Philip. *The Feeling Intellect*. Chicago, IL: University of Chicago Press, 1991.

Reisman, David. *The Lonely Crowd: A Study of the Changing American Character*. New Haven, CT: Yale University Press, 2001, orig. 1950.

Ritzer, George. *Explorations in the Sociology of Consumption : Fast Food, Credit Cards and Casinos*. London: SAGE, 2001.

Roberts, Deotis. *Liberation and Reconciliation: A Black Theology*. Philadelphia, PA: Westminster, 1971.

Robinson, John A.T. *The New Reformation*. Philadelphia, PA: Westminster Press, 1965.

Rorty, Richard, ed. *The Lingustic Turn: Recent Essays in Philosophical Method*. Chicago, IL: University of Chicago Press, 1967.

———. *Philosophy and the Mirror of Nature*. Princeton, NJ: Princeton University Press, 1979.

———. *Truth, Politics and Postmodernism*. Assen: Van Gorcum, 1997.

Rowan, Carl. *South of Freedom*. Baton Rouge: Louisiana State University Press, 1997.

Rowley, Hazel. *Tete-a-Tete: Simone de Beauvoir and Jean-Paul Sartre*. San Francisco: HarperCollins, 2005.

Saiving, Valerie. "The Human Situation: A Feminine View," *The Journal of Religion* 40/2 (1960).

Sarkar, Sahotra, ed. *Science and Philosophy in the 20th Century*. New York: Garland Press, 1996.

Schneider, Dorothy and Carl J. *American Women in the Progressive Era, 1900–1920*. New York: Facts on File, 1993.

Schultze, Quentin J. *Televangelism and American Culture: The Business of Popular Religion*. Grand Rapids, MI: Baker Book House, 1991.

Sellars, Wilfred. *Science Perception and Reality*. London: Routledge and Kegan Paul, 1963 [orig.1956].

———. *Philosophical Perspectives*. Springfield, IL: Charles Thomas Publishers, 1967.

Sernett, Milton C. *Bound for the Promised Land: African American Religion and the Great Migration*. Durham, NC: Duke University Press, 1997.

Singleton, Carl, ed. *Sixties in America*, 3 vols. Pasadena, CA: Salem Press, 1999.

Sitkoff, Harvard. *The Struggle for Black Equality: 1954–1992*. New York: Hill and Wang, 1993.

Sluga, Hans and David Stern, eds. *The Cambridge Companion to Wittgenstein*. Cambridge: Cambridge University Press, 1996.

Smith, Barry. *Austrian Philosophy: The Legacy of Franz Brentano*. Chicago, IL: Open Court, 1994.

Sontag, Susan. *Styles of Radical Will*. New York: Picador, 2002 [orig. 1966].

Sowell, Tom. *Race and Culture: A World View*. New York: Basic Books, 1994.

Stadler, Friedrich. *The Vienna Circle: Studies in the Origins, Development, and Influence of Logical Empiricism*, trans. Camilla Nielsen et al. Vienna: Springer, 2001.

Stoper, Emily. *The Student Nonviolent Coordinating Committee: The Growth of Radicalism in a Civil Rights Organization*. New York: Carlson Press, 1989.

Stout, Jeffrey. *The Flight from Authority: Religion, Morality and the Quest for Autonomy*. Notre Dame, IN: University of Notre Dame Press, 1981.

Stuckey, Sterling. *Slave Culture: Nationalist Theory and the Foundations of Black America*. New York: Oxford University Press, 1987.

Sweet, Leonard, ed. *The Evangelical Tradition in America*. Macon, GA: Mercer University Press, 1984.

———. "The 1960s: The Crises of Liberal Christianity and the Public Emergence of Evangelicalism," in George Marsden, ed. *Evangelicalism and Modern America*. Grand Rapids, MI: Eerdmans, 1984.

Tipton, Steven. *Getting Saved From the Sixties*. Berkeley: University of California Press, 1981.

Tong, Rosemarie Putnams. *Feminist Thought: A More Comprehensive Introduction*, 2nd edn. Boulder, CO: Westview Press, 1998.

Tracy, David, "On Naming the Present," *Concillium*, no. 2 (1990).

Trilling, Lionel. *Freud and the Crisis of Our Culture*. Boston: Beacon Press, 1955.

Trotter, Joe William. *The Great Migration in Historical Perspective: New Dimensions of Race, Class and Gender*. Bloomington, IN: Indiana University Press, 1991.

Tye, Larry. *Rising from the Rails: Pullman Porters and the Making of the Black Middle Class*. New York: Henry Holt and Co., 2004.

Van Buren, Paul. *The Secular Meaning of the Gospel*. New York: The Macmillan Co., 1963.

Viorst, Milton. *Fire in the Streets: America in the 1960s*. New York: Simon and Schuster, 1979.

Weinstein, Allen, and Frank Gatell, eds. *The Segregation Era: 1863–1954*. New York: Oxford University Press, 1970.

Weisbrot, Robert. *Freedom Bound: A History of America's Civil Rights Movement*. New York: Norton, 1990.

Wells, David F. *No Place for Truth: Whatever Happened to Evangelical Theology*? Grand Rapids, MI: Eerdmans, 1993.

———. *Losing our Virtue: Why the Church Must Recover its Moral Vision*. Grand Rapids: Eerdmans, 1998.

West, Cornel. *The American Evasion of Philosophy*. Madison, WI: University of Wisconsin Press, 1989.

———. *Prophetic Fragments*. Grand Rapids, MI: Eerdmans, 1991.

———. *Beyond Eurocentrism and Multiculturalism*. Monroe, ME: Common Courage Press, 1993.

———. *Prophetic Thought in Postmodern Times*. Monroe, ME: Common Courage Press, 1993.

———. *Race Matters*. Boston: Beacon Press, 2001.
Whitfield, Stephen J. *Death in the Delta: The Story of Emmett Till*. New York: Free Press, 1988.
Whyte, William H. *The Organization Man*. Philadelphia: University of Pennsylvania Press, 2002 [orig. 1956].
Williams, Michael. *Groundless Belief: An Essay on the Possibility of Epistemology*, 2nd edn. Princeton, NJ: Princeton University Press, 1999 [orig. 1977].
Winter, Gibson. *Being Free: The Possibilities of Freedom in an Overorganized World*. London: MacMillan, 1970.
Wittgenstein, Ludwig. *Philosophical Investigations*, eds G.E.M. Anscombe and R. Rhees, trans. G.E.M. Anscombe. Oxford: Blackwell Publishers, 1953.
———. *Tractatus Logico-Philosophicus*, trans. D.F. Pears and B.F. McGuinness. London: Routledge and Kegan Paul, 1961. First German edition, 1921.
Wolin, Sheldon. "The Destructive Sixties and Postmodern Conservatism," in Stephen Macedo, ed. *Reassessing the Sixties: Debating the Political and Cultural Legacy*. New York: Norton, 1997.
Wolterstorff, Nicholas. "An Engagement with Rorty," *Journal of Religious Ethics* 31/1 (2003).
Wuthnow, Robert. *The Struggle for America's Soul: Evangelicals, Liberals and Secularism*. Grand Rapids, MI: Eerdmans, 1989.
———. *God and Mammon in America*. New York: Free Press, 1994.

Index